Contents

Preface

This text is not written as most texts. It is written, intentionally, with unfilled spaces: with ideas raised, with arguments suggested, with problems noted but without elaboration. Spaces may be filled with additional readings, lectures, and/or class discussion and debate. I have done this to allow teachers to adapt it to their own styles of teaching. Far too often, texts provide too much information, making sure that every question is answered. While perhaps comforting on some levels, this approach seems uninspiring, less conducive to learning, and unchallenging to teaching. Such an approach leaves nothing for professor or students to grapple with, either individually or collectively.

It does seem necessary to explain this book further, by saying what it is and is not. It was intended to be comprehensive in scope, but not exhaustive in content. Thus, do not expect to find all relevant case work cited here, all issues covered completely, all questions fully explained, etc.

This is an introductory, undergraduate text. The job of such a book is multiple: to inform at an initial level, to open new doors a little way, and to open old doors more widely. It is to pique curiosity and stimulate continued study at more advanced levels. The book's aim is to offer possibilities.

A number of people helped make this book a possibility for me, and to them and those whom I may inadvertently slight in the following list, I give my heartfelt thanks. First, to Patty Coleman for suggesting that I write this book. There is no doubt that if she had not planted the seed and then prodded thereafter, there would be no book today. Second, to La Salle University for granting me a semester leave to work on the book. Thanks to the birth of my son, the leave was not used as productively as it could have been, but it was nevertheless greatly appreciated. Third, to Alison Bricken, the initial editor at Praeger who took on this work, and to Ann Keifer, her successor, who patiently supported my delayed efforts. Fourth, to Naomi Timson for her tireless typing efforts. Fifth, and finally, to my parents, Jane and Alan Otten, the two best editors any writer could ever hope to have.

Women's Rights and the Law

1

Introduction

The law embodies the story of a nation's development through many centuries, and it cannot be dealt with as if it contained only the axioms and corollaries of a book of mathematics. In order to know what it is, we must know what it has been, and what it tends to become. We must alternately consult history and existing theories of legislation. But the most difficult labor will be to understand the combination of the two into new products at every stage. The substance of the law at any given time pretty nearly corresponds, so far as it goes, with what is then understood to be convenient.

Oliver Wendell Holmes, Jr.
The Common Law (1891)

SETTING THE STAGE

Has the law, over time, treated women and men similarly? When we look at how the law has delimited the economic, social, political, and personal lives of females and males in American society, do we see comparable pictures? Honest answers to these questions—debated frequently and, certainly, currently—must be that the two sexes have not been treated similarly, let alone equally. Over the centuries, mothers have not been given the same options as fathers; wives have not been given the same "rights" as husbands; female professionals have not been given the same benefits and opportunities as male professionals. And the list of disparities could go on. Why these disparities have prevailed—and continue to prevail—despite inroads in resolving the differences, is at the heart of the debate.

The debaters have argued the subject from a variety of approaches, though the most common has been predominantly discursive. This method is not to be faulted; an understanding of all subjects is strengthened by a multifaceted approach. Yet this method seems to weaken whatever position it sets forth by its failure to present, in the original form, the very subject under examination: the law. It seems reasonable that if we want to understand not only the *how* of the law's treatment and definition of the status of women, but also the *why* of that treatment, we must look beyond the musings of others and directly at the source; we must look at the law. Only in this way can we learn exactly what was said, and to some extent, why it was said. And only then can each of us, individually and from our own perspective, begin to understand and to "know."

But what do we want to know or, perhaps more aptly put, need to know, and what law should we examine? Each of these questions is open to a variety of answers, and the answers given would no doubt reflect the biases of the respondent. The answers given here, therefore, and the answers that drive the course and substance of this book, are presented not as "truths" but as "possibles," thus offering more fuel for the debate.

WHICH LAW?

In order to uncover the law's image and treatment of women over time, from our early colonial days to the present, we could look at any number of different laws: the laws of municipalities, the laws of states, the laws of the federal government, or the laws of regulatory agencies. We could examine the laws as they sit on the books, or we could watch them in action as they are applied and argued in court and then subsequently used in everyday life. Looking at all these possibilities, however, is overwhelming, almost impossible, and hardly desirable. Some parameters on our study are necessary, and the limits that have been set reflect the goal of our inquiry.

If we define the goal as understanding how the law has structured women's position in American society, whether the aim has been to keep them in check and control or to open the doors to all possibilities, then only one law appears appropriate. That law is the law of the courts. We must examine the laws that have been applied in everyday life, have been found unfair, and consequently have been challenged in a court of law and as a result subjected to judicial review. A law that has never been challenged leaves women's position sketched in only vaguely; it is the challenge and the discourse that accompanies it that really defines her place. It is much like a TV warranty sitting idly in your drawer: until the TV goes bad, you really don't know the full scope of its protection.

To understand a law's "real" function, we must look at a law that has been challenged in a court and, as a result of that challenge, has been interpreted. The court gives the explanation of the law's what, why, and legality. It is this interpretation that clearly tells society just how, or whether, the law should be put into practice and function.

But, just as laws come at all levels of government, so do courts, and so once again, a choice must be made: Which court's interpretations will we look at? Remembering that the goal is to understand the status of women in *American* society, the choice becomes easy. Rather than turning to the decisions of the court of any individual state that, constitutionally, can influence behavior only within the confines of that state, it seems reasonable to turn to the court whose decisions control and influence the law of all of the United States, the U.S. Supreme Court. Thus, this book will examine laws that have been appealed all the way to the highest court in the land, and it will include challenges to both state and federal law.

The selected cases to be reviewed, from the late 1700s to today, deal with "women's issues" (an egregious misnomer, as is explained below), as well as with other issues that have helped to define the political, economic, social, and legal position of women throughout the history of our country. Including all the Supreme Court cases addressing these issues during this time period would, however, be both unnecessary and unruly. Instead, this book reviews a sampling of influential cases representing major issues covering the dominant concerns in women's lives—home, health, and professional and economic standing. The cases have been selected for their importance and their ability to paint the evolving picture of women's position in American society. For the most part, the cases are presented in their original form, albeit excerpted, an approach that allows each reader to draw her/his own interpretation and conclusion.

Although this book's continued focus is on understanding how the law has defined women's position in society, the process—sometimes explicitly, sometimes implicitly—also uncovers the law's definition of men's position in society. It appears that for centuries the law, and those who have applied and interpreted it, have viewed males and females as flip sides of a coin. Consistent with that view, the law's treatment of the sexes has taken on a somewhat Hegelian flavor; when it said "no" to women, it was saying—again sometimes explicitly, sometimes implicitly—"not no" (if not, in fact, "yes") to men. Thus, in looking at the law and what it has to say about women, we are actually seeing what it has to say about men as well.

WHAT DO WE NEED TO KNOW?

Having determined what law will be the object of review, we must next identify the basic questions to ask. The answers will give us the knowledge we need to determine how the law has treated women and men. Understanding is a piecemeal process; we arrive at it as the end result of pooling together small nuggets of knowledge. The small nuggets result from asking, again and again, at each stage of analysis, certain key questions; a larger understanding comes from answering more universal questions that flow, logically, from the process of collecting the nuggets.

There are any number of little questions, some of which could apply to case after case, others of which might be specific to a particular issue under consideration. Two questions, however, should consistently drive the reader's critical thinking and awareness when perusing the pages that follow. They are as follows:

1. What is the nature of the law's response to women and men?
2. What is the rationale for that response?

Answering the first question should not be difficult. It is relatively easy to determine the nature of the law's response and whether it has treated males and females differently or similarly. It is even easier to determine the content of that treatment. The second question, searching out the reasoning underlying this treatment, involves far more problems but is even more essential to answer, for it is the reasoning that allows us to see the Court's broader concept of women's role in society. It is this reasoning, too, that partially enables us to anticipate the Court's position for the future. The Supreme Court's decisions to some degree reflect the thinking and tone of American society in general, but at the same time they set forth ideas that American society then uses to reshape its own beliefs and practices. The Court's decisions are the pace car, if you will, for society's attitudes and behavior.

But looking at the Court's words and language brings us to another level of analysis: the rationale behind what the justices said. We need to know not only what the justices said but their underlying thinking as well. For example:

- What is the legal basis for the decision in each case?
- In presenting their decision, did the justices call on societal, biological, historical, or legal dictates?
- Did the justices believe their decision was beneficial or harmful to society, women, men, and/or children?
- Did the decision seem to reflect naivete? maliciousness? sincerity?

If, at each step in the review of women's legal history, we address these questions and others that may come up, it should be possible at the end to answer the following, more universal questions.

- To what degree did and does the Constitution of the United States protect women?
- Despite seeming gains in status and legal protection, has the status of women really improved and are women better protected legally now than before?
- What, in fact, is the actual status of women as defined by the ultimate law of the United States?
- Do the decisions of the Supreme Court reflect a consistency in the Court's thinking as regards women and their "rightful" position in society?
- When addressing issues related to women's rights, have the Supreme Court justices engaged in social activism or strict judicial interpretation?

- If the former, has it been reflective of the temperament of society or the ideologies of individual justices?
- Do the decisions of the Supreme Court rely on or reflect the knowledge gained through careful, scholarly research, thereby, perhaps, reflecting reality rather than bias?

To help answer these questions, the text of the Court's decisions will be supplemented with readings from the social sciences when available and appropriate. Via these two different but highly interrelated and complementary perspectives, it should be possible to gain a comprehensive understanding of the thinking and behavior that have controlled women's reality throughout our country's history.

VALUE-FREE READING

One final comment on this book: It is about much more than just the law and women. It is also about stereotyping and its effects on individuals and social welfare and development; it is about basic American values and how the law works to reinforce them; it is about the interplay of attitudes and law—the attitudes of legislators, judges, and the American public; and of course, the book is about changing roles and a changing American society. Fairness and justice come into play here, as does how we as a society have come to understand these concepts—at least as they pertain to women and men.

In order to see and appreciate all these threads and patterns, however, the reader must be attentive to *all* that is presented, not just that which is comfortable, familiar, and nonthreatening. Seeing and appreciating all of this requires an honest and *unbiased*, or value-free, reading and necessitates seeing both (or all) sides of each issue.

To do this—to be able to say, "Yes, I understand that position *intellectually*, but I cannot personally accept it as my interpretation of the evidence and as consistent with my own beliefs"—demands two things: first, a careful and comprehensive inventory of one's own biases, and second, constant work either to rid oneself of them or to be continuously conscious of them lest they interfere with the desired unbiased view. Only then does it become possible to build the most solid platform for any position you hold (or that your bias pushes you to hold). Arguments are strengthened when you understand the *actual* position of an opponent; then you can rebut that position with substantive counterpoints rather than by merely repeating a few much-used tenets of your own argument. Regardless of your own position, it is equally important to understand intellectually both the argument that says the law has bullied and abused women and the counterargument that says the law has protected women and their rightful sphere.

There are many who say that value-free learning and knowing are neither desirable nor possible. This may be true in practice but still does not negate the desirability of constant striving toward value-free understanding, if that is the goal. Critics say also that adherence to the belief in value-free knowledge is, in and of itself, a value-laden position. Obviously, that is true.

It is as value-laden a perspective as the position that opponents take in saying that it is better simply to put one's biases on the table and let the listener beware. But it is possible to argue that the content of learning and understanding that flows from each of these two positions is so qualitatively different that to call each a value-laden position is akin to describing both a dot-to-dot drawing and a Mary Cassatt painting as art. There is no question that if you view the world brightly through rose-colored glasses or darkly through sunglasses, whether or not you acknowledge up front that you are wearing them, your understanding is going to take on a tint. But only if you acknowledge that the enhancement is due to your glasses—and is not the reality—can you, if you desire, adjust your vision.

The real difference in the two perspectives may be one of semantics rather than substance; perhaps bias and interests are being confused. Was it bias or interest that influenced the topic for this book? Was it bias or interest that directed the selections included in this book? Bias would suggest lopsided readings, reflecting only those cases and articles that produced a picture of women consistent with the author's personal (read "biased") views. Interest would suggest readings of many persuasions in order to provide a rounded exploration of women and the law, regardless of whether it was consistent with the author's personal (read "biased") views.

For those who say the best way to deal with the bias that each of us has is to express it straightforwardly, let me state mine here and now. My bias is that everyone should attempt a value-free reading of what follows so that facts and reality, rather than prejudice and preconceived notions, can be added to each person's arsenal of ideas and understanding. If, however, the rosy glasses are more comfortable, please leave them on.

ASKING QUESTIONS

To help determine the exact color of the glasses we're wearing—if any—each of us must ask and answer a series of questions before proceeding any further. It is important that we at least be aware of our biases; whether we then wish to control them is another issue.

- *What are your own biases, conscious and unconscious*? In other words, what is the color of your glasses (since we all wear glasses)?
- *Which of these biases are really "yours"* and which have you simply gotten by osmosis from your parents, religion, neighborhood, and so on?
- *Given the results of your bias inventory, do you need to do any reevaluation?*
- *Can you understand that which you haven't personally experienced*? In other words, is there, in that end result of understanding, a difference between understanding gained simply intellectually and that gained experientially?

As this last question suggests, there is no doubt that experience shapes all of us. I raise issues that my parents' and grandparents' generations could not; for example, why can women not be on the firing line in combat zones? At the same time, my students are puzzled by the issues over which I still agonize, issues such as the use of sexist language. Experience shapes both our interests and our biases, as well as our understanding. But does that mean that in order to understand something, it must be experienced first-hand? Does that mean that in order to appreciate the negative consequences of discrimination, you must be a woman, an African American, or a Jew? These questions, along with those raised above about biases, are important ones that should be addressed before proceeding any further because the answers to these questions will greatly influence your reading and understanding of the rest of this book.

2

The Law, the Constitution, and the U.S. Supreme Court

The constitution doesn't always follow the flag, but the supreme court follows the iliction returns.

Finley Peter Dunne
The Supreme Court's Decisions

Since the core of this book is the text of U.S. Supreme Court decisions, it is important to have a general understanding of both the legal and sociological functions of the law and of the Supreme Court itself. Complicated and abstruse tomes have been written on both, but the goal of this book is simply to provide a context for understanding the consequence and implications of the decisions included in these pages.

Most people take the law for granted. They do not stop to think about its origins and sources or purpose and role in our society beyond the immediate, and obvious, role of prescribing the particular behavior it addresses. But the law does more than simply codify behavior and, thereby, define right and wrong for society. The law is also supposed to protect both society and its individual members from harm and to provide for social order and well-being. Yet another and often overlooked role, and perhaps the most important one in the context of an examination of the law's influence on the status of women, is that of "value patrol."

This is a role that might not come readily to mind for most individuals: the role of reflector and reinforcer of societal values and beliefs. With every enactment of a law, every official response to the violation of that law, every verdict, every sanction, and every judicial opinion, messages are being sent to all members of society. Those messages are this is what we value, this we do not. When, for example, a husband found guilty of battering his wife is given a sentence of only one year while a convicted burglar receives a sentence of five years, society has been sent a clear message as to whether the woman or the stolen property is more highly valued. And when, for example, as happened in the early 1980s in Philadelphia, a judge chastised a defendant accused in an attempted rape case for having picked an "unattractive girl" and later, in a subsequent interview, described the victim as "coyote ugly," society is again sent a clear message.[1]

It would seem that once enumerated, the law's functions are very straightforward. They do, however, raise some perhaps less than straightforward questions that are important to consider, especially as antecedent to an investigation of the law's impact on women. It might be argued that these questions are better raised at the end of such an investigation, rather than at its beginning, but raising them at both ends seems even better. Asking them now at the beginning will lead to less-informed answers, no doubt, but also to a heightened sensitivity in reading all that follows. This sensitivity, in turn, should lead to a far more informed response when the questions are introduced once again at the end of the book. So consider the following:

- It has often been alleged, especially by conflict theorists, that one of the law's functions is to protect the powerful—their interests and values, their definitions of right and wrong—against the interests and values of the powerless. *Has protecting the interests of the powerful (men) from the powerless (women) been one of the law's functions in regard to women*?
- Another of the enumerated functions of law is to protect all from harm. In fact, some argue that the primary thrust of our law is the promise to protect each person from the harm others would unjustifiably and inexcusably inflict upon her/him. *Has our law kept this promise to women*? Or, for example, in saying that a raped or abused woman was "asking for it" or that a worker who is sexually harassed is "misreading things," have the interpreters of the law reneged on that promise to women?
- Given that the law seeks only to prevent and punish manifest or serious harms, and not those that are hidden or less serious, *how effective is the law as a tool for redress for women? Can the law, in reality, protect women? Can it protect them by itself—be their panacea—or can it do that only in conjunction with other areas of social life, such as education and religion*?

Once again, it may not be possible here and now to give as informed an answer to these questions as one might like, yet having asked them here may ensure that they will be carried with each reader as s/he progresses through the book.

THE PROCESS OF DUE PROCESS

Unlike the role of law in our society, which, it can be argued, is often murky both in theory and in practice, the sources of law are relatively straightforward. Everyone who has taken high school social studies knows that laws are made at each level of government—local, state, and federal. They are created, predominantly, via statutory enactments[2] passed by each government's legislative body (i.e., city council, county council, state legislature, Congress). Laws also derive from the rules and regulations of government regulatory bodies, such as the Occupational Safety and Health Administration or the Environmental Protection Agency. Laws are also embodied in constitutions, arguably the most important source of laws. Constitutions are important not only for the express laws they contain (and often these are few) but also for the guidelines they establish for the creation, content, and application of laws created by governing bodies. The federal constitution and the constitutions of the states contain stipulations about what can and cannot be done in a wide variety of areas, as well as other stipulations about how laws should and should not be applied.

It is in the application of laws where, once again, the subject of law gets complex. Though much time is expended at all levels of government in developing laws that are thought to be clear and precise, things may be less certain when it comes time to apply these same laws. For example, when a constitution says that "all men are created equal," is the word *men* being used in its narrow meaning of "all males" or in its generic meaning of "all human beings" (though not all believe that *males* can have such a meaning)? Or, when, in the 1890s, the Wyoming legislature discussed giving the vote to "ladies," rather than to "women," was it aware of the implied differences?

Or, by way of another type of example, some people argue that the original intent of affirmative action laws was to help pull people out of poverty by forcing open entry-level jobs previously closed. Yet the application of these laws has forced open the doors to board rooms, medical suites, and law offices as well. Is this outcome a lawful or unlawful extension of affirmative action? Other cases may simply raise questions as to whether the law under challenge is a good or bad law. Does it achieve what its sponsors wanted? Does it still work in present-day society? When these questions arise, and they occur, as noted before, at all levels of government, someone needs to evaluate the law in light of the specific concerns it raises. Ultimately, the diviners of good/bad, lawful/unlawful, clear/not clear are supreme courts.

Just as the federal government rests upon a constitution, so does each state. And for each state, as for the federal government, there is a supreme court (though not necessarily so titled). The constitution and supreme court of each state are the final arbiters of all legal matters that arise within the territorial confines of that state. Decisions made by a state supreme court are binding on *all* who operate within the confines of that state; the decisions of one state's supreme court are not, however, binding in other states or on other states' supreme courts. It is true that some supreme courts, in framing decisions, may look to precedents established by other states' courts, and subsequently even cite those decisions in their own, but there is absolutely no legal obligation to do so. The only supreme court whose rulings are binding on every state is the Supreme Court of the United States in Washington.

MARBURY V. MADISON

The United States Supreme Court (the Court) is the final appellate court for the entire country,[3] its rulings spelling out the laws for all citizens, not merely those of one particular jurisdiction. All Americans and all courts must abide by its dictates. As the final adjudicator in our land, it makes the definitive determination in two very important areas, which were set forth in the landmark case of *Marbury v. Madison* (1803).

The Court, in this case, established for itself two broad areas of authority. First, it said that it is the Court's responsibility to declare what the law means and, in so doing, to interpret the Constitution of the United States. Second, it said it is the Court's responsibility to determine which laws or acts are in conflict with the Constitution of the United States, or, to use the language of *Marbury*, to determine which laws or acts are "repugnant" to the Constitution and, therefore, must be declared null and void. Under the reasoning in *Marbury*, judicial interpretation of the Constitution and judicial review of the actions of other branches of government are the Court's responsibility.

In exercising this responsibility, however, the Court does not necessarily take up any and every legal question that arises anywhere in the United States. Rather, in carrying out this appellate function derived from *Marbury*, the Court hears only a select group of cases. To qualify for this elite group, a case must involve a federal question. In other words, a case must either challenge a federal law or allege that some practice or law violates a basic constitutional right.

Cases generally come to the Supreme Court in one of two ways (as will become apparent, subsequently, in reading the cases). When a state law or practice is challenged as violating a constitutional right, the case will travel through the state system first, beginning with a hearing in the lowest appropriate state court and continuing through to the state's highest court. A case appealed from a state supreme court goes directly to the U.S. Supreme Court, which does not, however, necessarily accept all cases brought on appeal. An appellant to the high court files a *petition for a writ of certiorari*, which puts forth the claim that the state system violated the appellant's constitutional rights. The petition is either accepted (which means that at least four justices agreed to hear the case) or denied. If the case is accepted, it is then put on the Court's docket to be heard at a later date; if the petition is denied, the state supreme court's decision stands.

There is, however, an alternative to a denied *writ*. Appellants can try a second path to the Supreme Court by going to a federal district court, the lowest court in the federal system. There they can either charge that the state violated a constitutional right or they can simply challenge the procedure used by the state. If this alternative avenue is followed, then the case may later, after a district court decision, be appealed to a federal circuit court of appeals. And after a hearing and decision there, one side or the other may be in the position to seek review by the Supreme Court.

When a federal law is challenged, the process is much more straightforward. The case usually begins in the federal district court, is appealed to the circuit court, and ends in the Supreme Court.

Regardless of the route a case takes to get to the Supreme Court, the process after arrival is the same. In hearing cases, the U.S. Supreme Court sits as a panel of all nine justices: the Chief Justice and eight associate justices.[4] When the Court accepts a case for review, the case comes surrounded with written material. Attorneys for both the plaintiffs and defendants always file fat briefs for the Court's information, and additional material may be submitted as well: transcripts of lower court decisions, briefs by other interested parties (*amici curiae*, or "friends of the court"), and so on. Usually, though not always, there is oral argument before the Court in which each side makes a formal statement and justices may question the presenter. No decision is rendered at the time the case is argued, however; that decision, made by simple majority vote, comes much later, after the justices have met privately and discussed and debated the case among themselves.

In reaching a decision, an unwritten rule suggests that the Court should decide a case on the narrowest issues possible, using the narrowest rule/law/interpretation possible. The Supreme Court is generally not out to be a path breaker, an attitude that continually reinforces the precedent of settling a case on the basis of the least controversial issue and in the least novel and controversial way that still is sure to address the claim. (This approach will become readily apparent in reading the Court's decisions.) An appellant's claim can be addressed either by reversing the lower court's decision, by affirming that decision, or by a combination that affirms some parts and reverses others. If the Court reverses all or part of the lower court's decision, the case is generally remanded to that court with instructions to reconsider the case and decide it anew in light of the Supreme Court's ruling. If the Court affirms, the decision of the lower court is binding.

The Court's decision—and, therefore, its position—is reflected in two ways: its vote (for example, eight in favor and one dissenting, or five in favor and four dissenting) and its written opinions.[5] The vote is, obviously, the key factor since it determines the outcome of the case and at the same time gives some indication of just how solidly the justices support that outcome. The closer the vote, the less agreement among the nine justices.

It is the opinion (or opinions) that truly reveals the underpinnings of the Court's position. The *majority opinion* sets forth the official thinking of the court; it constitutes the precedent for the future. Even the footnotes attached to the majority opinion have the weight of *holding*. As Lief Carter, a professor of law, noted, the majority opinion must "harmonize the legal, factual, and normative elements in the case,"[6] which is a difficult undertaking. The author of the majority opinion is selected from among those justices voting in the majority. If the Chief Justice is among that group, he assigns the task of writing the opinion to whomever he wishes (including himself); if he is not among the majority, the senior justice of the majority group either writes the opinion or assigns it to another.[7] Any justice who is in favor of the majority outcome but does not support the majority reasoning may write a *concurring opinion* in which s/he puts forth her/his own reasoning. Concurring opinions do not have the weight of precedent.

Justices not agreeing with the majority may also write opinions indicating the rationale for their dissent and critiquing the legal reasoning of the majority. These opinions often provide opponents of the majority decision with powerful arguments for subsequent use in court cases and legislative proceedings. Again, one justice may write the opinion for the group of dissenters, or each may write her/his own. *Dissenting opinions*, like concurring opinions, have no weight of precedent.

Finally, it is possible that a justice may concur in part and dissent in part. This may occur when a justice agrees with the majority in part of its decision but not all of it, or agrees with part of the rationale behind the decision but not all of it. Justices who find themselves in this position may opt to write their own opinions.

A problem may arise when there is a majority vote but no majority opinion. For example, eight of the nine justices may vote to void a law, but four have one line of reasoning for their vote and four have another. In such a case, there is no holding and what exactly is established as precedent becomes a matter of great debate. Such a situation occurred in the 1972 decision of *Furman v. Georgia* when, in a five-to-four decision, the judges declared the death penalty unconstitutional. Nine different opinions were written in that case, and the only point of majority agreement was that the death penalty constituted cruel and unusual punishment. Each of the five majority justices offered a different legal rationale for his decision.

THE WEIGHT OF OPINIONS

Far more than in the actual vote, it is in the opinions themselves—whether they are majority, dissenting, or concurring—that the Supreme Court exercises its sociological role and becomes the final arbiter of American values. The vote conveys limited information; the opinions tell all. The reasoning set forth in the opinions, especially in the majority or official court opinion, presents the justification for the vote and, in so doing, explicitly or implicitly identifies the elements that are important to Americans and American society.

Thus, when in 1961 the Court ruled that women should not be required to serve on juries (but that men should), the unanimous vote certainly told the country that women need not serve. The opinion, however, told us far more—that the court believed women need not serve because American society still thought that a woman's proper place was in the home tending children and husband, not in the courtrooms being exposed to the evils and ugliness of life. And when in 1991 the Court ruled that health clinics receiving federal monies could not inform pregnant women of the option of having an abortion, many learned something more. As a consequence of the rationale voiced in the majority opinion, they learned that American society was willing to endorse different treatment of rich and poor women and does not believe that women need to know all their options in order to make informed decisions.

The underlying value statements made by each of these Supreme Court opinions, as well as numerous others, must be viewed as so damaging to the chances of equality for women and so demeaning of their abilities and needs that they cannot afford to be overlooked by merely glancing at the Court's vote. There is no question that when the Court identifies what is repugnant to the Constitution and what is not, its decisions identify as well exactly what American society values and exactly what it does not. Thus, the decisions of the Supreme Court, in its all-important role of arbiter and reinforcer of societal values, must always be read at two levels—the explicit and the implicit. Only when these two levels are considered and examined can the true power of the Court be understood.

Although Supreme Court decisions are surely the ultimate voice on any given issue at any given time, there is seldom such a thing as a *final* decision for all time. Interpretation of the Constitution is a constantly evolving process, one that allows the law to reflect the changing needs of a changing society. The present conservative Supreme Court gives evidence of this process, with its reversal of defendant rights granted during the tenure of the Warren Court and in its present chipping away of the 1973 *Roe v. Wade* decision legalizing abortion. During the 1970s, the Court first declared the death penalty unconstitutional and then, a mere four years later, declared it constitutional. And although the Supreme Court normally practices *stare decisis* (allowing an earlier decision to stand) and is not in the habit of regularly reversing earlier Court decisions, it has done so in the past and will, no doubt, do so again in the future. As the late Justice William O. Douglas, a moving force on the Court for almost forty years, noted:

> The place of *stare decisis* in constitutional law . . . is tenuous. A judge looking at a constitutional decision may have compulsions to revere past history and accept what was once written. But he remembers above all else that it is the Constitution which he swore to support and defend, and not the gloss which his predecessors may have put on it. So he comes to formulate his own views, rejecting some earlier ones as false and embracing others. He cannot do otherwise unless he lets men long dead and unaware of the problems of the age in which he lives do his thinking for him.[8]

NOTES

1. Bissinger, H.G. & Daniel R. Biddle. January 27, 1986. "Defendants' Fates Sometimes Decided Out of the Public Eye." *The Philadelphia Inquirer*, A1.

2. Some jurisdictions still recognize common law; however, the federal government and the majority of states do not.

3. Although the U.S. Supreme Court is also a court of original jurisdiction, such cases make up only a small portion of its work load. The majority of Supreme Court time is spent exercising its appellate function.

4. On comparatively rare occasions, the Court may not sit with the full complement of nine justices. At times it may be necessary for a justice to disqualify her/himself for some legal (e.g., conflict of interest) or personal reason. Minimally, six justices must sit, with an obvious preference for the full complement of nine.

5. In a few cases, there is no written decision by the Supreme Court, only its vote.

6. Carter, Lief. 1985. *Contemporary Constitutional Lawmaking*. New York: Pergamon, pg. xvii.

7. The Chief Justice is referred to as "he" only because as of this writing the Chief Justice is and has been historically male.

8. Douglas, William O. 1949. *The Record of the Association of the Bar of the City of New York*, 4: 153-154.

3

Women and Men, Girls and Boys: Separate and Equal?

The law is a sort of hocus-pocus science.

Charles Macklin
Love à la mode

What often seems to appear in Supreme Court decisions, according to the few examples cited thus far, is an affirmation of long-held stereotypical notions of female and male. And, it could easily be argued, this attachment to stereotypical understandings leads to the continuation of sex discrimination on the part of the courts, society, family, friends. In order to understand that argument fully, however, or to be able to advance or counter its validity, one must first be aware of the content of those stereotypical images and their origins and consequences. In addition, one must understand just what constitutes sex discrimination. Thus,there are still some pivotal questions that should be answered before moving on to reading the actual Court decisions. They are these:

- What is sex discrimination?
- What is its origin?
- What are its consequences?
- Does equal treatment mean/necessitate the same treatment?

To aid in answering these questions, any number of readings could be used. Two are offered here, not as definitive sources of answers but rather as starting points for discussion.

UNDERSTANDING WHAT'S BENEATH THE PROCESS

The first reading is an excerpt from two chapters in *The Natural Superiority of Women* by Ashley Montagu,[1] one of this country's most respected anthropologists and the author and/or editor of several myth-debunking books. Montagu was one of the rare early and vocal male feminists of this century. He recognized early on what so many have yet to comprehend: the liberation of one sex is indeed the liberation of both. Montagu offers the following sage admonition:

The truth will make men free as well as women, for until women are freed from the myths that at present impede their progress, no man can be free or mentally completely healthy. The liberation of woman means the liberation of man.[2]

In the excerpt that follows, Montagu provides food for thought on both the origins and consequences of sex discrimination. Pay particular note to the last paragraph of chapter 2 and the repetition of that idea in the third chapter.

Ashley Montagu: Chapter 2: The Subjection of Women[3]

Why is it that in most of the cultures of which we have any knowledge, women are considered to be a sort of lower being, a creature human enough but not quite so human as the male; certainly not as wise, not as intelligent; and lacking in most of the capacities and abilities with which the male is so plentifully endowed?

How has it come about that women have occupied a position of subjection to men in almost all the cultures of which we have any knowledge?

Mankind is several million years old. So is womankind. Since we know practically nothing directly about the social life of our early ancestors, the following discussion must, to a large extent, be conjectural. But if, with all the necessary qualifications of caution, we were to judge from what we know of the social life of existing nonliterate (often miscalled "primitive peoples"), we should have to conclude that for the greater part of the several million years men have, on the whole, been dictatorial, unfair, and quite unkind to women. During their long period of subjection, women have been treated as chattels, slaves, housekeepers, economic advantages, and sexual conveniences; indeed, throughout a great part of the world they are still so treated.

How did this relationship between the sexes come about?

There are certain biological facts of pertinence here—I should say not the biological facts so much as the interpretations that have been given to them. Because women bear children and nurse them, they are forced to be much more sedentary than men.... Women stay at home to nurse and care for their children, to prepare food. Men leave the hearth for the hunt.

. . . let us consider the consequences of the different roles played by each of the sexes, roles arising from the fundamental biological sexual differences relating to reproduction, always remembering that we are discussing the roles of the sexes during the long phase of man's food gathering and hunting stage of development.

First, the female is rendered sedentary, even though before becoming a mother she may have been as mobile as any man or boy. Thus her experience becomes limited to her domestic duties, and she is confined to her home territory. She is the food-gatherer; her husband is the hunter. . . . Between caring for her children, food gathering, preparing meals, and performing other domestic activities, little time is left her for any other kind of experience.

The male, on the other hand, while he may be quite highly domesticated, is nevertheless called upon to exercise his ingenuity very much more frequently, and in a more varied manner, than the female. As a consequence of his hunting activities, he acquires a great deal of the kind of experience that almost never falls to the lot of the female. He learns to read tracks and signs of the presence of animals or men; . . . he learns a great deal about the habits and ways of animal and plant life, about the weather, and about the rocks and other materials from which his implements will be made, and numerous other details associated with a hunting economy. Because he is the hunter, he knows best what implements serve him most effectively in the hunt, and it is he who is the inventor and maker of hunting implements. . . . The general myth is that it is the male who provides most of the food in the food-gathering-hunting society, but the truth is that some 80 percent of it is provided by the female. The men hunt, women do not, for they are far too occupied with their domestic duties; and furthermore, in many cultures they are actively discouraged from engaging in activities considered the exclusive prerogative of males—just as males are excluded from engaging in activities considered the exclusive preserve of females.

We see, then, that the division of labor between the sexes has its origin in the biologically determined different functions of male and female. This does not mean that the male is biologically more active or that he is biologically designed to be a hunter; it *does* mean that these roles are the *social consequences* of the biologically determined reproductive differences between the sexes [emphasis in the original]. It is an error to assume that the female is by nature sedentary whereas the male is by nature active and mobile. . . .

The socially observed differences in activity between the sexes, it cannot be doubted, are to a large extent acquired rather than inherited. In short, these activity differences do not represent first nature, though they may become second nature. First nature is the biological equipment of potentialities with which one is born; second nature is what one's culture and society make of one, the habits one acquires.

. . . . The division of labor between the sexes represents a *cultural* expression of biological differences. The variety of cultural forms that this expression may take in different societies is enormous; what may be considered women's work in one may be deemed men's work in another. In some cultures men and women may engage in common activities that in other cultures are strictly separated along sexual lines. The important point to grasp is that the prescribed roles assigned to the sexes are not determined biologically but largely culturally. . . .

The biological differences between the sexes obviously provide the grounds upon which are based the different social roles the sexes are expected to play. But the significance of the biological differences is often interpreted in such a manner as to convey the appearance of a natural connection between conditions that are, in fact, only artificially connected, that is, by misinterpretation. For example, in almost all cultures pregnancy, birth, and nursing are interpreted by both sexes as handicapping experiences; as a consequence women have been made to feel that by virtue of their biological functions they have been biologically, naturally, placed in an inferior position to men. But as we today well know, these biological functions of women are only minimally, if at all, handicapping.

It is worth paying some attention to the significance of the fact that in the fundamental role in which one would have thought it all too obviously clear that women were the superiors of men, namely, in their ability to bear and bring up children, women have been made to feel that their roles are handicapping ones. . . . In almost all societies birth seems to have been culturally converted into a very much more complex, difficult, and handicapping process than it in fact is. In general it would seem that the more complex a society becomes, the more it tends to complicate the process of birth; one result of this is seen in the cultures of the Western world where women have been made to spend anything from ten days to three weeks in "confinement," as the reduction to helplessness so appropriately used to be called. With the advent of "natural childbirth," women are finding childbirth far from unpleasant and far from handicapping. . . .

Childbirth and nursing do introduce additional activities into the life of the female, but such activities do not necessarily constitute disadvantages. In comparison with certain forms of masculine mobility, and under certain social conditions, such activities *may* be disadvantages, and it would be wrong to underestimate them. It would, however, be equally wrong to overestimate such disadvantages; yet this has been done, and I believe the evidence strongly indicates that it has been deliberately, if to some extent unconsciously, done. If one can turn childbirth into a handicapping function, then that makes women so much more inferior to the sex that suffers from no such handicap. Persons who resort to such devices are usually concerned not so much with the inferiorities of others as with their own superiority. If one happens to be lacking in certain capacities with which the opposite sex is naturally endowed, and those capacities happen to be highly, if unacknowledgedly, valued, then one can compensate for one's own deficiency by devaluing the capacities of others. By turning capacities into handicaps, not only can one make their possessors feel inferior, but anyone lacking such capacities can then feel superior for [the] very lack of them.

Ludicrous as the idea may appear to some, the fact is that men have been jealous of women's ability to give birth to children, and they have even envied their ability to menstruate; but men have not been content with turning these capacities into disabilities, for they have surrounded the one with handicapping rituals and the other with taboos that in most cases amount to punishments. . . .

The very terms we use when we speak of male and female roles in reproduction, . . . make women subservient addenda to men and reflect the ignorance and prejudice that have characterized the dominant male attitudes regarding the female. The male "fertilizes," "fecundates," or "impregnates" the female. The truth, however, is quite otherwise. The process of reproduction is not one-sided; its antecedent condition is the fusion of two cells, the female ovum and the male sperm. It is not that an ovum is rendered fertile by the sperm but that ovum and sperm together contribute to the initiation of those further processes that result in the development of the conceptus. . . .

Man's jealousy of women's capacity to bear children is nowhere better exhibited than in the Old Testament creation story in which man is caused to give birth (from one of his ribs) to women:

> And the rib, which the Lord God had taken from man, made he a woman, and brought her unto the man.

> And Adam said, This is now bone of my bones, and flesh of my flesh: she shall be called Woman, because she was taken out of Man (*Genesis*, 2).

We begin to see, then, how it may have come about that childbirth as well as menstruation were converted from perfectly healthy natural phenomena into a handicap and a "curse." Men project their unconscious wishes upon the screen of their society and make their institutions and their gods in the image of their desires. Their envy of woman's physiological powers causes them to feel weak and inferior, and fear is often added to jealousy. An effective way for men to protect themselves against women, as well as to punish them, is to depreciate their capacities by depreciating their status. One can deny the virtues of women's advantages by treating them as disadvantages and by investing them with mysterious or dangerous properties. By making women objects of fear and something to be avoided as unclean, one can lower the cultural status of women by simple inversion. Their biological advantages are demoted to the status of cultural disadvantages, and as cultural disadvantages they are then converted into biological disadvantages. Once this is achieved, there need be no end to the belief in the cultural and biological disadvantages of these traits.

It is not here being suggested that this sort of thinking occurs, except occasionally, on the conscious level; the suggestion is that it does occur on the unconscious level, a suggestion for which there is a very great deal of evidence, mainly of an anthropological and psychoanalytic nature, of the kind that has already been mentioned. . . .

Owing to the enlarging experiences that fall to the male in consequence of his roles as the hunter and maker of implements, he develops certain highly valued traits and skills. These are a broad experience and varied knowledge of an environment larger than that which the female experiences, the increase in knowledge which such experience brings, and the ability to make things that the female is not called upon to make, especially hunting implements. It will readily be seen that such traits immediately give their possessor an advantage over their non-possessor. It will also be readily understood why it is that men, under such conditions, consider women their inferiors and themselves incomparably more important, for while it is woman's work to concern herself with the preservation of the individual, men are concerned with no less than the perpetuation of the race. Were it not for the basic support that men provide for the family (so they consider), the race would die out. Even though this is, and always has been, a highly questionable proposition, such, nevertheless, has always been the opinion of the "head of the family." It is an open question whether the real holder-together and support of the family in the psychological, if not entirely in the material sense, has not always been the wife and mother. However that may be, he who pays the piper calls the tune, and the head of the family has always demanded the respect due to a superior person, and it has been given him—but always at the cost of making all other members of his family feel inferior. And, indeed, by comparison everyone else in the family *was* inferior, for the wife possessed no such skills as her husband, nor was she anywhere nearly as knowledgeable about so many of the things her husband had experienced; furthermore, he was bigger and stronger than she. The children, of course, were even more inferior to their father than was their mother, and they would naturally grow up having no doubt of the mother's inferiority to their father.

Thus everyone, including Mother, would be convinced that Father was a superior person and that Mother was at best a mere second-rater. Everyone drew the erroneous conclusion from the cultural facts that these differences of superiority and inferiority were biologically determined; women, it was assumed, were naturally inferior to men, and that was that. And, in reality, to the present day, women have remained inferior to men practically everywhere in the world for much the same reasons that they were, from the earliest times, first discovered to be inferior: *They were practically never given equal opportunities with men to develop their capacities; the opportunities for the development of their intelligence and tribal skills were severely restricted by what was traditionally considered permissible to women; they were prejudged rather than fairly judged; and they were condemned to a servitude from which they could never emerge unless granted the opportunity to do so* [emphasis in the original].

. . . At any rate, where the sexes are concerned, the factors of size and power, added to other prerogatives and statuses, put the male decidedly in the position of dominance. Women have been so long conditioned in the environment of masculine dominance that they have come to expect the male to be dominant and the female subservient. The psychologic subservience of the female has assumed innumerable ramifications in almost all human societies and constitutes yet another illustration of the effects of the cultural differentiation of the sexes. . . .

. . . there is a remarkable parallel between the phenomena of race prejudice and the prejudice against women. This is nicely illustrated by an editorial comment on a woman's suffrage meeting held in Syracuse, New York. The editorial appeared in the New York *Herald*, in the issue of 12 September 1852, and was probably written by the elder Bennett. Among other things, the editorial said:

> How did women first become subject to man, as she now is all over the world? By her nature, her sex, just as the negro is and always will be to the end of time, inferior to the white race and, therefore, doomed to subjection; but she is happier than she would be in any other condition, just because it is the law of her nature. . . .

How often do men mistake their prejudices for the laws of nature! . . .

When men understand that the best way to solve their own problem is to help women solve those that men have created for women, they will have taken one of the first significant steps toward its solution. And what is woman's greatest problem? Man. For man has created and maintained her principal difficulties, and until man solves his own difficulties there can be no wholly satisfactory solution of woman's. . . .

Chapter 3: Biological Facts and Social Consequences

. . . The long training of men in securing obedience through the use of force is almost certainly related to the ease with which men fall back upon this means of compelling attention and securing obedience.

I am not writing an indictment of man. I am writing part of the story of man trying to be human. Men have been confused and scared for a long time, and like most scared and confused creatures conscious of their physical superiority to the opposite sex or to members of their own sex they are likely to take on something of the character of the bully. . . .

Because, by virtue of his greater physical power, man has been able to determine the fate and development of woman, men and women have come to assume that it was natural for men to do so, and both have come to mistake their prejudices for the laws of nature. That men may bully women into a position of subservience is not a biological fact but a cultural one, a cultural misuse of a biological condition. This is a very different thing from saying that women are biologically determined to occupy a subservient relation to the male and that the male is biologically determined to keep the female in such a subservient position. Female subservience is a culturally, *not* a biologically, produced condition. It is one of the consequences of the misuse of masculine power.

At this juncture it may be useful to [look at] some of the presumed social consequences of the biological differences between the sexes, thereby enabling us to perceive ... some of the biological pegs upon which men have hung the cultural disabilities of women. . . .

I am not the first to suggest, and I am sure I shall not be the last, that the male's drive in work and achievement may actually be the consequences of his recognition of his biological inferiority with respect to the female's creative capacity to conceive and create human beings. One of the ways in which the male may compensate for this biological inferiority is by work and by achievement. By keeping the means of making a livelihood almost exclusively a masculine prerogative, men have unconsciously, as well as consciously, been able to satisfy themselves that they are by nature the "breadwinners," the pillars of society, and the guarantors of the race. Hence, the great opposition to women when they begin to enter into "competition" with men in earning a living. Married men, in particular, frequently object to their wives' working; they consider it, somehow, a reflection upon themselves. They fear it will be said that they are unable to support their family. "My wife doesn't have to work. Why should she?" The arguments will be familiar to the reader, whether married or not.

Let men honestly ask themselves why they object to women working, particularly their wives, even though they may be largely free of those domestic duties that would otherwise keep them at home. Some quite illuminating answers might begin to break through the barrier of the unconscious. A wife, or almost any woman, working for a living, particularly in a field considered the special preserve of the male, is held by many males to constitute a challenge to their masculinity. When the question comes up of the employment of a woman in some position that has hitherto been filled by a male, masculine reactions are often very revealing. The violence of the emotion and the irrational behavior that many males have exhibited, and many still continue to exhibit on such occasions, indicate how profoundly they are disturbed by the idea of women working outside the home.

The male, in all societies, is at greater risk than the female. As Ritchie has pointed out, "The female, as she grows older and develops, has before her in more or less continuous relationship, the model of her mother. The male, as he grows through life, begins his life also in primary relationship to a maternal object but he has to give it up, he has to leave off identification with the mother, he has to take on the full male role. Males have to switch identification during development, and all sorts of things can go wrong in this." And, unfortunately, they frequently do. The male has a much more difficult time than the female in growing up and separating himself from the loving mother and in identifying himself with a father with whom he is nowhere nearly as deeply involved as he remains with the mother. This often puts a strain upon him. The switch in identification he is called upon to make results in something of a conflict. This he usually seeks to resolve by, in part, rejecting the mother and relegating her to a status inferior to that into which he has, so to speak, been thrust.

Masculine antifeminism can be regarded as a reaction-formation designed to oppose the strong unconscious trend towards mother-worship. . . .

Marriage, that "ghastly public confession of a strictly private intention," as some Victorian once put it, used to be the one institution by means of which the female could be securely kept in her place. Men used to be able to work and to create without feeling challenged by their own wives. Wives used to stay at home, have babies, and look after them and the "breadwinner" too. God was in his Heaven and all was right with the world.

. . . Men have resisted the "intrusion" of women into their workday world to the last ditch, and many are still doing it. Why? May it not be that such men feel that the working woman constitutes a threat to their belief in themselves as the pillars of society? to the foundations upon which society rests, the "creators" of civilization? May it not be that men don't want their fears and insecurities about women disturbed? . . .

The origin of the English word "woman" indicates that the female's very right to social existence was determined in the light of her secondary relationship to the male, for the word was originally "wifman," that is, "wife-man," the wife of the man; in the fourteenth century the *f* was dropped and the word became "wiman," and later on "woman." Men unconsciously have desired to keep women in a secondary position, and all the rationalizations they have offered for keeping her there have avoided the statement of their motivation, because in most cases they have not consciously been aware of the nature of that motivation. Men must work and women must spin, because if women stop spinning and start working, man's claim to "creativity" and indispensability as breadwinner is undermined—and this he must resist.

Some motivations seem to be even clearer with respect to achievement or creativity proper. If men cannot conceive, become pregnant, and bear a child, they can conceive great ideas and great works, gestate them, and be delivered of them in the form of all the things that make up our complex civilization: art, science, philosophy, music, machinery, bridges, dams, automobiles, kitchen gadgetry, and the million and one things men create and women buy. How often have we heard men exclaim, "That's my baby," when they have been referring to some product of their creation, whether it be an idea or an object? True enough, it is a way of speaking and may represent merely an analogical expression. Perhaps, and perhaps not. "These are the children of my brain," is another such expression. "I want to nurse this idea," is yet another. And there are many more. Why, it may be asked, should men use such expressions when in practically every other instance they use purely masculine phraseology and take great pains to avoid anything suggestive of the feminine? To be "pregnant with ideas," to be "delivered of a great idea," to "give birth to a plan"—may not these and other obstetrical expressions possibly indicate, when used by males, an unconscious desire to imitate the biological creativity of the female? The conversion process takes the form: "Well, if I can't create and give birth to biological babies, I can, at least, create and give birth to their social equivalents." Man's drive to achievement can, at least in part, be interpreted as an unconsciously motivated attempt to compensate for the lack of biological creativity. Witness how men have used their creativeness in the arts, sciences, and technologies as proof of their own superiority and the inferiority of women!

The fact is that men have had far greater opportunities for this kind of cultural creativity than women, and in this respect they have had a far more profoundly motivated drive to achieve than women. The evidence strongly suggests that were women motivated by as strong drives to achieve as men, and afforded equal opportunities to do so, they would at least be every bit as successful as men. Because women are for some time yet likely to remain, on the whole, less strongly motivated than men, I think it probable that men will continue to show a higher frequency of achievement, *not* because they are naturally superior but because their opportunities will remain greater, and because, among other things, they are overcompensating for a natural incapacity—the incapacity to bear babies.

The second excerpt comes from Letty Cottin Pogrebin's book *Growing Up Free: Raising Your Child in the 80s*.[4] Pogrebin, one of the early editors of the original *Ms* magazine, talks of the process of learning the stereotypes for both females and males, as well as some of the consequences of such stereotypes. In so doing, she takes a different course to address Montagu's concern with the ramifications of "psychologic subservience" and his recognition that sexism harms both sexes.

Letty Cottin Pogrebin: Girls and Boys: What's the Difference?

How can one dismiss the two distinct sexual essences that are distilled in every school of human thought: anthropology's hunter and childbearer, philosophy's masculine and feminine principles, religion's Man and Helpmeet, psychology's Oedipus Complex and Penis Envy, not to mention such age-old sexual dichotomies as carnal/spiritual, Science/Mysticism, and Yin/Yang?

And what about the polarities that inspire art and passion? Soft/strong in the poet's sonnet, light/dark in the painter's portrait, subject/object in the lover's pursuit—each seems to borrow its aesthetic tension from the original attracting "opposites," male and female.

Whether or not such expressions are the cause or the effect of sex differences, do we really want to live without them? Maybe the French are right: *Vive la difference*. So why not leave well enough alone?

Because it isn't well enough or good enough. In fact, the cult of sex differences hurts both sexes. It creates a gender caste system with reasoning that leaps from

the two sexes are different,
to
the two sexes are opposites,
to
one sex is better than the other.

Differences and "opposites" seem to cry out for hierarchical evaluation, which is where the trouble starts. When Dr. Samuel Johnson was asked who is more intelligent, men or women, he replied, "Which man and which woman?" But that respect for human individuality has been rare through the centuries. Most people find it easier to generalize, to earmark group traits and make sure everyone acts accordingly.

By instructing a child to *act* like a girl or *act* like a boy, the cult of sex differences says, "Conform," "Pretend," "Act"; it does not say "Be your best self." It makes children imposters within their own sex and strangers to their "opposites." It decrees a half-life for a girl and a half-life for a boy. In short, the cult of sex differences cheats children. . . .

Here come the "buts". . . .

"But how will my son know he's a boy unless he learns all the ways he's different from a girl?" And vice versa.

"But my daughter might turn out masculine if we don't teach her to be feminine." And vice versa.

In a society that favors either/or simplifications, such concerns make sense. But stop and think for a moment and they become suspect: Why do sex differences alone inspire such paranoia? Parents show absolutely no concern about teaching children about everything *else* they're different from. No one asks, "How will my son know he's different from a dog, or my daughter know she's a person, not a houseplant?" No one worries that without intervention children might think they are chairs.

Such rudimentary lessons in identity are considered unnecessary because humanness is perceived to be a "felt reality." Obvious. Basic. Certain. After humanness, being female or male is the most salient fact in every person's who-am-i or what-am-i profile.

If adults were not so hypertense about "femininity" and "masculinity," the same knowingness, the same "felt reality" that is taken for granted about one's human identity would develop in connection with one's gender identity. Since the anatomical, biological, and physical sex differences are among the most visually obvious human characteristics, gender is one of the earliest concepts children understand. By the time they can talk, they know girls from boys as surely as they know humans from dogs, chairs, and houseplants.

A child learns that she is a girl or he is a boy sometime between eighteen months and three years of age, a period considered critical for the establishment of gender identification. During these months, children learn their gender label by hearing the word girl or boy applied to themselves over and over again. ("What a good boy you are!" "That's my brave little girl." And so on.) At the same time they learn to generalize sex labels by organizing information they see and hear about other people. ("He's a nice man." "She's a friendly woman." "Look, that boy is running after that girl!") We may not know exactly how children organize all this information but we do know how the sequence progresses.

By interviewing thousands of children—asking such questions as "Is this a girl doll or a boy doll?" "Are you a boy or a girl?" "Is this a picture of a woman or a man?"—developmentalists have been able to trace the stages of gender comprehension.

At twenty-four months, many children were not quite sure of their own gender but could identify the women and men even if the pictured females had short hair or wore trousers. By age three, almost all children were aware of their own sex as well as other people's.

In the three-year old's mind, however, gender identity is still subject to a childhood phenomenon known as "magical thinking," the belief that under certain conditions, things can turn into other things on whim; for example, a cat could become a dog if its whiskers were cut off.

Ask a three- or four-year old girl, "Could you turn into a boy if you wore a boy-style haircut or boy's clothing?" and she will nod confidently. By age five she may equivocate; sometimes gender is stable, other times not. But ask her at age six and she'll think you've lost your mind.

Once the concept of "gender constancy" is absorbed, the healthy child knows that each person's sex is unchanging; the girl knows that she was a girl when she was a baby, will remain a girl no matter what she wears or does or plays with, will become a woman, not a man, when she grows up, and a mother, not a father, if she has a child. This knowledge becomes a "felt reality" to children at about the same time that their minds make the link between genital differences and the girl-boy labels that go with them.

Once *core gender identity* has been established, it is "probably the most entrenched, unchangeable psychic structure in the human psyche." *So invincible are feelings of boyness or girlness after the critical period that if a child with male genitals somehow believes himself to be a girl* (parental and medical ignorance or ambiguous infant genitals have created such error in sex assignment), *it is easier to surgically change his body to match his belief than to try to psychologically change his gender identity to match his body*. (And the same is true for incorrectly assigned girls.)

With normal children under normal circumstances, once core gender identity is established, there is no reason why children should not spend the rest of their lives exploring the infinite variations of their who-am-I profiles. In a nonsexist society, that open vista would stretch out before us all. But in our present culture, the facts of biological and physical sex differences and the "felt reality" of gender identity are overlaid with layers and layers of irrelevant sex-linked rules.

It is not enough today to *be* a girl or *be* a boy; one must *play the part* of a girl or boy. Society reintroduces "magical thinking" in a new guise: Watch out, child; the haircut may not change her into a boy but it can make her *masculine*. The whiskers don't make the tomcat male, but without them he might turn *feminine*. Watch Out.

How sex differences can be touted as "natural" . . . and at the same time must be hammered into us, is one of sexism's craziest contradictions. Nevertheless, the hammering is accomplished by a catechism of sex role rules and regulations expressed in absolutes and extremes and embodied in the sex role stereotype.

Literally, a stereotype is a printing block from which pages of type can be duplicated. The essential "permanence and unchangeableness" of these blocks are the features that have come to symbolize rigidity and regularity.

Stereotypes oversimplify human complexity. They bang people into shape with a cultural sledgehammer that flattens the wonder of individuals into monotonous group characteristics.

Stereotypes assert themselves through caricature, name-calling, and idolatry: "Poles are dumb," "Children are destructive," "Blacks are lazy." All stereotypes are "a substitute for intimacy"—and sex stereotypes, in particular, are a *barrier* to intimacy. One doesn't describe a friend or lover in lumpish generalizations. . . .

Because stereotypes are by definition extravagant overstatements blunt enough to be understood by children, they are also blunt enough to advertise their intent. What sex role stereotypes tell children and the rest of us is this:

Boys Are Better.
Girls Are Meant to Be Mothers.

These two messages—male supremacy and compulsory motherhood—are the raw essentials of a patriarchal system. In order for the system to perpetuate itself, children must be trained to play their proper roles and to believe the system natural and just.

Male supremacy—the paradigm for white supremacy or any oppressive form of hierarchy—begins at home. Big Daddy is in charge in the family, and some men are expected to be in charge of other men (and all women) in the corporations, universities, governments, and playing fields of the nation. Boys, therefore, must be trained to become men who can exercise their rightful power and believe themselves worthy of it. Girls must be trained to admire and depend upon the men who exercise power, and to believe themselves unworthy of controlling their own or others' destinies.

Because male power is to be spread across all of public life, boys must be motivated to produce in all arenas—business, policy, art, academia, everywhere. Not only are the females to stay out of the action in those arenas, but they are themselves to be incentives that motivate males to strive for power, the sexual and ornamental rewards that the male controls and sometimes marries. As a wife, "his woman" further rewards him with offspring (she "gave" him a son) to carry on his name, the continuity of the patriarchal line, and to provide the larger patriarchal system with workers, soldiers, and more mothers. (History shows that in wartime and during periods of decreasing population and underemployment, motherhood has been vigorously promoted and abortion and contraception are more likely to be made illegal.)

For this gender arrangement to come into being, girls must learn to see themselves as sexual entities after puberty and be motivated to be mothers after marriage. Only when she is under male control (married) can a woman be exalted in motherhood (unwed mothers are not) and her child be officially recognized ("illegitimate" babies are not). A girl must be so well trained that she relinquishes the desire to *produce*—business, policy, art, and so on—in favor of *reproducing*. When she succumbs to the definition of her optimum self as Mother legitimatized by marriage, she locks male supremacy into place.

As Simone de Beauvoir has said, woman's "creation results only in repeating the same Life in more individuals," whereas man "remodels the face of the earth, he creates instruments, he invents, he shapes the future." Man transcends. Woman repeats. Or, as I have chosen to formulate it for purposes of this discussion: *Boys Are Better. Girls Are Meant to Be Mothers.* That's how children see it.

Thus, vastly oversimplified, we have the intent of sex stereotypes and the hidden agenda of sex roles. The name of the game is power and one's relationship to it: Someone wins because someone else loses. All the players learn the rules in childhood. The objective of the game for boys is to grow up to be President. The objective of the game for girls is to grow up to have a baby. For him, the one and only pinnacle position; for her, a destiny available to every female of every species on the face of the earth.

There is nothing wrong with the stereotype of the attractive young woman who becomes a mother—other than the fact that she is the *only* woman a girl is supposed to become.

There is nothing wrong with the fearless leader stereotype either, except that since it cannot be fulfilled by 99,999 out of 100,000 males, it dooms most boys and men to a deep sense of "masculine" failure, which must then be relieved by reaffirmation of the one manageable component of the male stereotype: superiority over women.

Whoever he is and however he performs, at least he can feel strong if she is weak. Her "femininity" and his "masculinity" have been made such a seesaw of opposites that if she refuses to be powerless she "emasculates" him. His sex role and his phallic potency rise and fall in unison. If she agrees to be powerless, his "masculinity" rises and from his full height on the seesaw, he looks down and proclaims her "a real woman."

This dynamic springs from the original fallacy:

The two sexes are different;
the two sexes are opposites;
one sex is better than the other.

Making sure that boys know they are better and that girls accept lesser status and eventual reproductive duty is the basic agenda of patriarchy and the conscious or unconscious foundation of sex role learning.

FEMALE AND MALE STEREOTYPES

Pogrebin points out some of the assumptions underlying the standard female and male stereotypes that abound in all segments of society. And although these assumptions and images do not necessarily differ from the myths and stereotypes relied upon by the sex-caste system of the legal arena, it is important to see specifically how the legal arena transforms those fictitious notions for its own end. Pointing them out now will make them easier to spot in subsequent readings.

Although the following is not an all-inclusive listing, the most common stereotypes and their immediate consequences are:

- The female's role in life is that of wife and mother and there are no others. The implication is that these roles are so important that she should do nothing that would infringe upon them.
- Related to this is the idea that the female must be encapsulated within the home if, in fact, she is to carry out her dual role of wife and mother. As Talcott Parsons, an eminent American sociologist, explains it, she is the expressive (i.e., emotional, nurturing, etc.) end of the axis, concerned only with the intrafamilial operations while the male is the instrumental end negotiating (for the family) with the outside world.[5] She is the internal caregiver who provides care by emotional—not monetary— support and runs the household, not the world. The implication is that she need not be concerned with or involved in extrafamilial affairs.
- Again, related to this but producing a different set of consequences is the idea that women are biological captives. (This is related because, after all, it is her biology that creates her role as mother.) According to this stereotype, women are gripped by biological forces beyond their control; they are not in control of themselves. The clear implication is that women are not be to trusted because they are irresponsible, emotional, and so on.
- Flowering from these concepts blooms the notion of her inferiority, an inferiority based on many components: her delicacy, passivity, innocence and naivete, timidity. Those who hold this notion cite as evidence her supposed fear of the outside world. Recall Montagu's hunters who learn the geography of their region in order to survive and thereby make the unknown the known; for the females, the geography remains the unknown. The implications here, of course, are that woman needs protection and guidance.
- And, finally, the stereotypes depict females as impulsive and nonanalytic, acting intuitively, illogically, nonrationally, and so on. The implications here are similar to those above: females are untrustworthy, in need of guidance, and so forth.

None of these stereotypes is unique to the legal arena; their relevance to the law is that these images have very real and important consequences when relied upon as the basis for legal pronouncements. It is, therefore, important to scrutinize just how these images appear and are used in Supreme Court decisions.

Two of the four questions raised at the beginning of this section—what are the origins and consequences of sex discrimination—have been addressed. Two—what is sex discrimination and whether equal means same—have been left hanging, but intentionally so. Interrelated, these as yet unanswered questions provoke answers that may be harder to pin down, answers that may change as more knowledge is gained. These are pervading questions that deserve to be asked and answered constantly until definitive answers are achieved.

One final point needs to be raised. Although sex discrimination affects men and women at a very individual and personal level, it is not solely an individual phenomenon but also a *social* phenomenon. Sex discrimination affects society. Because of its blanket effect, it is important to look at the consequences of sex discrimination for *all* of society, not simply the consequences for one individual or a handful of individuals. This perception of discrimination is often misunderstood, leading to a general emphasis on the consequences of sex discrimination at the individual level and a false distinction between "good" and "bad" discrimination. Some discrimination, such as affirmative action, may help a group or individuals achieve some advantage and therefore is theoretically considered "good"; some discrimination, such as excluding classes of people from getting certain jobs, holds back individuals or groups and therefore is theoretically considered "bad."

This seems to be spurious reasoning. May it not be true that even discrimination that ends up benefiting a person or group—and, therefore, could be called "good"—is, in fact, bad, since it perpetuates stereotypical attitudes and treats people as members of a class rather than as individuals? Moreover, may it not be true that all discrimination, regardless of its consequences for individuals, is bad for society? Lawyer David Cole, in an article looking at the effects of gender perspectives—male definitions of right and wrong, male-made laws, male judges, and so forth—on outcomes in sex discrimination cases rightly questions the validity of the notion of "benign" discrimination. He says:

> "Benign" discrimination refers to discrimination against women that is motivated, at least superficially, not by animus but by paternalistic protectionism. In the typical example, women are relieved of a duty, barred from a profession, or afforded a benefit on the presumption that women need protection. The very term "benign" discrimination is an oxymoron that reflects a radical difference in gender perspectives. Men see it as "benign"; women feel it as discrimination.[6]

Is there really such a thing as "good" discrimination? Perhaps the answer depends upon how one answers the two questions of what is sex discrimination and whether *equal* means *same*. If discrimination is simply a matter of differentiation and discernment, then perhaps there might be good and bad discrimination. But if discrimination takes on the role of elevating one individual or group at the cost of lowering another, then all discrimination is bad, none good, for, as Montagu points out:

> The truly superior person doesn't need to lord it over anyone; it is only the inferior person who, in order to feel that he is superior, must have someone to look down on. The genuinely superior person looks neither up nor down; he looks straight at you.[7]

NOTES

1. Montagu, Ashley. 1952. *The Natural Superiority of Women*. New York: Collier, 1974, 3rd edition.

2. *Ibid.*, pg. 10.

3. Montagu, pp. 11-44 (footnotes excluded).

4. Pogrebin, Letty Cottin. 1980. *Growing Up Free: Raising Your Child in the 80s*. New York: McGraw-Hill, pp. 8-9, 30-33, 40-42 (footnotes excluded).

5. Parsons, Talcott. 1964. *Social Structure and Personality*. New York: Free Press.

6. Cole, David. 1984. Strategies of Difference: Litigating for Women's Rights in a Man's World. *Law and Inequality*, 2(33):33-96, pg. 38, footnote 12.

7. Montagu, pg. 10.

4

No Women Allowed: The Early History

In view of the Constitution, in the eyes of the law, there is in this country no superior, dominant, ruling class of citizens. There is no caste here. Our Constitution is color blind. In respect of civil rights, all citizens are equal before the law. The humblest is the peer of the most powerful.

Supreme Court Justice John Marshall Harlan
dissenting opinion, *Plessy v. Ferguson*, 1896

ORIGINAL INTENT: THE DECLARATION OF INDEPENDENCE AND CONSTITUTION SAY NO WOMEN ALLOWED

At some early stage in our lives, most, if not all, of us—either in school or by osmosis—learn the preamble to the Constitution of the United States. This is the document that established what we, as a country, were, are, and should be. It is the document that, in essence, sets the tone for the country.

The preamble to this august document begins as follows: "We the People of the United States, in Order to form a more perfect Union, . . ." Most of us, unless we had been exposed to some more critical thinkers, were led to believe that "we" meant "all": all colors, all religions, all sexes, and so on. And, the same, of course, must be said about the Declaration of Independence, the document that incorporated into our legacy the notion that all men are created equal and are endowed with certain inalienable rights. We learn this declaration in our early school years. We understand it as our statement of divorce from an unfair and unjust ruler, while simultaneously charting the course for our new country. We are led to believe that its reference to "men" was generic, rather than sex specific—that it encompassed all the colonists, women as well as men.

Unfortunately, however, many of us learn later in life—when we experience sneers and discrimination—that the "we" of the Constitution's "we the people" and the "all men" of the Declaration of Independence in no way included everyone. "We" and "all men" in fact meant "some," and women were those left out. This exclusion, moreover, does not appear to be an oversight but rather a deliberate and calculated decision.

In fairness to our forebears, however (this is not offered as excuse, but simply as historical background and fact), they were merely following automatically a mode of thinking based on centuries of similar thinking and practice. (Here, it is hoped, the explanation cum excuse of "that's the way things have always been done" will be recognized as an easy but far from legitimate line of reasoning.) With the introduction of feudalism in the thirteenth century, and the fief's replacement of the family as the important legal and economic unit, women were no longer valued for their economic productivity. Instead, with this loss of status, women became valued solely for their procreative abilities—namely the ability, as wives, to produce legitimate heirs, thereby enhancing men's status, since a man's status was directly proportionate to his property and number of heirs. As part of this valuation process that established a woman's worth only as a wife and mother, laws were passed defining single women as "surplus labor." These laws were accompanied by additional legislation setting women's wages lower than those of males. Even when such laws were not on the books, it became practice to pay women lower wages. Thus, women were either forced to exist at a marginal level of subsistence or to engage in one of the three traditional arenas for single women to enter: domestic service, prostitution (as the sole or supplemental source of income), or marriage. (The composition of this triad should not go unappreciated.)

This was the legacy from our Anglo-Saxon forebears, whose society—and legal system—served as the model for the social and legal structure of our country. Since the terms derive from a heritage that included a statement by the leading eighteenth century jurist, Sir William Blackstone, that husband and wife were one and that one was the husband, it should not be surprising to learn that the "we" and "all" do <u>not</u>, in fact, mean "everyone." The surprise is that anyone with a knowledge of history might think otherwise.[1] In so much of the historical evidence of the pre- and post-Revolutionary periods, the intent of the founding men[2] to exclude women seems clear. Even Thomas Jefferson, until fairly recently thought by so many to be a strong champion of fairness and justice, was explicit in his intention to exclude women from government and from the protections such government might provide. When queried as to whether the word *men* was being used in an inclusive sense, thereby incorporating women as well, Jefferson noted the following: "Were our state a pure democracy, there would still be excluded from our deliberations. . . women, who, to prevent depravation of morals and ambiguity of issues, should not mix promiscuously in gatherings of men."[3]

THE ADAMS LETTERS

Where this intentional omission of women is best evidenced is in the exchange of letters among Abigail and John Adams (soon to be the second president of the country) and a few of their friends. John was away from home over a number of years, drafting the Declaration of Independence; Abigail was at home managing family life and affairs. Their letters make clear the prevailing gender stereotypes of the time. But even more important, if any doubts linger as to whether the omission of women was one of oversight or intent, John's bemused, if not in fact condescending, dismissal of Abigail's plea for consideration of "the ladies" should wipe them out.

Abigail and John Adams: Remember the Ladies[4]

Abigail Adams to Isaac Smith, Jr.
Braintree April the 20 1771

Dear Sir

I write you, not from the Noisy Buisy Town, but from my humble Cottage in Braintree, where I arrived last Saturday and here again am to take up my abode.

"Where Contemplation p[l]umes her rufled Wings
And the free Soul look's down to pitty Kings."

Suffer me to snatch you a few moments from all the Hurry and tumult of London and in immagination place you by me that I may ask you ten thousand Questions, and bear with me Sir, tis the only recompence you can make for the loss of your Company.

From my Infancy I have always felt a great inclination to visit the Mother Country as tis call'd and had nature formed me of the other Sex, I should certainly have been a rover. And altho this desire has greatly diminished owing partly I believe to maturer years, but more to the unnatural treatment which this our poor America has received from her, I yet retain a curiosity to know what ever is valuable in her. I thank you Sir for the particular account you have already favourd me with, but you always took pleasure in being communicatively good.

Women you know Sir are considered as Domestick Beings, and altho they inherit an Eaqual Share of curiosity with the other Sex, yet but few are hardy eno' to venture abroad, and explore the amaizing variety of distant Lands. The Natural tenderness and Delicacy of our Constitutions, added to the many Dangers we are subject too from your Sex, renders it almost imposible for a Single Lady to travel without injury to her character. And those who have a protecter in an Husband, have generally speaking obstacles sufficent to prevent their Roving, and instead of visiting other Countries; are obliged to content themselves with seeing but a very small part of their own. To your Sex we are most of us indebted for all the knowledg we acquire of Distant lands. As to a Knowledg of Humane Nature, I believe it may as easily be obtained in this Country, as in England, France or Spain. Education alone I conceive Constitutes the difference in Manners. Tis natural I believe that every person to have a partiality for their own Country. Dont you think this little Spot of ours better calculated for happiness than any other you have yet seen or read of. Would you exchange it for England, France, Spain or Ittally? Are not the people here more upon an Eaquality in point of knowledg and of circumstances—there being none so immensly rich as to Lord it over us, neither any so abjectly poor as to suffer for the necessaries of life provided they will use the means. . . .

Abigail Adams to John Adams
Braintree March 31 1776

—I long to hear that you have declared an independancy—and by the way in the new Code of Laws which I suppose it will be necessary for you to make I desire you would Remember the Ladies, and be more generous and favourable to them than your ancestors. Do not put such unlimited power into the hands of the Husbands. Remember all Men would be tyrants if they could. If perticuliar care and attention is not paid to the Laidies we are determined to foment a Rebelion, and will not hold ourselves bound by any Laws in which we have no voice, or Representation.

That your Sex are Naturally Tyrannical is a Truth so thoroughly established as to admit of no dispute, but such of you as wish to be happy willingly give up the harsh title of Master for the more tender and endearing one of Friend. Why then, not put it out of the power of the vicious and the Lawless to use us with cruelty and indignity with impunity. Men of Sense in all Ages abhor those customs which treat us only as the vassals of your Sex. Regard us then as Beings placed by providence under your protection and in immitation of the Supreem Being make use of that power only for our happiness.

John Adams to Abigail Adams
Ap. 14. 1776

As to Declarations of Independency, be patient. Read our Privateering Laws, and our Commercial Laws. What signifies a Word.

As to your extraordinary Code of Laws, I cannot but laugh. We have been told that our Struggle has loosened the bands of Government every where. That Children and Apprentices were disobedient—that schools and Colledges were grown turbulent—that Indians slighted their Guardians and Negroes grew insolent to their Masters. But your letter was the first Intimation that another Tribe more numerous and powerfull than all the rest were grown discontented.—This is rather too coarse a Compliment but you are so saucy, I wont blot it out.

Depend upon it, We know better than to repeal our Masculine systems. Altho they are in full Force, you know they are little more than Theory. We dare not exert our Power in its full Latitude. We are obliged to go fair, and softly, and in Practice you know We are the subjects. We have only the Name of Masters, and rather than give up this, which would compleatly subject Us to the Despotism of the Peticoat, I hope General Washington, and all our brave Heroes would fight. I am sure every good Politician would plot, as long as he would against Despotism, Empire, Monarchy, Aristocracy, Oligarchy, or Ochlocracy.

Abigail Adams to Mercy Otis Warren
Braintree April 27 1776

He is very sausy to me in return for a List of Female Grievances which I transmitted to him. I think I will get you to join me in a petition to Congress. I thought it was very probable our wise Statesmen would erect a New Government and form a new code of Laws. I ventured to speak a word in behalf of our Sex, who are rather hardly dealt with by the Laws of England which gives such unlimited power to the Husband to use his wife Ill.

I requested that our Legislators would consider our case and as all Men of Delicacy and Sentiment are averse to Excercising the power they possess, yet as there is a natural propensity in Humane Nature to domination, I thought the most generous plan was to put it out of the power of the Arbitrary and tyranick to injure us with impunity by Establishing some Laws in our favour upon just and Liberal principals.

I believe I even threatned fomenting a Rebellion in case we were not considered, and assured him we would not hold ourselves bound by any Laws in which we had neither a voice, nor representation.

In return he tells me he cannot but Laugh at My Extrodonary Code of Laws. That he had heard their Struggle had loosned the bands of Government, that children and apprentices were dissabedient, that Schools and Colledges were grown turbulant, that Indians slighted their Guardians, and Negroes grew insolent to their Masters. But my Letter was the first intimation that another

Tribe more numerous and powerfull than all the rest were grown discontented. This is rather too coarse a complement, he adds, but that I am so sausy he wont blot it out.

So I have help'd the Sex abundantly, but I will tell him I have only been making trial of the Disintresstedness of his Virtue, and when weigh'd in the balance have found it wanting.

It would be bad policy to grant us greater power say they since under all the disadvantages we Labour we have the assendancy over their Hearts.

And charm by accepting, by submitting sway.

Abigail Adams to John Adams
B[raintre]e May 7 1776

I can not say that I think you very generous to the Ladies, for whilst you are proclaiming peace and good will to Men, Emancipating all Nations, you insist upon retaining an absolute power over Wives. But you must remember that Arbitrary power is like most other things which are very hard, very liable to be broken—and notwithstanding all your wise Laws and Maxims we have it in our power not only to free ourselves but to subdue our Masters, and without voilence throw both your natural and legal authority at our feet—

"Charm by accepting, by submitting sway
Yet have our Humour most when we obey."

John Adams to James Sullivan
Philadelphia, 26 May, 1776

It is certain, in theory, that the only moral foundation of government is, the consent of the people. But to what an extent shall we carry this principle? Shall we say that every individual of the community, old and young, male and female, as well as rich and poor, must consent, expressly, to every act of legislation? No, you will say, this is impossible. How, then, does the right arise in the majority to govern the minority, against their will? Whence arises the right of the men to govern the women, without their consent? Whence the right of the old to bind the young, without theirs?

But let us first suppose that the whole community, of every age, rank, sex, and condition, has a right to vote. This community is assembled. A motion is made, and carried by a majority of one voice. The minority will not agree to this. Whence arises the right of the majority to govern, and the obligation of the minority to obey?

From necessity, you will say, because there can be no other rule.

But why exclude women?

You will say, because their delicacy renders them unfit for practice and experience in the great businesses of life, and the hardy enterprises of war, as well as the arduous cares of state. Besides, their attention is so much engaged with the necessary nurture of their children, that nature has made them fittest for domestic cares. And children have not judgment or will of their own. True. But will not these reasons apply to others? Is is not equally true, that men in general, in every society, who are wholly destitute of property, are also too little acquainted with public affairs to form a right judgment, and too dependent upon other men to have a will of their own? If this is a fact, if you give to every man who has no property, a vote, will you not make a fine encouraging provision for corruption, by your fundamental law? Such is the frailty of the human heart, that very few men who have no property, have any judgment of their own. They talk and vote as they are directed by some man of property, who has attached their minds to his interest.

Upon my word, Sir, I have long thought an army a piece of clock-work, and to be governed only by principles and maxims, as fixed as any in mechanics; and, by all that I have read in the history of mankind, and in authors who have speculated upon society and government, I am much inclined to think a government must manage a society in the same manner; and that this is machinery too. . . .

Your idea that those laws which affect the lives and personal liberty of all, or which inflict corporal punishment, affect those who are not qualified to vote, as well as those who are, is just. But so they do women, as well as men; children, as well as adults. What reason should there be for excluding a man of twenty years eleven months and twenty-seven days old, from a vote, when you admit one who is twenty-one? The reason is, you must fix upon some period in life, when the understanding and will of men in general, is fit to be trusted by the public. Will not the same reason justify the state in fixing upon some certain quantity of property, as a qualification?

The same reasoning which will induce you to admit all men who have no property, to vote, with those who have, for those laws which affect the person, will prove that you ought to admit women and children; for, generally speaking, women and children have as good judgments, and as independent minds, as those men who are wholly destitute of property; these last being to all intents and purposes as much dependent upon others, who will please to feed, clothe, and employ them, as women are upon their husbands, or children on their parents. . . .

> Depend upon it, Sir, it is dangerous to open so fruitful a source of controversy and altercation as would be opened by attempting to alter the qualifications of voters; there will be no end of it. New claims will arise; women will demand a vote; lads from twelve to twenty-one will think their rights not enough attended to; and every man who has not a farthing, will demand an equal voice with any other, in all acts of state. It tends to confound and destroy all distinctions, and prostrate all ranks to one common level.

The reliance on stereotypes, on the part of both Abigail and John Adams, is readily apparent. And one of those stereotypes that John certainly did not question was commonly shared throughout colonial America: Women are physically, economically, and socially dependent, and thus their political and economic position should be one of dependence. It was a stereotype that would haunt and handicap women for centuries.

WOMEN ARE DEPENDENT

It was this stereotype (as well as the apparent fear of losing power and control) that John Adams and his colleagues used to justify not giving the vote to women. Women's failure to gain the vote (at least not for over a century and a quarter) was certainly damaging to them politically, but it also served to solidify the image of women as dependent, with equally damaging economic, legal, and political consequences.

The questions of whom to enfranchise and how to do so were of great concern to the framers of the Declaration of Independence and the Constitution. After all, the revolution was fought and independence sought over the issue of representation. According to historian Andrew Sinclair (1965), women had been legally eligible to vote in many of the colonies when they were still part of England, although there is no record of any woman ever excercising that right; moreover, even though the right had not been exercised, subsequent colonial legislatures took it away after independence was won. After the beginning of the revolutionary war, two colonies—New Jersey (1776) and Virginia (1779)—restored laws giving women the right to vote, but they, too, eventually repealed them.[5] Sinclair suggests that the legislatures' initial gesture of enfranchisement was one of haste and expediency rather than one of ideological statement or commitment; repeal, on the other hand, was the product of thought and consideration, and the true reflector of attitudes and ideas. And what that reflection revealed was once again the image of women as dependent.

In fact, according to Joan Gundersen (1987), where legislation had existed in the colonies allowing women to vote, it applied only to women who were property owners, and, therefore, independent. But when it became apparent that women were being brought to the polls by men and thus could be assumed not to be independent, *all* women lost the vote, for the additional assumption that operated was that all women married and were, therefore, one with, and dependent upon, their husbands.

This identifies another important and related assumption that dominated this period of our history: adult women were married. In actuality, as we know, not all were. But as suggested earlier—and echoing Harriet Taylor's[6] statement that women became wives and mothers because no other careers were open to them—marriage was, sadly, an economic and survival necessity for women and, frequently, the only option available. The legal status of women in colonial times (and, in fact, until not so long ago) was determined by their marital status. If adult women were single, they could draft binding legal contracts, bring and defend lawsuits, and become the legal guardian of their children. If married, however, their husbands controlled them, their children and, for the most part, their property. Without their husbands' consent, they were unable to make contracts, deeds, or wills or to sue another person (Bergold, 1976).

FAMILY LAW

Two common family law systems operated in colonial America, and it was these two systems that decided legal issues concerning women since their position in society was defined only via their relationships with family, either as wives or daughters. These two family law systems directed women's relationship to their property and their husbands.

The most prevalent system was the common law, inherited from England. It established that on marriage, a woman's husband acquired her personal property and the right to control whatever real property she brought with her. In addition, any earnings or property acquired during marriage belonged to each spouse, with each having an equal interest in it, but with the husband having exclusive control over it. Women had no right to allowances or wages and no claim of joint ownership in the then-rare eventuality of divorce.

The second, and less common, system, found in Louisiana and other territories originally controlled by France or Spain, was the so-called community property system. Under this system, each spouse was the owner of half the earnings of the other and half of all property acquired during the marriage (except gifts and inheritances). The husband managed and disposed of the property during marriage, but women were entitled to some ownership upon divorce.

It is indicative of the sentiments of the times that the law chose either to ignore a woman completely or to keep her firmly locked in her dependent roles of wife and mother. The law of our early history rarely addressed women who were not married, looking upon an adult single woman as an aberration and exception, and, therefore, not worthy of attention. When the law did choose to address women, it worked to rule out any public role, thereby ensuring her encapsulation in the home; however, the law simultaneously refused to regulate the domestic sphere. Hence the law ensured not only her encapsulation in the home but also the fact that she would be dominated there. This is well evidenced by the protest that Lucy Stone, ardent feminist and abolitionist, and her husband-to-be, Henry Blackwell, felt necessary to incorporate as part of their wedding vows in Massachusetts in 1855.

Lucy Stone and Henry Blackwell: Marriage Protest[7]

While acknowledging our mutual affection by publicly assuming the relationship of husband and wife, yet in justice to ourselves and a great principle, we deem it a duty to declare that this act on our part implies no sanction of, nor promise of voluntary obedience to such of the present laws of marriage, as refuse to recognize the wife as an independent, rational being, while they confer upon the husband an injurious and unnatural superiority, investing him with legal powers which no honorable man would exercize, and which no man should possess. We protest especially against the laws which give to the husband:

1. The custody of the wife's person.
2. The exclusive control and guardianship of their children.
3. The sole ownership of her personal, and use of her real estate, unless previously settled upon her, or placed in the hands of trustees, as in the case of minors, lunatics, and idiots.
4. The absolute right to the product of her industry.
5. Also against laws which give to the widower so much larger and more permanent an interest in the property of his deceased wife, than they give to the widow in that of the deceased husband.
6. Finally, against the whole system by which "the legal existence of the wife is suspended during marriage," so that in most States, she neither has a legal part in the choice of her residence, nor can she make a will, nor sue or be sued in her own name, nor inherit property.

We believe that personal independence and equal human rights can never be forfeited, except for crime; that marriage should be an equal and permanent partnership, and so recognized by law; that until it is so recognized, married partners should provide against the radical injustice of present laws, by every means in their power.

We believe that where domestic difficulties arise, no appeal should be made to legal tribunals under existing laws, but that all difficulties should be submitted to the equitable adjustment of arbitrators mutually chosen.

Thus reverencing law, we enter our protest against rules and customs which are unworthy of the name, since they violate justice, the essence of law.

(Signed) Henry B. Blackwell
Lucy Stone.

A CHINK IN THE WALL: MARRIED WOMEN'S PROPERTY ACTS

Though not yet true in Massachusetts, as Stone and Blackwell make obvious, conditions had begun to improve slightly in the mid-1800s in some areas of the country, with the introduction of "married women's property acts." These acts proved to be an important vehicle through which women were able to gain some reforms and access to due process claims prior to the twentieth century (Hoff-Wilson, 1987). These new laws, which gave women various rights—ranging from joint standing with her husband as guardian of their children to a claim of control over her property and earnings during her husband's life and after his death—marked the beginning of the move away from the Blackstonian view of woman as one with her husband. By the end of the nineteenth century, every state had some form of a married women's property act.[8] Had such a law been on the books at the time of Lucy Stone's marriage, her protest might not have been necessary.

Women did not, however, sit back and assume the battle won with the passage of the first few married women's property acts. They kept on fighting. They lobbied legislatures for such acts in the states that didn't have them and began crusading for equal treatment outside the home, for the right to vote and equal access to jobs. They tried to foment that rebellion that Abigail Adams had promised if women were not treated justly. These rebellious attempts did not always produce the results women wanted; indeed, when the courts finally started responding to women's suits, the response was usually in direct opposition to what had been sought. Pushing and fighting and lobbying were telling important tales about the social, economic, and legal plight of women.

WOMEN AND BLACKS: SEPARATE AND UNEQUAL

Two important historical events helped define this period in women's struggle to obtain just and legal recognition. One was the coalescing of the women's rights movement, as represented by the Seneca Falls convention of 1848; the other was the abolitionist movement and the ensuing Civil War. These should not be viewed as separate influences because the concerns and work of these two movements were very much interrelated.

There were strong similarities in standing and in the remedies sought: the *Dred Scott*[9] case of 1857 had made it clear that blacks were no more considered "people" than were women. Yet the relationship that existed between abolitionists and feminists (many feminists were ardent abolitionists as well, though the reverse did not necessarily apply) was neither easy nor equal. The antislavery cause had far broader appeal than did the women's movement and was received with more respect and credibility. Many abolitionists did not want the two causes mixed for fear of tainting their own goals by association with the women's movement. An example of the lengths to which some carried this concern was the abolitionist leaders' request to Lucy Stone, an equally staunch abolitionist and feminist, not to preach both causes on the same platform. She agreed to speak in favor of women on weekdays and in support of abolition on weekends (Schneir, 1972).

But the concern was not completely one-sided. At a women's convention in Ohio in 1851, some attendees objected to allowing abolitionist-feminist Sojourner Truth to speak, fearing that their cause would be harmed by association with the abolitionists' battle. (She not only spoke but won the crowd as well.)

This tension—and, more importantly, the norm of excluding women from public life—was evidenced at the 1840 world antislavery convention where women delegates were denied seats. Lucretia Mott and Elizabeth Cady Stanton met at this convention and in reaction to being denied participation began plans for a women's rights organization. Due to other responsibilities and concerns, however, nothing came of their interest until July 1848, when they placed an advertisement in the *Seneca County Courier* (N.Y.) announcing a women's rights convention within the week.

Despite the short notice, about three hundred people attended the convention, chaired by Lucretia Mott's husband, James Mott. (Note the irony of a man chairing the first meeting of a women's rights group.) At this meeting, the Declaration of Sentiments and Resolutions, considered by many to be the most important document of the nineteenth century women's movement, was read and passed, though not without some difficulty. All but one of the twelve resolutions, which for the most part addressed such general concerns as a woman's right to equality and access to whatever station in life "her conscience shall dictate," passed unanimously. The twelfth, which addressed women's enfranchisement, passed only after an impassioned plea from Frederick Douglass, the great abolitionist and feminist.

What is noteworthy about the Seneca Falls Declaration of Sentiments, beyond its content, is the form it took. Here are the first three paragraphs.

Seneca Falls Declaration of Sentiments

> When, in the course of human events, it becomes necessary for one portion of the family of man to assume among the people of the earth a position different from that which they have hitherto occupied, but one to which the laws of nature and of nature's God entitle them, a decent respect to the opinions of mankind requires that they should declare the causes that impel them to such a course.
>
> We hold these truths to be self-evident: that all men and women are created equal; that they are endowed by their Creator with certain inalienable rights; that among these are life, liberty, and the pursuit of happiness; that to secure these rights governments are instituted, deriving their just powers from the consent of the governed. Whenever any form of government becomes destructive of these ends, it is the right of those who suffer from it to refuse allegiance to it, and to insist upon the institution of a new government, laying its foundation on such principles, and organizing the powers in such form as to them shall seem most

> likely to effect their safety and happiness. Prudence, indeed, will dictate that governments long established should not be changed for light and transient causes; and accordingly all experience hath shown that mankind are more disposed to suffer, while evils are sufferable, than to right themselves by abolishing the forms to which they were accustomed. But when a long train of abuses and usurpations, pursuing invariably the same object evinces a design to reduce them under absolute despotism, it is their duty to throw off such government, and to provide new guards for their future security. Such has been the patient sufferance of the women under this government, and such is now the necessity which constrains them to demand the equal station to which they are entitled.
>
> The history of mankind is a history of repeated injuries and usurpations on the part of man toward woman, having in direct object the establishment of an absolute tyranny over her. To prove this, let facts be submitted to a candid world.[10]

The document then went on to offer supporting evidence for the claim of the preceding paragraph by identifying a litany of wrongs that women had suffered and to suggest, in the twelve resolutions, the requisite corrective measures. The similarity of the wording in this declaration to that of the earlier one was not accidental, but was contrived in an effort to give legitimacy to what many might view as rebellious assertions (Kerber, 1977; Sinclair, 1965). It was done purposely, historian Linda Kerber suggests, in an effort to defuse hostility and to make the claims of this new fledgling group as self-evident as the claims made by the fledgling group that coined the original phrases four score years before. That it did not meet with as much success as its predecessor should be obvious.

SETBACKS

Why it did not work, why the Seneca Falls Declaration of Sentiments and Resolutions did not prove to be the rallying cry needed to set the women's movement on a successful track can be explained in any number of ways from internal conflicts to external resistance. Clearly, there was resistance, resistance on the part of men but resistance on the part of some women too. In 1853, at a women's rights convention, a man strongly criticized the declaration as unjustly blaming men for the plight of women. His remarks led William Lloyd Garrison, another staunch feminist and abolitionist, to rise in defense of the sentiment that men were, indeed, the responsible and guilty perpetrators of the injustices women alleged. In extemporaneous remarks, Garrison said the following:

William Lloyd Garrison: Intelligent Wickedness[11]

I believe in sin, therefore in a sinner; in theft, therefore in a thief; in slavery, therefore in a slaveholder; in wrong, therefore in a wrong-doer; and unless the men of this nation are made by woman to see that they have been guilty of usurpation, and cruel usurpation, I believe very little progress will be made. To say all this has been done without thinking, without calculation, without design, by mere accident, by a want of light; can anybody believe this who is familiar with all the facts in this case? Certainly, for one, I hope ever to lean to the charitable side, and will try to do so. I, too, believe things are done through misconception and misapprehension, which are injurious, yes, which are immoral and unchristian; but only to a limited extent. There is such a thing as intelligent wickedness, a design on the part of those who have the light to quench it, and to do the wrong to gratify their own propensities, and to further their own interests. So, then, I believe, that as man has monopolized for generations all the rights which belong to woman, it has not been accidental, not through ignorance on his part; but I believe that man has done this through calculation, actuated by a spirit of pride, a desire for domination which has made him degrade woman in her own eyes, and thereby tend to make her a mere vassal.

It seems to me, therefore, that we are to deal with the consciences of men. It is idle to say that the guilt is common, that the women are as deeply involved in this matter as the men. Never can it be said that the victims are as much to be blamed as the victimizer; that the slaves are to be as much blamed as the slaveholders and slave-drivers; that the women who have no rights, are to be as much blamed as the men who have played the part of robbers and tyrants. We must deal with conscience. The men of this nation, and the men of all nations, have no respect for woman. They have tyrannized over her deliberately, they have not sinned through ignorance, but theirs is not the knowledge that saves. Who can say truly, that in all things he acts up to the light he enjoys, that he does not do something which he knows is not the very thing, or the best thing he ought to do? How few there are among mankind who are able to say this with regard to themselves. Is not the light all around us? Does not this nation know how great its guilt is in enslaving one-sixth of its people? Do not the men of this nation know ever since the landing of the pilgrims, that they are wrong in making subject one-half of the people? Rely upon it, it has not been a mistake on their part. It has been sin. It has been guilt; and they manifest their guilt to a demonstration, in the manner in which they receive this movement. Those who do wrong ignorantly, do not willingly continue in it, when they find they are in the wrong. Ignorance is not an evidence of guilt certainly. It is only an evidence of a want of light. They who are only ignorant, will never rage, and rave, and threaten, and foam, when the light comes; but being interested and walking in the light, will always present a manly front, and be willing to be taught and be willing to be told they are in the wrong.

Take the case of slavery: How has the anti-slavery cause been received? Not argumentatively, not by reason, not by entering the free arenas of fair discussion and comparing notes; the arguments have been rotten eggs, and brickbats and calumny, and in the southern portion of the country, a spirit of murder, and threats to cut out the tongues of those who spoke against them. What has this indicated on the part of the nation? What but conscious guilt? Not ignorance, not that they had not the light. They had the light and rejected it.

How has this Woman's Rights movement been treated in this country, on the right hand and on the left? This nation ridicules and derides this movement, and spits upon it, as fit only to be cast out and trampled underfoot. This is not ignorance. They know all about the truth. It is the natural outbreak of tyranny. It is because the tyrants and usurpers are alarmed. They have been and are called to judgement, and they dread the examination and exposure of their position and character.

Women of America! you have something to blame yourselves for in this matter, something to account for to God and the world. Granted. But then you are the victims in this land, as the women of all lands are, to the tyrannical power and godless ambition of man; and we must show who are responsible in this matter.

Male resistance alone, however, cannot be blamed for the derailment of the feminist cause. But male resistance, along with the Civil War and the activities of the abolitionist movement leading up to the war, can certainly together be blamed for the feminists' failure to gain much ground.

During the years of the abolitionist movement and the Civil War, many women put their feminist concerns on hold and campaigned solely for emancipation of the slave. They were hoping, by so doing, to establish strong ties with the abolitionists and gain good will to be drawn on later in support of the feminist cause. Not only did this strategy fail but this tactic also gave rise to factional fights within women's groups, for many other women were displeased by the downplaying of women's concerns (Sinclair, 1965).

The fact was that many women believed that supporting the abolitionist efforts was more than simply a ploy to gain support for the women's movement later. They felt that there was a strong and legitimate case to be made for advocating both causes simultaneously and thus making explicit the parallel positions in society of women and slaves.

This theme did seem to run throughout the public addresses and private statements of many abolitionist-feminist leaders and others. Dolly Madison, wife of the fourth president of the United States and herself a southerner, is alleged to have observed that a southern wife was the chief slave of the harem. The parallels between woman and slave were developed at the podiums of both abolitionists and feminists. Elizabeth Cady Stanton draws the parallel clearly in her 1860 address to the New York state legislature, imploring that body to pass, finally, a married women's property act.

Elizabeth Cady Stanton: A Married Woman's Property Act[12]

You who have read the history of nations, from Moses down to our last election, where have you ever seen one class looking after the interests of another? Any of you can readily see the defects in other governments, and pronounce sentence against those who have sacrificed the masses to themselves; but when we come to our own case, we are blinded by custom and self-interest. Some of you who have no capital can see the injustice which the laborer suffers; some of you who have no slaves, can see the cruelty of his oppression; but who of you appreciate the galling humiliation, the refinements of degradation, to which women (the mothers, wives, sisters, and daughters of freemen) are subject, in this the last half of the nineteenth century? How many of you have ever read even the laws concerning them that now disgrace your statute-books? In cruelty and tyranny, they are not surpassed by any slaveholding code in the Southern States; in fact they are worse, by just so far as woman, from her social position, refinement, and education, is on a more equal ground with the oppressor.

Allow me just here to call the attention of that party now so much interested in the slave of the Carolinas, to the similarity in his condition and that of the mothers, wives, and daughters of the Empire State. The negro has no name. He is Cuffy Douglas or Cuffy Brooks, just whose Cuffy he may chance to be. The woman has no name. She is Mrs. Richard Roe or Mrs. John Doe, just whose Mrs. she may chance to be. Cuffy has no right to his earnings; he can not buy or sell, or lay up anything that he can call his own. Mrs. Roe has no right to her earnings; she can neither buy nor sell, make contracts, nor lay up anything that she can call her own. Cuffy has no right to his children; they can be sold from him at any time. Mrs. Roe has no right to her children; they may be bound out to cancel a father's debts of honor. The unborn child, even, by the last will of the father, may be placed under the guardianship of a stranger and a foreigner. Cuffy has no legal existence; he is subject to restraint and moderate chastisement. Mrs. Roe has no legal existence; she has not the best right to her own person. The husband has the power to restrain, and administer moderate chastisement.

Blackstone [author of *Commentaries on the Laws of England*] declares that the husband and wife are one, and learned commentators have decided that that one is the husband. In all civil codes, you will find them classified as one. Certain rights and immunities, such and such privileges are to be secured to white male citizens. What have women and negroes to do with rights? What know they of government, war, or glory?

The prejudice against color, of which we hear so much, is no stronger than that against sex. It is produced by the same cause, and manifested very much in the same way. The negro's skin and the woman's sex are both *prima facie* evidence that they were intended to be in subjection to the white Saxon man. The few social privileges which the man gives the woman, he makes up to the negro in civil rights. The woman may sit at the same table and eat with the white man; the free negro may hold property and vote. The woman may sit in the same pew with the white man in church; the free negro may enter the pulpit and preach. Now, with the black man's right to suffrage, the right unquestioned, even by Paul, to minister at the altar, it is evident that the prejudice against sex is more deeply rooted and more unreasonably maintained than that against color. . . .

Just imagine an inhabitant of another planet entertaining himself some pleasant evening in searching over our great national compact, our Declaration of Independence, our Constitutions, or some of our statute-books; what would he think of those "women and negroes" that must be so fenced in, so guarded against? Why, he would certainly suppose we were monsters, like those fabulous giants or Brobdingnagians of olden times, so dangerous to civilized man, from our size, ferocity, and power. Then let him take up our poets, from Pope down to Dana; let him listen to our Fourth of July toasts, and some of the sentimental adulations of social life, and no logic could convince him that this creature of the law, and this angel of the family altar, could be one and the same being. Man is in such a labyrinth of contradictions with his marital and property rights; he is so befogged on the whole question of maidens, wives, and mothers, that from pure benevolence we should relieve him from this troublesome branch of legislation. We should vote, and make laws for ourselves. Do not be alarmed, dear ladies! You need spend no time reading Grotius, Coke, Puffendorf, Blackstone, Bentham, Kent, and Story to find out what you need. We may safely trust the shrewd selfishness of the white man, and consent to live under the same broad code where he has so comfortably ensconced himself. Any legislation that will do for man, we may abide by most cheerfully. . . .

Now do not think, gentlemen, we wish you to do a great many troublesome things for us. We do not ask our legislators to spend a whole session in fixing up a code of laws to satisfy a class of most unreasonable women. We ask no more than the poor devils in the Scripture asked, "Let us alone." In mercy, let us take care of ourselves, our property, our children, and our homes. True, we are not so strong, so wise, so crafty as you are, but if any kind friend leaves us a little money, or we can by great

> industry earn fifty cents a day, we would rather buy bread and clothes for our children than cigars and champagne for our legal protectors. There has been a great deal written and said about protection. We, as a class, are tired of one kind of protection, that which leaves us everything to do, to dare, and to suffer, and strips us of all means for its accomplishment. We would not tax man to take care of us. No, the Great Father has endowed all his creatures with the necessary powers for self-support, self-defense, and protection. We do not ask man to represent us; it is hard enough in times like these for man to carry backbone enough to represent himself. So long as the mass of men spend most of their time on the fence, not knowing which way to jump, they are surely in no condition to tell us where we had better stand. In pity for man, we would no longer hang like a mill-stone round his neck. Undo what man did for us in the dark ages, and strike out all special legislation for us; strike the words "white male" from all your constitutions, and then, with fair sailing, let us sink or swim, live or die, survive or perish together.

But lest the reader see the thinking of Stanton and Garrison as the work of impassioned and, therefore, perhaps less than fully rational pleaders, here is yet one more passage. This excerpt, from an 1883 Supreme Court decision in *Civil Rights Cases*, 3 S.Ct. 18 (1883), was written by Justice Joseph P. Bradley (a justice who played a not insignificant role in the definition of women's position in America) and is viewed as the definitive American description of the "badges of slavery." Concerned only with slavery in this case, Justice Bradley drew no parallels to women; that is left to each individual reader to do. Said Justice Bradley [*Civil Rights Cases*, 3 S.Ct. 18, 29 (1883)]:

> The long existence of African slavery in this country gave us very distinct notions of what it was, and what were its necessary incidents. Compulsory service of the slave for the benefit of the master, restraint of his movements except by the master's will, disability to hold property, to make contracts, to have a standing in court, to be a witness against a white person...were the inseparable incidents of the institution...Congress...undertook to wipe out these burdens and disabilities, the necessary incidents of slavery, constituting its substance and visible form; and to secure to all citizens of every race and color...those fundamental rights which are the essence of civil freedom, namely the same right to make and enforce contracts, to sue, be parties, give evidence, and to inherit, purchase, lease, sell and convey property, as is enjoyed by white citizens.

If the parallels are not immediately apparent, remember the words of Lucy Stone, Elizabeth Cady Stanton, and Henry Blackwell. And read now the less emotional and more factual picture drawn by Sinclair (1965:4):

> Early American women were almost treated like Negro slaves, inside and outside the home. Both were expected to behave with deference and obedience towards owner or husband; both did not exist officially under the law; both had few rights and little education; both found it difficult to run away; both worked for their masters without pay; both had to breed on command, and to nurse the results. . . . The only slavemaster was the free sane white male. Outside his jurisdiction lived the despised of society, free Negroes, spinsters, widows, and the inhabitants of the wilderness.

Thus, we see clearly where all women—from the expected standard of the wife and mother to the aberration of the single female—stood in the hierarchy created by white "sane" males.

CONCLUSION

Although the feminist movement had only limited success for most of the nineteenth century, the abolitionist movement scored significant gains. As a result of the Civil War and the Thirteenth, Fourteenth and Fifteenth Amendments to the Constitution, slavery was outlawed, blacks were given (at least on paper) the right to vote, and blacks were granted (theoretically at least) equal protection under the law. These were important advances, even though it is doubtful that the hearts and minds of most white Americans changed very much.[13] But women won practically nothing. Their slavery did not end, they did not get the vote, and, as time quickly told, they were not to receive equal protection. It was also clear that the hearts and minds of most men and many women had not changed on the question of women's rights any more than on the rights of black people.

As women began in this country, so they entered the last quarter of the nineteenth century: absent rights, enfranchisement, and equal protection—but hopeful. They were hopeful, as they had been when they looked to the Declaration of Independence and the Constitution and saw promise and potential, that the gains made by black men would quickly be used to improve their own position. They were soon to learn what Lucy Stone had long known but only voiced in 1855: "Disappointment is the lot of woman."

NOTES

1. There are, nonetheless, a few people, such as historian Joan Hoff-Wilson, who suggest that the use of words such as *we*, *people*, and *elector* left open the possibility for the inclusion of women in the reach of the Declaration of Independence and the Constitution. That is, she says, until 1894, when the Supreme Court made it clear that *person* meant *male*. [Hoff-Wilson, Joan. 1987. "The unfinished revolution: Changing legal status of U.S. women."

Signs, 13(1): 7-36.] It seems, however, that there is ample historical evidence to support this same conclusion one hundred years earlier.

2. There is no need to dicker about the choice of words here because there were only men involved in framing the crucial documents that shaped this country. Fifty-six men, no women, signed the Declaration of Independence; thirty nine men, again, no women, signed the Constitution.

3. Gruberg, Martin. (1968) *Women in American Politics*, Oskosh, Wis.: Academia Press, pg 4.

4. "'Remember the ladies': Abigail Adams vs. John Adams." In *The Feminist Papers: From Adams to de Beauvoir*, ed. A. Rossi. New York: Bantam Books, 1973, 9-15. Cited with original spelling and punctuation.

5. Sinclair asserts that colonial law was less exclusive than laws passed by the newly independent country. As evidence, he cites the fact that a number of colonies and territories that joined the Union much later did give women suffrage.

6. Harriet Taylor was an early feminist, as well as the long-time companion and eventual wife to and very strong influence upon feminist John Stuart Mill.

7. "Marriage of Lucy Stone under protest." 1855. In *Feminism: The Essential Historical Writings*, ed. M. Schneir. New York: Vintage Books, 1972, pp. 104-105.

8. For easy access to an example of a married women's property act, see "Married Women's Property Act, New York, 1860," in *Feminism: The Essential Historical Writings*, ed. M. Schneir. New York: Vintage Books, 1972, pp. 122-124.

9. *Dred Scott v. John F. A. Sandford*, SC (19 How) 691 (1857). See especially page 700.

10. "Declaration of sentiments and resolutions, Seneca Falls." In *Feminism: The Essential Historical Writings*, ed. M. Schneir. New York: Vintage Books, 1972, pp. 77-78. For a complete rendering of the "Declaration and resolutions," see same, pp. 77-82.

11. Garrison, William Lloyd. 1853. "Intelligent wickedness." In *Feminism: The Essential Historical Writings*, ed. M. Schneir. New York: Vintage Books, 1972, pp. 87-89.

12. Stanton, Elizabeth Cady. 1860. "Address to the New York State Legislature, 1860." In *Feminism: The Essential Historical Writings*, ed. M. Schneir. New York: Vintage Books, 1972, pp. 117-121.

13. Sinclair and other historians claim that black men got the vote not because the country desired this, which it desired no more than giving the vote to women, but rather because of political expediency. With blacks voting in the South, legislators from the North and West could dominate the South; giving women the vote could create no such political benefits for the lawmakers who then controlled Congress. (Sinclair, 1965: 186).

5

The Writing on the Wall: No Constitutional Protections for Women

No higher duty, or more solemn responsibility, rests upon this court than that of translating into living law and maintaining this constitutional shield deliberately planned and inscribed for the benefit of every human being subject to our Constitution—of whatever race, creed, or persuasion.

Supreme Court Justice Hugo L. Black
Chambers v. Florida, 1938.

Because their movement had so paralleled and intertwined with the abolitionist movement, feminists hoped that their gains would mirror those being made by blacks in the post-Civil War era. In their lobbying efforts around the country, feminists urged that the post-Civil War amendments to the Constitution should extend rights, privileges, and protections to women as well as to blacks. They would soon learn that this was not to be.

THE FOURTEENTH AMENDMENT

Of the three Reconstruction amendments, only one—the Fourteenth—held the possibility of including women in its scope. Phrased in the most general of terms, it did not offer what feminists had wanted. It proved, nevertheless, to be one of the most important amendments for women ever passed. Although it did not appear so initially, it was to play an absolutely central role in women's rights litigation over the next century and beyond.

Ratified in 1868 as the middle of the three Reconstruction amendments, the Fourteenth Amendment—among other things—forbade the abridgment of citizens' rights by, in essence, making the Bill of Rights applicable to the states. Until the passage of this amendment, only the federal government was obliged to abide by those first ten amendments. The Fourteenth Amendment broadened the Bill of Rights protections, making all state governments also obliged to respect them.

Of the five sections of the amendment, only the first two have proven to have import for women's struggle for equality. And of these, the first is the more important and has played a continuing role in the fight for women's rights. Often referred to as the "equal protection clause," the first section says the following:

> All persons born or naturalized in the United States, and subject to the jurisdiction thereof, are citizens of the United States and of the State wherein they reside. No State shall make or enforce any law which shall abridge the privileges or immunities of citizens of the United States; nor shall any State deprive any person of life, liberty, or property without due process of law; nor deny to any person within its jurisdiction the equal protection of the laws.

It is this section of the Fourteenth Amendment that has often been used over the past century as justification for asking the Supreme Court to consider women's rights cases (as well as many others). In citing this section, plaintiffs can claim that some privilege, immunity, or right has been denied without due process or that there has been some denial of equal protection.

It is little wonder that the women of the 1860s should have felt cheered when they read this section of the Fourteenth Amendment—but only if they did not read beyond it. Continuing to section 2 makes it clear that disappointment lay ahead. Section 2, which spells out the basis on which congressional and state legislative representatives are to be apportioned within states, is important here not for its general content but for its specific language. The language of the first section of the Fourteenth Amendment made no reference to sex, but referred always to "citizen" or "person," thus leading women to hope that citizen and person were sex neutral. The second section, however, dashes this hope. Although at the outset it talks about apportioning on the basis of the number of "persons" in a state, the provision goes on to make three separate references to voting and apportionment based on "male inhabitants" or "male citizens." The term *female citizens* never appears, lending credence to the argument that the Fourteenth Amendment and, therefore, the Constitution, applied only to males. Women—and the country—did not have long to wait for confirmation of the accuracy of this understanding.

Five years after the passage of the Fourteenth Amendment, in 1873—and one day before one of the most famous decisions in the history of women's rights litigation—the Supreme Court decided the *Slaughter-House Cases* [83 US (16 Wall.) 394 (1873)]. In this case, the butchers' association challenged a Louisiana law that gave a monopoly to one slaughterhouse, requiring that all slaughtering and preparing of meat for eating be done at that one house. Individual butchers were allowed to do their own slaughtering there but were obliged to pay a fee to the slaughterhouse.

The association challenged the law, using both the Thirteenth and Fourteenth Amendments as justification. Arguing that the law created involuntary servitude, the association said this was in violation of the Thirteenth Amendment's proscription of slavery. Alleging an abridgment of their privileges and immunities as citizens, as well as both a denial of equal protection of the law and a taking of their property without due process, the association argued that the Louisiana statute was also in violation of the Fourteenth Amendment.

At first glance, this case would appear to have nothing to do with women's claims for legal protection and social standing, and indeed much of the decision is irrelevant. One portion, however, had major ramifications for the women's rights movement of the period. In deciding the *Slaughter-House Cases*, the Court was called upon to give for the first time (as noted by Justice Samuel F. Miller, who wrote the majority opinion in the five to four decision) its interpretation of the Thirteenth and Fourteenth Amendments. And that interpretation nailed the coffin shut on any ill-placed hopes women had held for the Fourteenth Amendment.

The coffin nails came from one pronouncement: Justice Miller's statement that the Reconstruction amendments showed such a "unity of purpose" that there could be no doubt as to their true intent. As to the Thirteenth Amendment, he continued, it had no other purpose than to free the slaves and to prevent all forms of servitude in the future. It was, he argued, intended as reinforcement of President Lincoln's Emancipation Proclamation, since many people had been afraid that if the proclamation were left to stand alone, it might be subject to erosion. The Fourteenth Amendment, he went on, was passed to ensure that the states wishing to rejoin the Union not only recognized the abolition of slavery but also would not pass restrictive laws continuing the pre-Civil War pattern of unfair hardships on blacks. These conditions would be ensured, he said, if the returning southern states ratified the Fourteenth Amendment prior to regaining full status in the Union. And finally, he said, the Fifteenth Amendment had been passed to ensure that blacks could be fully secure in their person and property, a guarantee that could not exist without suffrage. He concluded the Court's interpretation of these three amendments by stating the following (*Slaughter-House Cases*, 1873: 81):

> In the light of the history of these amendments, and the pervading purpose of them, ..., it is not difficult to give a meaning to [the equal protection] clause. The existence of laws in the states where the newly emancipated negroes resided, which discriminated with gross injustice and hardship against them as a class, was the evil to be remedied by this clause. . . .
>
> We doubt very much whether any action of a state not directed by way of discrimination against the negroes as a class, or on account of their race, will ever be held to come within the

> purview of this provision. It is so clearly a provision for that race and that emergency, that a strong case would be necessary for its application to any other.

It is hard to imagine, after Miller's seemingly airtight decision, how anyone—female or male—could continue harboring any hope that the Fourteenth Amendment was meant to operate in the general manner suggested by its language. But lest there was a lingering hope that women, somehow, might be able to seize a sliver of the Fourteenth Amendment's protections, the answer came the very next day.

THE BEGINNING OF THE LEGAL STRUGGLE: THE END OF THE NINETEENTH CENTURY

Myra Bradwell had wanted to go to college, but the limited availability of colleges open to women in the mid-1800s had precluded the possibility. Instead, she followed the stereotypical female path: She became a teacher. Subsequently, after marrying a lawyer, she began studying law in order to be able to assist her husband, <u>not</u> because she had any career designs of her own. Eventually, however, she decided that she did, indeed, want to be a lawyer. She studied, passed the exam for entrance to the Illinois bar, and met all the necessary qualifications; nevertheless, the Illinois Supreme Court refused to admit her.

The court based its refusal on the fact that as a married woman she was ineligible to practice law since married women could not make binding contracts except through their husbands. She, however, showing her strong spirit and determination, filed a supplemental brief designed to make the court reveal its true reason for denying her admission. Their response confirmed what she had long suspected: She was refused admission solely on the basis of her sex. With that ruling, the case was on its way to the Supreme Court of the United States.

Matthew Carpenter, Bradwell's attorney, argued the case before the Supreme Court in January 1873, three months before the Court handed down the *Slaughter-House Cases* decision. Thus, he was working in uncharted terrain, and the error of his thinking, in hindsight, is quite evident. Whether or not this made a difference in the ultimate Court decision is open only to speculation, obviously. The case that Carpenter and Bradwell built rested on the allegation that her civil rights had been abridged: She had been denied access to the bar not because of any lack of qualifications but solely because of her status as a married women. That, Carpenter argued, was a denial of the protection granted under the Fourteenth Amendment, which stated that no privileges and immunities granted citizens of the United States should be abridged.

In pointing this out, Carpenter declared that "[o]f course women, as well as men, are included in this provision and recognized as citizens" [*Bradwell v. Illinois*, 83 U.S. (16 Wall.) 442 (1873): 443]. This being so, he continued, the question was not whether or not women were citizens and, therefore, entitled to the protections granted citizens, but rather what constituted a privilege and immunity that could not be abridged.

Pursuing that line of thought in his oral argument, Carpenter conceded straight off that the right to vote was not such a privilege, since the very amendment that talks about abridgment also indicates that participation in a "rebellion, or other crime" can constitute grounds for denying the vote to citizens.

But since the amendment says nothing about admission to the bar, he sought to establish that admission was protected because it pertained to the choice of avocation. And on that right, he pointed out, the Supreme Court had been clear. Carpenter noted that the Court had earlier declared that "in the pursuit of happiness, all avocations, all honors, all positions are alike open to everyone, and that in the protection of these rights all are equal before the law" (*Bradwell*, 1873: 444). Obviously believing that this citation was insufficient support for his position, however, Carpenter went on to cite additional precedents showing that the Court had held that law, medicine, and clerical avocations were open to all.

Having thus established to his satisfaction that avocations—including that of the practice of law—were protected Fourteenth Amendment privileges, he acknowledged that the pursuit of such avocations might not necessarily be without "entrance" requirements but insisted that a person's sex was not one of those. "[A]nd while the legislature may prescribe qualifications for entering upon this pursuit," he said, "it cannot, under the guise of fixing qualifications, exclude a class of citizens from admission to the bar" (*Bradwell*, 1873: 444). If the latter occurred, Carpenter argued, what was operating was a prohibition to, rather than a qualification for, entrance. He concluded by stating once again his belief that the Fourteenth Amendment operated to protect all citizens, regardless of race, sex, or marital status, and that pursuit of employment was a protected privilege.

The Court, in an eight-to-one decision (with Chief Justice Salmon P. Chase the lone dissenter), did not accept Bradwell's and Carpenter's argument and upheld the lower court's decision. In fact, in writing the opinion for the Court (an opinion joined in by three other justices), Justice Miller (the same justice who authored the opinion in the *Slaughter-House Cases*) did not even address the broad question of women's rights as citizens. Rather, he focused on the narrow legal issues of Bradwell's standing as a citizen of the state of Illinois, which the Court agreed she had under the Fourteenth Amendment, and then on the question of whether admission to a state bar was a constitutionally protected privilege or immunity. And on the latter question, the Court concluded that it was not a constitutionally protected privilege since admission to the bar was a matter for individual states to determine. Referring to the *Slaughter-House Cases*, Miller wrote:

> unless we are wholly and radically mistaken in the principles on which those cases are decided, the right to control and regulate the granting of license to practice law in the courts of a state is one of those powers which are not transferred for its protection to the Federal government, and its exercise is in no manner

> governed or controlled by citizenship of the United States in the party seeking such license. (*Bradwell*, 1873:445)

Thus, the Court nicely side-stepped the whole issue of women's access to avocations—in this case the particular avocation of the law—by defining the concern at hand to be a matter of states' rights and not women's rights. As a subject left to state discretion, it did not fall under the umbrella of the Fourteenth Amendment.

LEGAL REASONING OR BIASES?

Since *Bradwell*, one of the most famous decisions in the history of women's rights, did not advance those rights, the reader may be a bit puzzled at its inclusion here. There is nothing momentous or impressive, at least in the context of the struggle for women's rights, in Justice Miller's opinion. The more important opinion—the one of social and historical influence and the one that no doubt expressed the sentiment of the day—was not the majority opinion but the concurring opinion. Authored by Justice Joseph P. Bradley and endorsed by two colleagues, it agreed with the decision that the state court was correct in denying Bradwell the right to practice law. Justice Bradley went further, however, and agreed with the lower court's reasoning that denial should be on the basis of sex. In so doing, he addressed a portion of the broader question of the rights of women. In one of the most frequently quoted concurring decisions, Justice Bradley stated the following:

Bradwell v. Illinois
83 U.S. (16 Wall.) 442 (1873)
Justice Bradley, concurring

> The claim . . . assumes that it is one of the privileges and immunities of women as citizens to engage in any and every profession, occupation or employment in civil life.
>
> It certainly cannot be affirmed, as a historical fact, that this has ever been established as one of the fundamental privileges and immunities of the sex. On the contrary, the civil law, as well as nature herself, has always recognized a wide difference in the respective spheres and destinies of man and woman. Man is, or should be, woman's protector and defender. The natural and proper timidity and delicacy which belongs to the female sex evidently unfits it for many of the occupations of civil life. The constitution of the family organization, which is founded in the divine ordinance, as well as in the nature of things, indicates the domestic sphere as that which properly belongs to the domain and functions of womanhood. The harmony, not to say identity, of interest and views which belong or should belong to the family institution, is repugnant to the idea of a woman adopting a distinct and independent career from that of her husband. So

> firmly fixed was this sentiment in the founders of the common law that it became a maxim of that system of jurisprudence that a woman had no legal existence separate from her husband, who was regarded as her head and representative in the social state; and, notwithstanding some recent modifications of this civil status, many of the special rules of law flowing from and dependent upon this cardinal principle still exist in full force in most states. One of these is, that a married woman is incapable, without her husband's consent, of making contracts which shall be binding on her or him. This very incapacity was one circumstance which the supreme court of Illinois deemed important in rendering a married woman incompetent fully to perform the duties and trusts that belong to the office of an attorney and counselor.
>
> It is true that many women are unmarried and not affected by any of the duties, complications, and incapacities arising out of the married state, but these are exceptions to the general rule. The paramount destiny and mission of woman are to fulfill the noble and benign offices of wife and mother. This is the law of the Creator. And the rules of civil society must be adapted to the general constitution of things, and cannot be based upon exceptional cases.
>
> The humane movements of modern society, which have for their object the multiplication of avenues for woman's advancement, and of occupations adapted to her condition and sex, have my heartiest concurrence. But I am not prepared to say that it is one of her fundamental rights and privileges to be admitted into every office and position, including those which require highly special qualifications and demanding special responsibilities. In the nature of things, it is not every citizen of every age, sex, and condition that is qualified for every calling and position. It is the prerogative of the legislator to prescribe regulations founded on nature, reason, and experience for the due admission of qualified persons to professions and callings demanding special skill and confidence. This fairly belongs to the police power of the state; and, in my opinion, in view of the peculiar characteristics, destiny, and mission of woman, it is within the province of the legislature to ordain what offices, positions, and callings shall be filled and discharged by men and shall receive the benefit of those energies and responsibilities, and that decision and firmness which are presumed to predominate in the sterner sex.
>
> For these reasons I think that the laws of Illinois now complained of are not obnoxious to the charge of abridging any of the privileges and immunities of citizens of the United States.

When the Supreme Court ruled against her, Bradwell decided not to continue efforts to gain admission to the state bar. Soon after the Court's decision, she did, however, get the state legislature to pass a law declaring it illegal to deny access to any profession because of an applicant's sex. Years later, as a result of her original application, she was admitted to the state bar of Illinois, as well as to the bar of the Supreme Court; however, she never practiced law. (She was not idle, though; she was the founder, editor, and business manager of *The Chicago Legal News*, the first weekly legal newspaper in the West, and she was also the founder of both state and national suffrage groups. Her two surviving children—one male, one female—both became lawyers.)

The decision and opinions in *Bradwell* are important because they sent a clear message on the status of women and what they could expect from the law. *Bradwell* is also important because it presents such a striking example of the foibles of juridical reasoning. The differences in the opinions of Justices Miller and Bradley rest not in ends, but in means. Not an uncommon occurrence in judicial opinions, these differences are ones deserving of careful consideration each time they happen. Justice Miller arrives at his conclusion by drawing a strict legal rationale: The states have the right to control access to the bar; hence the federal government may not intervene in the determination of qualifications. Justice Bradley, on the other hand, relies not on legal arguments but on stereotypical notions of women's role in life to justify denying Bradwell access to the bar. And then, almost as an afterthought, he makes a few legal points, noting the inability of married women to make binding contracts without their husbands' consent and bringing in the question of whether access to all occupations is one of those protected "privileges and immunities."

A question that must be asked is whether the decision to deny women the right to practice law—because that was the foreseeable result of the majority's decision—was based on sound legal reasoning or on biases which, as Montagu would say, masqueraded as the laws of nature? The objection that the majority opinion endorsed by implication in allowing the state court's decision to stand, and the objection that the concurring opinion made explicit, was that women could not be allowed to practice law because the law does not permit them to make binding contracts. But was this the Court's real concern, or was the Court really concerned with keeping women in their proper "sphere"?

The question of whether women could be lawyers—and the broader question of whether women could have access to all occupations in spite of their sex—was a battle that would continue to be waged for decades to come, dragging along with slow progress. But the question of defining women's other privileges and immunities would begin to take shape before the end of the decade.

THE RIGHT TO VOTE

Justice Miller's decision in the *Slaughter-House Cases*, his avoidance of the real issue in the *Bradwell* decision, and the pronouncements of Justice Bradley in the latter case make it a wonder that women ever went to court again. After all, a rather pointed message had been given: Women were not protected by the Fourteenth Amendment and women's rightful place—right by history and by nature—was not to be found seeking privileges and immunities in the civil sphere. Fortunately, though, some women of the period were not daunted. A mere two years after *Bradwell*, in February 1875, Virginia Minor went to court to challenge a Missouri law that denied her the right to vote simply because she was a woman. In the unanimous decision in *(Virginia) Minor (& Francis Minor, her husband) v. (Reese) Happersett* [S.C. 21 Wall. 162 (1875)], the Court made clear its thinking on the subject of what constituted the "privileges and immunities" that the Fourteenth Amendment protected for U.S. citizens.

Acknowledging that Virginia Minor had the necessary qualifications for voting in the state of Missouri, Reese Happersett, the registering officer, refused to register her solely because of her sex. Minor filed suit initially in St. Louis County claiming that the state constitution provision giving suffrage only to males was repugnant to the U.S. Constitution. One after the other, the hierarchy of all three state courts denied her claim. From the state courts, Minor took her challenge to the U.S. Supreme Court, arguing that there was a conflict in the constitutions of the state and the country. The right to vote, she asserted, was one of the privileges and immunities of all born or naturalized citizens, and the Fourteenth Amendment prohibited its abridgment.

Chief Justice Morrison R. Waite (the only justice <u>not</u> on the bench at the time of the *Bradwell* decision) wrote the opinion for the unanimous court, upholding the implicated section of the Missouri constitution. In addressing the question raised by Minor, of whether the Fourteenth Amendment allowed a female U.S. citizen to vote when the constitution of the state in which she resided said that only men could vote, Chief Justice Waite first asked this question: Were women citizens? He concluded that they were, and that it was not necessary to look to the Fourteenth Amendment to determine this answer. *But,* he continued, *citizen* simply meant the idea of membership in a group, and nothing more. He wrote (*Minor*, 1875: 165-170):

> There is no doubt that women may be citizens. They are persons, and by the Fourteenth Amendment "All persons born or naturalized in the United States and subject to the jurisdiction thereof" are expressly declared to be "citizens of the United States and of the State wherein they reside." But, in our opinion, it did not need this [Fourteenth] Amendment to give them that position. Before its adoption, the Constitution of the United States did not in terms prescribe who should be citizens of the United States or of the several States, yet there were necessarily such citizens without such provision. There cannot be a nation without a people. The very idea of a political community, such as a nation is, implies an association of persons for the promotion of their general welfare. . . .
>
> For convenience it has been found necessary to give a name to this membership. The object is to designate by a title the person and the relation he bears to the nation. For this purpose the words "subject," "inhabitant" and "citizen" have been used, and the choice between them is sometimes made to depend upon the form of the government. Citizen is now more commonly

> employed, however, and as it has been considered better suited to the description of one living under a republican government, it was adopted by nearly all of the States upon their separation from Great Britain, and was afterwards adopted in the Articles of Confederation and in the Constitution of the United States. When used in this sense it is understood as conveying the idea of membership of a nation, and nothing more. . . .
>
> But if more is necessary to show that women have always been considered as citizens the same as men, abundant proof is to be found in the legislative and judicial history of the country. . . . the records of the courts are full of cases in which the jurisdiction depends upon the citizenship of women, and not one can be found, we think, in which objection was made on that account. Certainly none can be found in which it has been held that women could not sue or be sued in the courts of the United States. Again; at the time of the adoption of the Constitution, in many of the States (and in some probably now) aliens could not inherit or transmit inheritance. There are a multitude of cases to be found in which the question has been presented whether a woman was or was not an alien, and as such capable or incapable of inheritance, but in no one has it been insisted that she was not a citizen because she was a woman. On the contrary, her right to citizenship has been in all cases assumed. . . .
>
> Other proof of like character might be found, but certainly more cannot be necessary to establish the fact that sex has never been made one of the elements of citizenship in the United States. In this respect men have never had an advantage over women. The same laws precisely apply to both. The Fourteenth Amendment did not affect the citizenship of women any more than it did of men. In this particular, therefore, the rights of Mrs. Minor do not depend upon the Amendment. She has always been a citizen from her birth, and entitled to all the privileges and immunities of citizenship. The Amendment prohibited the State, of which she is a citizen from abridging any of her privileges and immunities as a citizen of the United States; but it did not confer citizenship on her. That she had before its adoption.

Having confirmed women's status as citizens, Chief Justice Waite identified the real question that needed to be addressed: Is suffrage a privilege of citizenship? If so, he conceded, a state law that restricts it by sex would be unconstitutional. Noting that the Constitution does not identify specific "privileges and immunities," he looked elsewhere to determine if suffrage was intended to be included. He acknowledged that at the time the Constitution was ratified, suffrage was not added to the existing privileges and immunities of citizens, and he asked whether suffrage was then a right that came with citizenship of a state. His review of the constitutions of the states that had signed the U.S. Constitution (and all but Rhode Island had state constitutions) showed that in no state were all citizens allowed to vote; rather, each state limited the right based on age, sex, and/or wealth, and all states, with the possible exception of New Jersey, limited the right of suffrage to males. Thus, he concluded (*Minor*, 1875: 173):

> In this condition of the law in respect to suffrage in the several states, it cannot for a moment be doubted that if it had been intended to make all citizens of the United States voters, the framers of the Constitution would not have left it to implication. So important a change in the condition of citizenship as it actually existed, if intended, would have been expressly declared.

But Chief Justice Waite continued to pile on substantiation for the Court's position. Why, he asked, would the country have needed the Fifteenth Amendment if the Fourteenth Amendment protected suffrage as a right of citizenship? And why, when New Jersey had rescinded the right of women to vote in 1807, did the federal government not intervene? And why, when new states joined the Union and these states restricted suffrage to men, did the federal government not disallow their joining? The answer to all is plain, he determined: Suffrage was not a right of citizenship. And of this, he added, there can be no doubt.

> Certainly, if the courts can consider any question settled, this is one. For nearly ninety years the people have acted upon the idea that the Constitution, when it conferred citizenship, did not necessarily confer the right of suffrage. If uniform practice, long continued, can settle the construction of so important an instrument as the Constitution of the United States confessedly is, most certainly it has been done here. Our province is to decide what the law is, not to declare what it should be. (*Minor*, 1875: 177-178)

Having seemingly nailed this second coffin shut, Chief Justice Waite made an interesting, though uncharacteristic, move on the part of the Court. Playing just short of what some would see as judicial activism, he said the following (*Minor*, 1875: 178):

> We have given this case the careful consideration its importance demands. If the law is wrong, it ought to be changed; but the power for that is not with us. The arguments addressed to us bearing upon such a view of the subject may, perhaps, be sufficient to induce those having the power to make the alteration, but they ought not to be permitted to influence our judgment in determining the present rights of the parties now litigating before us. No argument as to woman's need of suffrage can be considered. We can only act upon her rights as they exist. It is not for us to look at the hardship of withholding. Our duty is at an end if we can find it is within the power of a State to withhold.
>
> Being unanimously of the opinion that the Constitution of the United States does not confer the right of suffrage upon anyone, and that the Constitutions and laws of the several States which commit that important trust to men alone are not necessarily void, we affirm the judgment of the court below.

Yet despite this slight encouragement, the laws excluding women from voting did not change for another forty-five years. Many explanations can be offered as to why it took so long for the change to occur. Clearly, the existing male power structure resisted change. In addition, however, as evidenced by the near defeat of the twelfth resolution at Seneca Falls, there was resistance within the feminist movement as well from those who found suffrage for women an extreme step at that time.

Perhaps the resistance lay in the fear of the possible results of suffrage; gaining the right to vote signals a qualitative change in the new voters' position and influence in society. Since one enormous qualitative change—the enfranchisement of the blacks—had recently been introduced in society, not everyone was ready for any more just yet. What had happened is that women once more suffered and were held in check while others benefited. It was an experience women would have again and again in their struggle for equal rights.

The Supreme Court had upheld the legality of denying women the possibility of economic power—through access to avocations. It had denied them the possibility of political power—through suffrage. The Court's twin actions firmly closed the gate on women's march toward equality. What the freed black man had won was not to be shared by women of any color for some time to come.

THE STRUGGLE CONTINUES: THE FIRST HALF OF THE TWENTIETH CENTURY

It is possible to say that the second half of the nineteenth century was concerned with trying to achieve basic rights for women—the right to control her earnings and her property, the right to go to college, the right to choose her occupation, and the right to vote. These years met with only a modicum of success, and so the first half of the twentieth century then became concerned with continuing the struggle to secure and refine these rights—gaining access to occupations, establishing the conditions of women's work environment, and obtaining the vote. The battle for this last right, although waged for decades, ended early in the twentieth century, with the ratification of the Nineteenth Amendment in 1920. Other battles—battles over what work she could do, where she could do it, for how long, and for how much—continued not only throughout the first half of the new century but are with us still today.

The dominant concern in women's rights litigation of the first half of the twentieth century involved rights in the workplace. Although some inroads had been made in employment opportunities—women were working in such areas as tobacco factories and foundries, meat-packing plants and offices—the changes were not smooth and not without setbacks. And although more diverse areas of employment had been opened to women, the underlying nature of the work was, for the most part, the same: unskilled and poorly paid. The case that came before the Court in 1908 addressed one of the more subtle impediments that women faced. Although men publicly dressed women in the guise of sheep who needed to be led and protected, women soon learned that in the workplace, men regarded them as threatening wolves. In writing laws that appeared to protect working women, men were actually protecting their own jobs and income.

By 1908, nineteen states (of the forty-six then in the Union) had protective labor laws that set maximum hours for working, prohibited working at night, or in some other way restricted working conditions. Until this time, state supreme courts had gone both ways in assessing the legality of these laws; some courts had upheld their validity, but others had ruled them invalid. But in 1905, the United States Supreme Court handed down a decision that questioned the constitutionality of protective legislation in general, and women's rights activists began the wait for just the "right" case to take to the Supreme Court to challenge the laws.

In the 1905 case of *Lochner v. New York* [25 S.Ct. 539 (1908)], the Court struck down a law that had restricted men from working in a bakery more than sixty hours a week or ten hours a day. In so ruling, the Court said that an individual's right to contract for work *was* one of the privileges protected by the Fourteenth Amendment. And then, using what was at that time the standard method of assessing when those Fourteenth Amendment protections were inviolate and when they were not, the Court applied the "rational reason" test. Used regularly in Fourteenth Amendment challenges, the test acknowledged that a rational reason for a law was sufficient ground for abridging a normally protected Fourteenth Amendment privilege or immunity. And the only rational reason, according to legal practice, lay in a state's lawful exercise of its police powers—its right to protect the health, safety, morals, and well-being of its citizens. Thus, if the law in question was a fair exercise of these powers—if its goal was in some way to protect the health, safety, general morals, and well-being of the public *and* there was a rational relationship between the law's intended goal and the law's prohibited behavior—then a Fourteenth Amendment privilege could be abridged in order to achieve what was seen as a "higher" good. If, however, the exercise of the police powers was found to be unreasonable or arbitrary, then the Fourteenth Amendment protections controlled because they were seen as the "higher" good, and the law was to be held invalid.

Applying this line of thinking, the Court found no reasonable grounds for the existence of the New York law. It stated that bakers were of reasonable intelligence and could protect themselves, and that "common knowledge" did not show that bakery work was harmful to health. The Court further noted that the interest of the public was not adversely affected by the behavior (i.e., the number of working hours) that the law attempted to curtail. Therefore, the Court ruled, the limitation of work hours was not a lawful exercise of New York's police powers and the law was invalid.

Although many regarded special laws protecting working women as beneficent legislation, others found them damaging both in restricting their working opportunities and in perpetuating the image of women as inferiors in need of special help. The case that tried to take advantage of the line of thinking established in *Lochner* and to challenge labor laws designed expressly to protect women came three years later. *Muller v. Oregon* [28 S.Ct. 324 (1908)] challenged an Oregon law that prohibited women from working more than ten hours a day in a laundry, factory, or mechanical establishment. Curt Muller, the owner of a laundry, required one of his supervisors to make a female employee work more than ten hours in one day. He was charged and found guilty of violating the state law and fined $10. Upon appeal, the state supreme court affirmed the lower court's ruling, and Muller then appealed the decision to the U.S. Supreme Court.

Some believe that *Muller* is best known for the "Brandeis brief"—a 113 page brief that Louis D. Brandeis, on his way to being one of the most eminent justices ever to sit on the Supreme Court of the United States, submitted in his role as co-counsel for Oregon. Thus, a comment or two on this brief is worthwhile.

Given the precedent of *Lochner*, Brandeis could have argued either of two ways in defense of the Oregon law. On the one hand, he could have argued to replace the "common knowledge" used in *Lochner*—the finding that bakery work involved no hazard to a worker's health—with the "common knowledge" that working at any job steadily for more than ten hours a day was dangerous to health. Or, on the other, he could have argued that the Court should make an exception to the *Lochner* doctrine of the individual's liberty to contract since the Oregon law was directed at women whereas the New York law pertained to men. Following this line, he could have argued that women needed "special protection" because there was something inherently different about them, their ability to bear children. Actually, Brandeis used both arguments but focused on that of the physical differences with special emphasis on women's biological *reproductive* role rather than her economic *productive* role.

Muller's counsel, in opposition, made a three-point argument. First, he charged that the law was unconstitutional because it violated Fourteenth Amendment protections of the pursuit of liberty and of a woman's right to make her own contract. Second, he alleged that the legislation was class legislation in that it did not apply equally to similarly situated people. And third, he said the law was an invalid exercise of the state's police powers because there was no reasonable connection between limiting women's work hours and the public's health, safety, or welfare.

Thus, the Court was faced with addressing the constitutionality of the law directly. Justice David J. Brewer wrote the unanimous opinion for the Court upholding the Oregon law as a valid exercise of the state's police power.

Muller v. Oregon
28 S.Ct. 324 (1908)
Justice Brewer, for the Court

> It is the law of Oregon that women, whether married or single, have equal contractual and personal rights with men. As said by [Oregon] Chief Justice Wolverton [cite omitted], after a review of the various statutes of the state upon the subject:
>
> "We may therefore say with perfect confidence that, with these three sections upon the statute book, the wife can deal, not only with her separate property, acquired from whatever source, in the same manner as her husband can with property belonging

to him, but that she may make contracts and incur liabilities, and the same may be enforced against her, the same as if she were a *feme sole.* There is now no residuum of civil disability resting upon her which is not recognized as existing against the husband. The current runs steadily and strongly in the direction of the emancipation of the wife, and the policy, as disclosed by all recent legislation upon the subject in this state, is to place her upon the same footing as if she were a *feme sole,* not only with respect to her separate property, but as it affects her right to make binding contracts; and the most natural corollary to the situation is that the remedies for the enforcement of liabilities incurred are made coextensive and coequal with such enlarged conditions."

It thus appears that, putting to one side the elective franchise, in the matter of personal and contractual rights they stand on the same plane as the other sex. Their rights in these respects can no more be infringed than the equal rights of their brothers. We held in *Lochner v. New York* [cite omitted] that a law providing that no laborer shall be required or permitted to work in bakeries more than sixty hours in a week or ten hours in a day was not as to men a legitimate exercise of the police power of the state, but an unreasonable, unnecessary, and arbitrary interference with the right and liberty of the individual to contract in relation to his labor, and as such was in conflict with, and void under, the Federal Constitution. That decision is invoked by plaintiff [Muller] in error as decisive of the question before us. But this assumes that the difference between the sexes does not justify a different rule respecting a restriction of the hours of labor. . . .

The legislation and opinions referred to in the margin [where Justice Brewer summarized Brandeis' listing of similar pieces of legislation and non-judicial pronouncements on the detrimental effects of women working long hours] may not be, technically speaking, authorities, and in them is little or no discussion of the constitutional question presented to us for determination, yet they are significant of a widespread belief that woman's physical structure, and the functions she performs in consequence thereof, justify special legislation restricting or qualifying the conditions under which she should be permitted to toil. Constitutional questions, it is true, are not settled by even a consensus of present public opinion, for it is the peculiar value of a written constitution that it places in unchanging form limitations upon legislative action, and thus gives a permanence and stability to popular government which otherwise would be lacking. At the same time, when a question of fact is debated and debatable, and the extent to which a special constitutional limitation goes is affected by the truth in respect to that fact, a widespread and long-continued belief concerning it is worthy of consideration. We take judicial cognizance of all matters of general knowledge.

It is undoubtedly true, as more than once declared by this court, that the general right to contract in relation to one's business is part of the liberty of the individual, protected by the 14th Amendment to the Federal Constitution; yet it is equally well settled that this liberty is not absolute and extending to all contracts, and that a state may, without conflicting with the provisions of the 14th Amendment, restrict in many respects the individual's power to contract. . . .

That women's physical structure and the performance of maternal functions place her at a disadvantage in the struggle for subsistence is obvious. This is especially true when the burdens of motherhood are upon her. Even when they are not, by abundant testimony of the medical fraternity continuance for a long time on her feet at work, repeating this from day to day, tends to injurious effects upon the body, and, as healthy mothers are essential to vigorous offspring, the physical well-being of woman becomes an object of public interest and care in order to preserve the strength and vigor of the race.

Still again, history discloses the fact that woman has always been dependent upon man. He established his control at the outset by superior physical strength, and this control in various forms, with diminishing intensity, has continued to the present. As minors, though not to the same extent, she has been looked upon in the courts as needing special care that her rights may be preserved. Education was long denied her, and while now the doors of the schoolroom are opened and her opportunities for acquiring knowledge are great, yet even with that and the consequent increase of capacity for business affairs it is still true that in the struggle for subsistence she is not an equal competitor with her brother. Though limitations upon personal and contractual rights may be removed by legislation, there is that in her disposition and habits of life which will operate against a full assertion of those rights. She will still be where some legislation to protect her seems necessary to secure a real equality of right. Doubtless there are individual exceptions, and there are many respects in which she has an advantage over him; but looking at it from the viewpoint of the effort to maintain an independent position in life, she is not upon an equality. Differentiated by these matters from the other sex, she is properly placed in a class by herself, and legislation designed for her protection may be sustained, even when like legislation is not necessary for men, and could not be sustained. It is impossible to close one's eyes to the fact that she still looks to her brother and depends upon him. Even though all restrictions on political, personal, and contractual rights were taken away, and she stood, so far as statutes are concerned, upon an absolutely equal plane with him, it would still be true that she is so constituted that she will rest upon and look to him for protection; that her physical structure and a proper discharge of her maternal functions—having in view not

> merely her own health, but the well-being of the race—justify legislation to protect her from the greed as well as the passion of man. The limitations which this statute places upon her contractual powers, upon her right to agree with her employer as to the time she shall labor, are not imposed solely for her benefit, but also largely for the benefit of all. Many words cannot make this plainer. The two sexes differ in structure of body, in the functions to be performed by each, in the amount of physical strength, in the capacity for long continued labor, particularly when done standing, the influence of vigorous health upon the future well-being of the race, the self-reliance which enables one to assert full rights, and in the capacity to maintain the struggle for subsistence. This difference justifies a difference in legislation, and upholds that which is designed to compensate for some of the burdens which rest upon her.
>
> We have not referred in this discussion to the denial of the elective franchise in the state of Oregon, for while that may disclose a lack of political equality in all things with her brother, that is not of itself decisive. The reason runs deeper, and rests in the inherent difference between the two sexes, and in the different functions in life which they perform.

At first glance, *Muller* appeared to be a very quiet decision, breaking little new ground. It was, however, anything but quiet. The decision was important, and loud, not only for its holding, but especially, as historian Leo Kanowitz (1969) has noted, for its language. The holding, obviously, decided the case at hand, and perhaps more important, it also advanced the principle that sex was a valid basis for enacting special legislation. This notion was subsequently used to restrict women's participation in any number of areas, from jobs to juries, to mention only two. But it was the language that Kanowitz really finds particularly damaging to the image of women, observing that "(t)he Court in *Muller* simply could not resist giving expression to some old-fashioned male supremacist notions" (153) in much the way that Justice Bradley's decision in *Bradwell* had done years earlier.

For many, then and now, viewing *Muller* in a negative light is difficult. After all, did the decision not protect women from having to work long and strenuous hours? But those who ask that question are not looking past the immediate tree to see the forest. It was the forest that created the mire that existed long into this century. In fact, it is possible to argue that women are still trying to recover from the negative impact of this seemingly positive, supportive decision, the theme of which Ruth Bader Ginsburg, a lawyer who brought many women's rights cases, labeled "benign preference."

The forest grew from the two clear conclusions that could be drawn from *Muller*:

- Women constitute a special category of citizens, and

- It is permissible to put special restrictions on women if it is for the future well-being of the race (underscoring, once again, the idea suggested earlier in this book: It is desirable to hold women in check so that others may progress.)

One negative consequence of this forest was that in those states where courts had struck down protective labor laws for women, legislatures introduced new protective laws. And though, as previously noted, it was argued that these laws were aimed at benefiting women since they "protected" them from harsh working conditions, the laws were, in actuality, a tremendous barrier. (And here one might ponder, once again, whether such a thing as "benign discrimination" can, indeed, exist.) What women lost far outweighed any benefit that might have accrued, for, most important, they lost the right to negotiate as independent, rational, clear-thinking individuals—a right clearly granted men in *Lochner*. And in exchange, they won perpetuation of the image of women as dependent, weak, in need of external protectors—a man, or, in this case, the state.

THE RIGHT TO EARN

But the image, at times, seemed one of convenience, pushed to the fore by legislatures and the courts when needed and ignored when that seemed expedient. When she needed the "protection" of a limited number of hours of work a week, she was dependent and weak, and the state acted as her protector. But when she needed the "protection" of a guaranteed minimum wage, she was capable of taking care of herself. In the post-*Muller* era, between 1912 and 1922, fifteen states passed minimum wage laws for women (and children)[8]; but by 1923 these laws would fall or be severely curtailed. In *Adkins v. Children's Hospital* [43 S.Ct. 394 (1923)], the Supreme Court, in a five-to-three decision (with Justice Brandeis taking no part), declared unconstitutional a District of Columbia law that allowed the establishment of minimum wages for women and children in an effort to protect them "from conditions detrimental to their health and morals." In so doing, the Court made it clear that the right to contract was not absolute; although it was the norm, "the existence of exceptional circumstances" could warrant infringement of that right. But interestingly, the Court did not then pursue a line of reasoning consistent with its past view of women and the "exceptional circumstances" that surround them. Rather, Justice George Sutherland, writing for the Court, harked back to the stereotypes of *Muller*, but not as their champion. Instead, he noted (*Adkins*, 1923: 399-400) the following about *Muller*'s findings on the inequality of the sexes:

> In view of the great—not to say revolutionary—changes which have taken place since that utterance in the contractual, political, and civil status of women, culminating in the Nineteenth Amendment, it is not unreasonable to say that these differences have now come almost, if not quite, to the vanishing point. In this aspect of the matter, while the physical differences

must be recognized in appropriate cases, and legislation fixing hours or conditions of work may properly take them into account, we cannot accept the doctrine that women of mature age, sui juris, require or may be subjected to restrictions upon their liberty of contract which could not lawfully be imposed in the case of men under similar circumstances. To do so would be to ignore all the implications to be drawn from the present day trend of legislation, as well as that of common thought and usage, by which woman is accorded emancipation from the old doctrine that she must be given special protection or be subjected to special restraint in her contractual and civil relationships.

Thus, the stage was set for attacking the statutes on grounds other than sex. This the Court did by saying that the statute was too vague; how could it be determined on a group basis, the Court asked, what level of wages was necessary to protect the health and morals of the widely divergent individual members of that group? (The Court did note that if women needed a minimum wage to protect their morals, so did men.) But the most egregious element of the law, in the view of the Court, was that it required the employer to make "an arbitrary payment for a purpose and upon a basis having no causal connection with his business, or the contract or the work the employee engages to do" (*Adkins*, 1923: 401). In other words, an employee was to be paid not in light of business profits or the quality and quantity of work she did, but solely in light of the needs of her health and moral well-being. And although the Court did note that in states with minimum wage laws, women's incomes were higher than before (the Court attributed this not to the laws but to unidentified other causes), the Court found that the statute exceeded the lawful exercise of a state's police powers and declared it unconstitutional.[9]

The fact that the Court had now ruled that women could negotiate wages but not hours extended the appearance that it was not really interested in female employees' welfare. After all, some of the most obvious immediate and tangible consequences of limited hours for women were the following:

- Lower take-home pay due to fewer hours worked;
- Lack of access to certain jobs that required longer hours or night work; and
- Restricted access to promotion because many higher-level jobs required experience in some of the work foreclosed to women because of the restrictions on their work hours.

And therein lies the *Muller* legacy, still battled in many quarters today. Women's progress in economic productivity was restricted in order to protect her social reproductivity. Her opportunity to compete openly and equally with men was foreclosed, and the continuation of occupational segregation endorsed. Laws that should have worked to protect workers of either sex ended up spawning a legacy of discriminatory employment practices against women.

But it should be emphasized that not only women were harmed here. For as is so often the case in the battle for women's rights, what really lies at stake is the battle for societal rights, women's and men's rights, or equal rights—whatever phrase is the most pleasing. Although at first glance it appears that she benefited from *Muller* and he did not, a second glance shows otherwise. In fact, each may have been equally harmed—ironically, treated equally in a sense—in that each suffered the consequences of the continuation of a sex and gender caste system. She got her hours curtailed; he was allowed to work long, excessive hours. She continued to be defined as dependent and in need of protection; he continued to bear the burden of having to labor without protection.

In the post-*Muller* decades, women made both little and great strides. The major stride, of course, was enfranchisement. But beyond the direct consequence of giving women the vote, the Nineteenth Amendment produced no immediate or major qualitative changes—as many had feared or hoped it might—in women's standing in the economy and in society. No snowball effect was forthcoming, no widespread reform, no noticeable change in attitudes. And although some additional cases involving women's rights went to the Supreme Court, progress and change were slow in coming.

In 1937, almost thirty years after *Muller*, women won, as previously noted, the protection of minimum wage laws. But forty years after *Muller* (and with fresh memories of how women labored capably and willingly during World War II to replace the men off fighting), the justices were still relying on the use of "common knowledge" (read "stereotypes") to support legal manipulations and maneuvers, still using language resplendent with male supremacist ideas, and still allowing the law to restrict the movement and progress of women in many facets of life.

A HINT OF CHANGE

Yet there was finally also just a hint of change. For what is refreshing in a case that came before the Court in 1948 is the way in which, for the first time, three justices challenged the real purpose of the law under review.

The case that evoked this challenge was *Goesaert v. Cleary* [69 S.Ct. 198 (1948)], at quick glance an example of *Muller* carried to an extreme; it questioned another facet of women's right to work and responded with stereotypical thinking to endorse the desired legal outcome. But it is the dissenting opinion by three justices that provides a point of interest, if not by itself, then as a foil to the official Court holding.

With only these three dissenters, the Court upheld a lower court decision sustaining a Michigan law that made it illegal for women to tend bar unless they were the wives or daughters of the male owner. In the following excerpts, Justice Felix Frankfurter's majority opinion reviews the background of the case sufficiently that no further background is needed here. It is important to note, however, one element of his opinion, which is its style, one not uncommon in judicial writings. Throughout the course of his opinion, Justice Frankfurter sends very clear signals as to what the Court will ultimately rule and why it is going to do so. This occurs long before the opinion actually arrives at the hinted outcome. Like bells that go off as harbingers of events to come, his hints deserve special attention. And of course, as suggested above, the dissenting opinion is equally notable. Here, first, are excerpts from Justice Frankfurter's majority opinion.

Goesaert v. Cleary
69 S.Ct. 198 (1948)
Justice Frankfurter, for the Court

As part of the Michigan system for controlling the sale of liquor, bartenders are required to be licensed in all cities having a population of 50,000, or more, but no female may be so licensed unless she be "the wife or daughter of the male owner" of a licensed liquor establishment. . . . [citation omitted] The claim, denied below . . . and renewed here, is that Michigan cannot forbid females generally from being barmaids and at the same time make an exception in favor of the wives and daughters of the owners of liquor establishments. Beguiling as the subject is, it need not detain us long. To ask whether or not the Equal Protection of the Laws Clause of the Fourteenth Amendment barred Michigan from making the classification the State has made between wives and daughters of owners of liquor places and wives and daughters of non-owners, is one of those rare instances where to state the question is in effect to answer it.

We are, to be sure, dealing with a historic calling. We meet the alewife, sprightly and ribald, in Shakespeare, but centuries before him she played a role in the social life of England [citation omitted]. The Fourteenth Amendment did not tear history up by the roots, and the regulation of the liquor traffic is one of the oldest and most untrammeled of legislative powers. Michigan could, beyond question, forbid all women from working behind a bar. This so despite the vast changes in the social and legal position of women. The fact that women may now have achieved the virtues that men have long claimed as prerogatives and now indulge in vices that men have long practiced, does not preclude the States from drawing a sharp line between the sexes, certainly in such matters as the regulation of the liquor traffic [citation omitted]. The Constitution does not require legislatures to reflect sociological insight, or shifting social standards, anymore than it requires them to keep abreast of the latest scientific standards.

While Michigan may deny to all women opportunities for bartending, Michigan cannot play favorites among women without rhyme or reason. The Constitution in enjoining the equal protection of the laws upon States precludes irrational discrimination as between persons or groups of persons in the incidence of a law. But the Constitution does not require situations "which are different in fact or opinion to be treated in law as though they were the same" [citation omitted]. Since bartending by women may, in the allowable legislative judgment, give rise to moral and social problems against which it may devise preventive measures, the legislature need not go to the full length of prohibition if it believes that as to a defined group of females other factors are operating which either eliminate or reduce the moral and social problems otherwise calling for prohibition. Michigan evidently believes that the oversight assured through ownership of a bar by a barmaid's husband or father minimizes hazards that may confront a barmaid without such protecting oversight. This Court is certainly not in a position to gainsay such belief by the Michigan legislature. If it is entertainable, as we think it is, Michigan has not violated its duty to afford equal protection of its laws. We cannot cross-examine either actually or argumentatively the mind of Michigan legislatures nor question their motives. Since the line they have drawn is not without a basis in reason, we cannot give ear to the suggestion that the real impulse behind this legislature was an unchivalrous desire of male bartenders to try to monopolize the calling.

It would be an idle parade of familiar learning to review the multitudinous cases in which the constitutional assurance of the equal protection of the laws has been applied. The generalities on this subject are not in dispute; their application turns peculiarly on the particular circumstances of a case. . . . Suffice it to say that "A statute is not invalid under the Constitution because it might have gone farther than it did, or because it may not succeed in bringing about the result that it tends to produce" [citation omitted].

Nor is it unconstitutional for Michigan to withdraw from women the occupation of bartending because it allows women to serve as waitresses where liquor is dispensed. The District Court has sufficiently indicated the reasons that may have influenced the legislature in allowing women to be waitresses in a liquor establishment over which a man's ownership provides control. Nothing need be added to what was said below as to the other grounds on which the Michigan law was assailed.

Judgment affirmed.

And now turn to the three-man dissenting opinion, Justices Douglas and Frank Murphy joining Justice Wiley B. Rutledge:

Goesaert v. Cleary
69 S.Ct. 198 (1948)
Justice Rutledge, dissenting opinion

While the equal protection clause does not require a legislature to achieve "abstract symmetry" or to classify with "mathematical nicety," that clause does require lawmakers to refrain from invidious distinctions of the sort drawn by the statute challenged in this case.

The statute arbitrarily discriminates between male and female owners of liquor establishments. A male owner, although he himself is always absent from his bar, may employ his wife and daughter as barmaids. A female owner may neither work as a barmaid herself nor employ her daughter in that position, even if a man is always present in the establishment to keep order. This inevitable result of the classification belies the assumption that the statute was motivated by a legislative solicitude for the moral and physical well-being of women who, but for the law, would be employed as barmaids. Since there could be no other conceivable justification for such discrimination against women owners of liquor establishments, the statute should be held invalid as a denial of equal protection.

The difference between the majority and minority opinions is not merely the readily apparent differences in legal interpretation; there is also a very different understanding of women's roles and place in society. Although Justice Frankfurter continues to endorse stereotypical views of women (by upholding a Michigan law so clearly resting on such stereotypes), he does at least acknowledge that women had experienced "vast changes." But then, rather than endorsing and furthering those changes (by, for example, saying that the Constitution requires that laws keep step with changes in societal standards), he reverts to the traditional condescending view of women, and allows the states to continue to "draw a sharp line between the sexes." Justice Rutledge and his fellow dissenters, on the other hand, do not bother to pepper their opinion with commentaries on the prerogatives of the sexes but rather seem to assume equality (or to feel the question irrelevant to deciding the case at hand) in their conclusion that the Michigan law denied equal protection.

But there is also a stark difference in the tone of these two opinions. Justice Frankfurter's opinion is almost dismissive of the women alleging discrimination and loss of rights, describing their case as "beguiling" and needing very little time to decide. Further, he is not willing "to give ear" to the possibility that the law reflected something other than chivalrous concern for women (itself a sexist position, endorsing her inferior, dependent position).

Justice Rutledge, on the other hand, starts out by calling the work of the law "invidious"—a word that anyone familiar with Fourteenth Amendment law knows sounds the death knell for any law so labeled. And he follows that remark not with a dismissive pat on the head for women but rather an accusing finger pointed at the legislature and the state for perhaps not acting with full integrity.

The question of the motivations of the legislature—which Justice Frankfurter takes on faith and Justice Rutledge questions—is important to consider. Was the law really "chivalrous," intended to protect a woman's well-being, or was it restrictive, intended to curtail her access to the more lucrative job of bartending and thereby protect men's monopoly on that job?

The fact that both the majority and dissenting opinions felt it necessary at least to raise the issue of the legislature's motivation highlights the need to question the real intent of any law, along with its undeniable and real consequence.

Unfortunately for women, however, dissenting opinions do not count in the eyes of the law, although they may portend things to come. Thus, it would be some time before women would see a majority opinion echoing Justice Rutledge—assuming equality of the sexes and questioning the motivations of state legislators.

CONCLUSION

The best way to understand the progress of the women's rights movement in the three-quarters of the century between 1873 and 1948 is to look at a toddler struggling to learn to walk: She stands up, falls down, tries it again and, perhaps, again; eventually she takes a step or two forward, totters, and once again falls backward. Although perhaps not quite as fraught as the toddler's, the "progress" on women's rights during these seventy-five years was extremely slow and costly.

For almost the first fifty years of the period, women remained firmly enslaved. In the first of many defeats, they were clearly told by the Court that they were not to benefit from the expansive mood of the country reflected in the Reconstruction amendments because those freedoms and protections were clearly meant only for black men. Throughout the ensuing years, the Court continued to buttress women's enslavement. The Court denied them the right freely to choose their occupation and to negotiate their own terms of employment or career paths. They were allowed to negotiate their own wages, but only because those negotiations would result in lower wages than they would have received if they had been protected by minimum wage laws. And for almost all of those fifty years, they could not vote.

During the next twenty-five years, some of the laws controlling women's rights did begin to change. Ultimately, women got the vote and gained the protection of minimum wage laws, other protective labor laws were applied to both sexes, and occupations previously closed to women began gradually to open. Nevertheless, the legacy of the old ways was slow to erode. No radical change in the position of women came with the vote. The legislative halls did not spill over with representatives (or lobbyists) championing the rights of women. Judicial opinions did not suddenly shed notions of chivalry and father-protector. The societal norm of setting women in only one "rightful" place—the home—did not instantaneously disintegrate. The economic position of women did not catch up to that of men. For as often is the case, even the few laws that changed were changed far more easily and readily than were the minds and attitudes of people. Change in attitude, change that could eventually force widespread change in the law, was still years away.

NOTES

1. The Thirteenth and Fifteenth Amendments completed the Reconstruction triplet. The Thirteenth, ratified in 1865, abolished slavery, and the Fifteenth, ratified in 1870, prohibited the denial of voting rights on the basis of race.

2. Obviously, the fifth section, giving Congress the power to enforce the provisions of the amendment, is of import; since it does no more than that, however, and extends no new rights, it is not considered here.

3. The *Slaughter-House Cases* was argued February 3-5, 1873, and the decision handed down on April 14, 1873. *Bradwell v. Illinois* [83 U.S. (16 Wall) 442 1873], the women's rights case, was argued January 18, 1873, and the decision handed down on April 15, 1873.

4. The first college to admit women was Oberlin, in 1833, its founding year. Others followed but slowly.

5. Information on Bradwell's personal life and accomplishments in this and subsequent paragraphs comes from Anonymous. 1971. Myra Bradwell (1931-1894). *Women's Rights Law Reporter*, 1(1): 5-6.

6. Here is evidence of the practice, noted in Chapter 1, of the Court's taking the narrowest and least controversial path for deciding a case. In *Bradwell*, the Court addressed none of the concerns Carpenter raised about discrimination on the basis of sex but addressed only the question of whether the federal or state government controlled access to the legal profession.

7. Twenty-one years later, the Supreme Court was still saying that admission to the bar was to be determined by each state and that the states could deny women entry into the legal profession. In *Ex parte Lockwood* (14 S.Ct. 1082 1894), the Court denied Belva Lockwood's challenge of a Virginia law that prohibited her admission to the bar because she was a woman. Citing *Minor* (see later in Chapter 5, "The Right to Vote") and *Bradwell*, the Court said that Virginia had the right to determine if the word *person* in the statute setting forth qualifications for admission to the bar included women or was restricted to men only. The absurdity of this ruling, and of the Virginia law, lies in the fact that Lockwood had been admitted to the District of Columbia bar in 1873 (the same year the Court ruled against Myra Bradwell) and was already, as the Supreme Court noted in its denial of her claim, a member of the bar of the Supreme Court. In fact, she was the first female member of that bar.

8. Levitan, Sar & Belous, Richard. 1979. *More than Subsistence: Minimum Wages for the Working Poor*. Baltimore, Md.: Johns Hopkins University Press.

9. Despite subsequent attempts to have minimum wage laws declared constitutional, this would not happen for another 14 years [*West Coast Hotel Co. v. Parrish*, 57 S.Ct. 578 (1937)]. That decision, in 1937, was quickly followed by the passage of the Federal Fair Labor Standards Act of 1938, which ensured both minimum wages and maximum hours.

6

The Dawning of Enlightenment

Even when laws have been written down,they ought not always remain unaltered.

Aristotle
Politics

INTRODUCTION

Compared to what had gone before, the second half of the twentieth century was to become, eventually, the glory days for women's rights. These years were not totally filled with glory, however, and some of it, like most glory, proved to be of a tenuous, if not fleeting, nature. It is doubtful that women's struggles, slow in coming as they were, will ever be likened to a thoroughbred's race, for the race has been far from fast and is far from won. And with the present composition of the Supreme Court, one not likely to change dramatically for decades, it is unlikely that complete victory is in sight; in fact, the greater probability for the near future is that penalty flags will be thrown down and extra yards added to the distance to the goal line.

The tide toward greater rights for women did not turn immediately with the step into the second half of the century. Sentiments endorsed by *Goesaert* did not, unfortunately, vanish like magic when the decade switched from the forties to the fifties. Not until the seventies, just a handful of years short of the nation's two hundredth birthday and just two decades short of the two hundredth birthday of the Bill of Rights, did enlightenment seem to dawn on the nation. Not until then did women begin to feel a countrywide, legal shift in attitudes. Until that time, the Supreme Court continued to endorse the stereotypical notions that had dominated legal pronouncements from the inception of this country.

THE END OF THE NAYSAYERS

The decision in *Hoyt v. Florida*, 82 S.Ct. 159 (1961), is important because it signals the end of a very long era. This was the last of the series of Supreme Court decisions endorsing the categorical denial to women of opportunities available to men, and like so many of its predecessors, it appeared to make that denial absolutely out of hand. Despite the fact that it came at the end of an era—or perhaps because it did end the era—the case is noteworthy for the strong stereotypical notions of a sex and gender caste system expressed in the opinion.

Hoyt challenged the long-standing norm of automatically excluding women from jury service, a duty that men had been obligated to perform since the passage of the Sixth and Seventh Amendments to the Constitution in 1791. Gwendolyn Hoyt killed her husband with a baseball bat during the heat of a marital battle over his alleged infidelity and his rejection of her attempts at reconciliation. Despite the defense of temporary insanity, which, defense attorneys argued, resulted from the mental anguish produced by both the infidelity and the refusal to reconcile, an all-male jury convicted her of second degree murder. Hoyt appealed her conviction, arguing that female jurors would have been more sympathetic in judging her. She claimed that the Florida law giving women absolute exemption from jury service *unless they expressly waived that privilege* (of nonservice) by registering with the clerk of the circuit court violated her Fourteenth Amendment rights both of a trial by her peers and of equal protection under the law. In a unanimous decision (though not a unanimous opinion), the Court rejected Hoyt's claim, thereby upholding the Florida state law and Hoyt's conviction. The official opinion, written by Justice John M. Harlan, is notable for what at best can be termed tautological reasoning and semantic games, and at worst for sexist reasoning and sleight of hand.

Justice Harlan began his opinion by reviewing the facts of the case and the law under challenge and acknowledged that Hoyt's attorneys had indeed demonstrated that only a "minimal" number of women had waived their exemption from jury duty. The remainder of his opinion, excerpted below, begins with his response to Hoyt's claim, which he labeled the "core" of her argument, that the nature of her crime especially warranted women jurors.

Hoyt v. State of Florida
82 S.Ct. 159 (1961)
Justice Harlan, for the Court

[T]hese premises misconceived the scope of the right to an impartially selected jury assured by the Fourteenth Amendment. That right does not entitle one accused of crime to a jury tailored to the circumstances of the particular case, whether relating to the sex or other condition of the defendant, or to the nature of the charges to be tried. It required only that the jury be indiscriminately drawn from among those eligible in the community for jury service, untrammeled by any arbitrary and systematic exclusions. . . . The result of [Hoyt's] appeal must therefore depend on whether such an exclusion of women from jury service has been shown.

I.

Several observations should initially be made. We of course recognize that the Fourteenth Amendment reaches not only arbitrary class exclusions from jury service based on race or color, but also all other exclusions which "single out" any class of persons "for different treatment not based on some reasonable classification" [cite omitted]. We need not, however, accept appellant's invitation to canvass in this case the continuing validity of this Court's dictum. . . that a State may constitutionally "confine" jury duty "to males." This constitutional proposition has gone unquestioned for more than eighty years in the decisions of the Court, . . . and had been reflected, until 1957, in congressional policy respecting jury service in the federal courts themselves. Even were it to be assumed that this question is still open to debate, the present case tenders narrower issues.

Manifestly, Florida's [statute] does not purport to exclude women from state jury service. Rather, the statute "gives to women the privilege to serve but does not impose service as a duty" [cite omitted]. It accords women an absolute exemption from jury service unless they expressly waive that privilege. This is not to say, however, that what in form may be only an exemption of a particular class of persons can in no circumstances be regarded as an exclusion of that class. Where, as here, an exemption of a class in the community is asserted to be in substance an exclusionary device, the relevant inquiry is whether the exemption itself is based on some reasonable classification and whether the manner in which it is exercisable rests on some rational foundation.

In the selection of jurors Florida has differentiated between men and women in two respects. It has given women an absolute exemption from jury duty based solely on their sex, no similar exemption obtaining as to men. And it has provided for its effectuation in a manner less onerous than that governing exemptions exercisable by men: women are not to be put on the jury list unless they have voluntarily registered for such service; men, on the other hand, even if entitled to an exemption, are to be included on the list unless they have filed a written claim of exemption as provided by law [cite omitted].

In neither respect can we conclude that Florida's statute is not "based on some reasonable classification," and that it is thus infected with unconstitutionality. Despite the enlightened emancipation of women from the restrictions and protections of bygone years, and their entry into many parts of community life formerly considered to be reserved to men, woman is still regarded as the center of home and family life. We cannot say that it is constitutionally impermissible for a State, acting in pursuit of the general welfare, to conclude that a woman should be relieved from the civic duty of jury service unless she herself determines that such service is consistent with her own special responsibilities.

Florida is not alone in so concluding. Women are now eligible for jury service in all but three States of the Union. Of the forty-seven States where women are eligible, seventeen besides Florida, as well as the District of Columbia, have accorded women an absolute exemption based solely on their sex, exercisable in one form or another. In two of these States, as in Florida, the exemption is automatic, unless a woman volunteers for such service. It is true, of course, that Florida could have limited the exemption, as some other States have done, only to women who have family responsibilities. But we cannot regard it as irrational for a state legislature to consider preferable a broad exemption, whether born of the State's historic public policy or of a determination that it would not be administratively feasible to decide in each individual instance whether the family responsibilities of a prospective female juror were serious enough to warrant an exemption.

Likewise we cannot say that Florida could not reasonably conclude that full effectuation of this exemption made it desirable to relieve women of the necessity of affirmatively claiming it, while at the same time requiring of men an assertion of the exemptions available to them. Moreover, from the standpoint of its own administrative concerns the State might well consider that it was "impractical to compel large numbers of women, who have an absolute exemption, to come to the clerk's office for examination since they so generally assert their exemption" [cite omitted].

Appellant argues that whatever may have been the design of this Florida enactment, the statute in practical operation results in an exclusion of women from jury service, because women, like men, can be expected to be available for jury service only under compulsion. In this connection she points out that by 1957, when this trial took place, only some 220 women out of approximately 46,000 registered female voters in Hillsborough County—constituting about 40 per cent of the total voting population of that county—had volunteered for jury duty since the limitation of jury service to males, . . . was removed . . . in 1949 [cite omitted].

This argument, however, is surely beside the point. Given the reasonableness of the classification involved in [Florida's statute], the relative paucity of women jurors does not carry the constitutional consequences appellant would have it bear. "Circumstances or chance may well dictate that no persons in a certain class will serve on a particular jury or during some particular period" [cite omitted].

We cannot hold this statute as written offensive to the Fourteenth Amendment.

II.

Appellant's attack on the statute as applied in this case fares no better.

In the year here relevant [Florida statutes] required the jury commissioners, with the aid of the local circuit court judges and clerk, to compile annually a jury list of 10,000 inhabitants qualified to be jurors. In 1957 the existing Hillsborough County list had become exhausted to the extent of some 3,000 jurors. The new list was constructed by taking over from the old list the remaining some 7,000 jurors, including 10 women, and adding some 3,000 new male jurors to build up the list to the requisite 10,000. At the time some 220 women had registered for jury duty in this county, including those taken over from the earlier list.

The representative of the circuit court clerk's office, a woman, who actually made up the list testified as follows as to her reason for not adding others of the 220 "registered" women to the 1957 list: "Well, the reason I placed ten is I went back two or three, four years, and noticed how many women they had put on before and I put on approximately the same number." She further testified: "Mr. Lockhart [one of the jury commissioners] told me at one time to go back approximately two or three years to get the names because they were recent women that had signed up, because in this book [the female juror register], there are no dates at the beginning of it, so we can't—i don't know exactly how far back they do go and so I just went back two or three years to get my names." When read in light of Mr. Lockhart's testimony, . . . it is apparent that the idea was to avoid listing women who though registered might be disqualified because of advanced age or for other reasons.

Appellant's showing falls short of giving this procedure a sinister complexion. It is true of course that the proportion of women on the jury list (10) to the total of those registered for such duty (some 220) was less than 5%, and not 27% as the trial court

> mistakenly said and the state appellate court may have thought. But when those listed are compared with the 30 or 35 women who had registered since 1952 [cite omitted] the proportion rises to around 33%, hardly suggestive of an arbitrary, systematic exclusionary purpose. Equally unimpressive is appellant's suggested "male" proportion which we are asked to contrast with the female percentage. The male proportion is derived by comparing the number of males contained on the jury list with the total number of male electors in the county. But surely the resulting proportion is meaningless when the record does not even reveal how many of such electors were qualified for jury service, how many had been granted exemptions. . . , and how many on the list had been excused when first called.
>
> This case in no way resembles those involving race or color in which the circumstances shown were found by this Court to compel a conclusion of purposeful discriminatory exclusions from jury service [cites omitted]. There is present here neither the unfortunate atmosphere of ethnic or racial prejudices which underlay the situations depicted in those cases, nor the long course of discriminatory administrative practice which the statistical showing in each of them evinced.
>
> In the circumstances here depicted, it indeed "taxes our credulity" [cite omitted], to attribute to these administrative officials a deliberate design to exclude the very class whose eligibility for jury service the state legislature. . . had declared only a few years before. . . . It is sufficiently evident from the record that the presence on the jury list of no more than ten or twelve women in the earlier years, and the failure to add in 1957 more women to those already on the list, are attributable not to any discriminatory motive, but to a purpose to put on the list only those women who might be expected to be qualified for service if actually called. Nor is there the slightest suggestion that the list was the product of any plan to place on it only women of a particular economic or other community or organizational group [cites omitted].
>
> Finally, the disproportion of women to men on the list independently carries no constitutional significance. In the administration of the jury laws proportional class representation is not a constitutionally required factor [cites omitted].
>
> Finding no substantial evidence whatever in this record that Florida has arbitrarily undertaken to exclude women from jury service, a showing which it was incumbent on appellant to make, (cites omitted), we must sustain the judgment of the Supreme Court of Florida. . . .

Though Justice Harlan's bottom-line decision represented the unanimous vote of the Court, only section II of his opinion represented a unanimous opinion. Chief Justice Earl Warren and two colleagues concurred only with that part of the opinion, noting that it could not be determined whether

Florida was, in fact, making a good faith effort not to discriminate against women in the performance of jury duty.

It should be easy to address the question of whether Justice Harlan's opinion, the last in a long line of similar opinions, reflects sound legal reasoning or a reliance on stereotypical notions to support desired legal outcomes. To facilitate analysis, ponder his response to Hoyt's claim that the ratio of males and females in the juror pools might not reflect women's "special" responsibilities but rather simply the fact that men are compelled to participate while women must volunteer. And in answering the question of whether the Court reached a "good" decision in *Hoyt*, consider, once again, the consequences of this decision. Women were granted a "privilege" by not being required to serve; men were denied that privilege. But isn't jury service more traditionally portrayed as a *responsibility* that *all citizens* should shoulder for their country? Aren't Americans always told that it is their civic duty to serve on juries, thereby upholding one of those basic promises of democracy forged centuries ago? What then is the image that unfolds, and the consequences of that image, when only men are required to bear yet another burden, while women are presumed too weak to do so?

THE TIDE BEGINS TO TURN—THE 1970s

It would be another fourteen years before the Supreme Court was to invalidate all remaining state laws that restricted jury duty on the basis of sex [see *Taylor v. Louisiana*, 95 S.Ct. 692 (1975)—ironically enough, an appeal by a man charged with rape], but only another ten years before men and women would begin to feel the Court's leveling of sex distinctions in other areas. From then on, far fewer of the Court's decisions endorsed a sex and gender caste mentality and far more of the decisions began to tear down that mentality. What is clearly important and apparent in the flood of decisions that began in the 1970s is the Court's growing recognition of exactly what it had claimed in *Hoyt* to be unable to see: an unfortunate atmosphere of prejudice and a long history of discriminatory administrative practice against women.

The causes of this change are open to much speculation. No single cause, or even several causes, can be conclusively given credit. But two pieces of Federal legislation enacted in the years between Hoyt and the next major piece of women's rights litigation certainly may have influenced some members of the Court. The Equal Pay Act of 1963 and the Civil Rights Act of 1964, most notably Title VII of the latter law, *appeared* to signal a major shift in national attitudes on both race and sex discrimination, and the Court could hardly ignore this entirely.

The Equal Pay Act of 1963 was conceived, according to Ruth Bader Ginsburg (1975), as a "women's remedy." It was, she contends, intended to redress compensation disparities between men and women engaged in the same or similar work. The Civil Rights Act of 1964 was a far broader ban on discrimination, but its Title VII is especially relevant here. Title VII forbids discrimination in the hiring, firing, and all other conditions of employment on the basis of race, religion, national origin, or sex. Ginsburg argues, however, that sex was included not as a good and heartfelt commitment to the equality of women but as a ruse that went awry. The ban on sex discrimination was added to the bill as a floor amendment by members of Congress who, she claims, believed that this addition would kill the entire act. (This is reminiscent of sentiments seen earlier in history that the specter of women's rights would automatically defeat any crusade with which it was linked.)

Certainly factors other than these two new laws were at work in producing a new Court approach, but whatever the reasons, change was indeed finally on the way.

1971: A LANDMARK YEAR

In 1971, before the Court officially signaled a change in attitude, two legal scholars—both *males*—examined the record of the judiciary in sex discrimination cases and concluded that it was abysmal.[1]

> [B]y and large the performance of American judges in the area of sex discrimination can be succinctly described as ranging from poor to abominable. With some notable exceptions, they have failed to bring to sex discrimination cases those judicial virtues of detachment, reflection and critical analysis which have served them so well with respect to other sensitive social issues. Particularly striking. . . is the contrast between judicial attitudes toward sex and race discrimination. Judges have largely freed themselves from patterns of thought that can be stigmatized as "racist"—at least their opinions in that area exhibit a conscious attempt to free themselves from habits of stereotypical thought with regard to discrimination based on *color*. With respect to *sex* discrimination, however, the story is different. "Sexism"—the making of unjustified (or at least unsupported) assumptions about individual capabilities, interests, goals and social roles solely on the basis of sex differences—is as easily discernible in contemporary judicial opinions as racism ever was. (Johnston & Knapp, 1971: 676)

The 1971 landmark decision of *Reed v. Reed*, 92 S.Ct. 251, brought an end to the sexist legacy cited by Johnston and Knapp, for while it was comparatively narrow in its reach, it was a harbinger of more extensive change brewing in the Supreme Court's response to sex discrimination cases. Monumental it may not have been, but fundamental it was. To be sure, the Court still refused to depart from reliance on its traditional equal protection clause standard and apply a "strict scrutiny" approach—the approach it had used successfully to reverse race discrimination cases. Nevertheless, for the first time, the Court required that a state be a bit more reasonable and a bit less arbitrary in its treatment of women.

The case of Sally and Cecil Reed is a short, sweet, and tide-turning case in the history of women's rights litigation. At the time the Reed's adopted son died, the couple was separated; each sought to become the administrator of the son's estate. Idaho probate court awarded the role to Cecil, under a state law stating that if several people were equally entitled—and father and mother were both so entitled—the court *must* prefer the male. (This was just one among several bases for preference; blood was another.) In ruling in favor of Cecil, the court did acknowledge that both Reeds were equally entitled under the law.

Sally appealed to an Idaho district court on the grounds that the law violated the equal protection clause; she, in essence, won. The court remanded the case to the probate judge for a determination of which person was in fact better qualified to administer the estate. Before the probate court had a chance to look at the case anew, however, Cecil appealed the district court decision to the state supreme court, which reversed the district court, and reinstated the probate court's original decision, making Cecil the administrator. The Idaho supreme court, in so doing, said that the state law was mandatory, leaving no room for discretion on the part of the probate court, and the law was not in violation of the equal protection clause. Sally then appealed to the U.S. Supreme Court.

What happened next is interesting both for what can be seen and for what is not seen. In her brief to the Supreme Court, Sally Reed alleged that the Idaho law, as well as all laws that discriminate against women, violated the equal protection clause of the Fourteenth Amendment, and she asked that the equal protection clause be considered under the more stringent Fourteenth Amendment standard—the "strict scrutiny" or "suspect criterion" measure—rather than the more lenient "reasonable relationship" test. (The differences between these two standards will be explained shortly.)

Despite the fact that the Supreme Court, in reaching its decision, completely ignored this request, the seed of a choice of standards by which to judge a sex discrimination case had been planted. And although the seed did not flower in this instance, it was to do so later. It is important, therefore, both for this and subsequent sex discrimination cases, to understand the substance and implication of Sally Reed's request and the Court's response.

When there is a claim of a violation of the equal protection clause, two determinations must be made (and judicial opinions often will dissect the determinations explicitly as part of their text). The first determination is a relatively easy and simple one; the second is complex and controversial.

As its first step in an equal protection challenge, a court must determine whether there are two groups of "similarly situated" people who are being treated differently. "Similarly situated," although the key phrase in this investigation, is a relatively easy determination to make. In fact, this determination was made, seemingly effortlessly, in *Muller* (female and male laundry workers), *Goesaert* (females who were the daughters and wives of bar owners and all other females), and *Hoyt* (female and male potential jurors). Once a court makes a positive finding that there are, indeed, two similarly situated groups of people, it must then ascertain that they are being treated differently (i.e., that different rules are being applied to each group). Then, if it establishes that similarly situated groups are in fact receiving different treatment, a court faces the second—and more difficult—determination.

As its second step, a court must determine the reason for the difference in treatment and whether that difference—that discrimination—is "invidious." The reason for requiring this second determination is straightforward: the Fourteenth Amendment does not prohibit all government discrimination but only that which is invidious. Whether a particular type of discrimination is or isn't invidious, however, is anything but straightforward, and it is this second, and complex, determination that courts generally have more trouble making in deciding equal protection challenges. The Supreme Court has developed two standards for making this determination, and a lower court's job is to decide which standard is the correct one to use in a given case and then to apply it. The two standards are "reasonable relationship" or "strict scrutiny."

REASONABLE RELATIONSHIP OR STRICT SCRUTINY

The "reasonable relationship" test, and the one applied without question to sex discrimination cases before 1971, is the less-stringent standard. Under this test, a law may be upheld as constitutional, and not in violation of the equal protection clause, if the mandate of the law bears a reasonable relationship to achieving a permissible legislative goal (e.g., the power of the police to protect public safety, discussed earlier). In order for something to be deemed reasonable, the classification of the two similarly situated groups and the subsequent difference in treatment must bear a "just and proper" relation to the goal being sought by the state. Neither classification may be arbitrary. (This line of reasoning has been apparent in the earlier decisions we have discussed.) As the less rigorous standard, it is thought to apply when "nonbasic" civil rights are allegedly being violated, and the burden of establishing the *absence* of a reasonable relationship rests with the person challenging the law.

The alternative to this standard is the "strict scrutiny" or "suspect criterion" test and is, as the names suggest, the more stringent of the two standards. Under this approach, a law may be upheld as constitutional and not in violation of the equal protection clause only if the government has some "compelling interest" for creating the difference in treatment between the two groups. "A "compelling interest" is far more difficult for the government to establish than a "reasonable relationship," and thus this test subjects a law to a much more intense level of review. It is, therefore, usually applied when a "basic" civil right is being claimed or the lines of difference are drawn on the basis of a "suspect class." (That is the precise legal term, although "suspect classification" might be more easily understood by the average person.) Thus, each time a law divides groups on the basis of a recognized suspect class—which race was but sex was not at the time of *Reed*, and still is not—the law must be subjected to the stricter standard of review. The burden of withstanding this stricter review and thus sustaining the law then switches to the law's supporters, who must establish a compelling affirmative justification for the law, a requirement that many deem impossible to meet. It was this standard, rather than the "reasonable relationship" standard—the standard used in all sex discrimination cases up until that date—that Sally Reed requested be applied to her challenge.

A third standard for reviewing equal protection challenges would be developed in 1976. Often referred to as "intermediate scrutiny," it was an outgrowth—and compromise—of the two primary standards for judging equal protection challenges. According to the Court, it flows logically from its predecessors, and will be explained later in the Court's decision in *Craig v. Boren*, 97 S.Ct. 451 (1976).

Before returning to *Reed*, and seeing how the Court passed judgment on the Idaho law and Sally Reed's request, reflect on the following. Males have been slow to see the imbalance that female feminists have always recognized—from Abigail Adams to the present. As lawyer David Cole observes, the difficulties women have experienced in having their concerns survive a review under either of the two basic standards is simply reflective of the inherent male bias in our laws. The traditional male perspective, he says, simply believes that since females are obviously different from males, they may therefore be treated differently. Further, and more important, he notes that the subjective experience of men becomes the "objective" reality—the "neutral normative standards"—by which women are judged to be different (Cole: 51). Clearly the thinking and attitude controlling sex discrimination cases until 1971, this attitude began to crumble somewhat in *Reed*.

In reading Chief Justice Warren E. Burger's unanimous opinion for the Court overturning the Idaho law, bear in mind that even while overturning the law, the Court did this without referring to Sally Reed's request to apply the stricter standard. And while reading, think about whether this was a good decision for this particular case and a good decision for future sex discrimination cases.

The Chief Justice began his opinion with a review of the history of the case in its course to the Court. He then gave the Court's decision.

Reed v. Reed
92 S.Ct. 251 (1971)
Chief Justice Burger, for the Court

. . . . Having examined the record and considered the briefs and oral arguments of the parties, we have concluded that the arbitrary preference established in favor of males by. . . the Idaho Code cannot stand in the face of the Fourteenth Amendment's command that no State deny the equal protection of the laws to any person within its jurisdiction.

Idaho does not, of course, deny letters of administration to women altogether. Indeed, . . . a woman whose spouse dies intestate has a preference over a son, father, brother, or any other male relative of the decedent. Moreover, we can judicially notice that in this country, presumably due to the greater longevity of women, a large proportion of estates, both intestate and under wills of decedents, are administered by surviving widows.

[The Idaho statute] is restricted in its operation to those situations where competing applications for letters of administration have been filed by both male and female members of the same entitlement class established by statute. In such situations, statute provides that different treatment be accorded to the applicants on the basis of their sex; it thus establishes a classification subject to scrutiny under the Equal Protection Clause.

In applying that clause, this Court has consistently recognized that the Fourteenth Amendment does not deny to States the power to treat different classes of persons in different ways [cites omitted]. The Equal Protection Clause of that amendment does, however, deny to States the power to legislate that different treatment be accorded to persons placed by a statute into different classes on the basis of criteria wholly unrelated to the objective of that statute. A classification "must be reasonable, not arbitrary, and must rest upon some ground of difference having a fair and substantial relation to the object of the legislation, so that all persons similarly circumstanced shall be treated alike" [cite omitted]. The question presented by this case, then, is whether a difference in the sex of competing applicants for letters of administration bears a rational relationship to a state objective that is sought to be advanced by the operation of [the Idaho statute].

In upholding the latter section, the Idaho Supreme Court concluded that its objective was to eliminate one area of controversy when two or more persons, equally entitled under statute, seek letters of administration and thereby present the probate court "with the issue of which one should be named." The court also concluded that where such persons are not of the same sex, the elimination of females from consideration "is neither an illogical nor arbitrary method devised by the legislature to resolve an issue that would otherwise require a hearing as to the relative merits . . . of the two or more petitioning relatives . . . " [cite omitted].

Clearly the objective of reducing the workload on probate courts by eliminating one class of contests is not without some legitimacy. The crucial question, however, is whether [the statute] advances that objective in a manner consistent with the command of the Equal Protection Clause. We hold that it does not. To give a mandatory preference to members of either sex over members of the other, merely to accomplish the elimination of hearings on the merits, is to make the very kind of arbitrary legislative choice forbidden by the Equal Protection Clause of the Fourteenth Amendment; and whatever may be said as to the positive values of avoiding intrafamily controversy, the choice in this context may not lawfully be mandated solely on the basis of sex.

> . . . The objective of [the statute] clearly is to establish degrees of entitlement of various classes of persons in accordance with their varying degrees and kinds of relationship to the intestate. Regardless of their sex, persons within any one of the enumerated classes of that section are similarly situated with respect to that objective. By providing dissimilar treatment for men and women who are thus similarly situated, the challenged section violates the Equal Protection Clause.

Chief Justice Burger's opinion clearly takes a reader through the analytical steps of a Fourteenth Amendment challenge, first determining whether there were two similarly situated groups being treated differently, and then, using the "reasonable relationship" test, assessing whether that difference in treatment was constitutional. And though disappointing because the opinion ignored completely (not even deigning to mention) Sally Reed's request to use the stricter standard, the ultimate conclusion reached by relying on the looser measure was a victory for her—and for women—in outcome and thinking. Striking down the Idaho law as an arbitrary and unreasonable differentiation in treatment of females and males was certainly a victory in outcome. But, as is true of every Supreme Court decision, perhaps the more important victory was the precedent established. In *Reed*, the Court announced a major change in position, departing from a position that had received full support as recently as ten years earlier. In *Hoyt*, the Court had endorsed as a reasonable government objective the automatic exclusion of women for historical <u>or</u> administrative purposes. Now, ten years later, the Court was saying that it was no longer "reasonable" to exclude women simply for administrative convenience. This, as will soon become apparent with subsequent decisions, was a major step toward fuller rights for women. And though the explicit rationale was important, the implications and underlying attitudes that were abandoned with this decision are equally important to recognize. In rejecting administrative ease as a justification for discrimination, the Court was withdrawing its support from the idea that women and men were *automatically* different and, therefore, could be subjected automatically to different treatment. Instead, the Court was now recognizing that though differences might exist, they could not be simply assumed. The differences could not be *assumed*, on the basis of stereotypes or on any other ground, to be true of an individual or of a class of people, but rather must be individually determined to see whether, <u>in fact</u>, they do exist in each individual case.

Although noteworthy in many respects, *Reed* was not noteworthy for bringing sex into the "suspect class" category. Justice William J. Brennan, a year later in a postscript to a case that addressed the question of whether unmarried couples had the same right to privacy as married couples in their use of contraceptives [*Eisenstadt v. Baird*, 92 S.Ct. 1029 (1972)], argued that the Court had not rejected Sally Reed's claim that sex was, like race and national origin, a suspect class. Rather, he said, there simply had been no need to take up that question. Given that the Idaho law could not pass constitutional review using the more lenient test of presenting a rational relationship between the law and intended outcome, Justice Brennan said, the Court had simply seen no reason to assess it by the stricter standard.

Neither result—the reliance on the looser standard and avoidance of testing the stricter one—is surprising given the Court's history of resolving cases at the lowest and least controversial plateau. By sticking to the old reliable standard (for which there was every legitimate legal reason) and not reaching for the untested (on women) standard (for which, again, there was every legitimate historical and sociopolitical reason to do so), the Court demonstrated its commitment to stick to the status quo unless absolutely necessary to do otherwise. And here, in the eyes of the Court, it was not absolutely necessary.

Although many saw *Reed* as a solid victory for women's rights in its decision to cast serious doubt on the viability of "administrative convenience" as a rationale for sex discrimination, others regarded it as only a minor gain in that it failed to address the question of sex as a suspect classification. A few commentators even saw it as no victory at all. For one thing, the detractors noted, the Idaho law had already been repealed before the Supreme Court even heard the case. For another, they said, by failing to change the standard for deciding sex discrimination cases, the Court had left challengers as the party required to prove that a law was unconstitutionally discriminatory. This, the detractors argued, was yet another example of the judicially endorsed burdens on the backs of American women.

It seems logically impossible, however, not to see *Reed*, and 1971, as at least a turning point. Just how sharp the turn was may be left for debate, but not too much time should be wasted on the matter; the Court appeared to be beginning to move.

1973-1975—AND *ROE V. WADE*

The movement, though, did not continue immediately with the next "women's rights" case that came to the Supreme Court. Hailed as a major victory for women, *Roe v. Wade* [93 S.Ct. 705 (1973)] was added, by feminists and nonfeminists alike, to the early win list in the history of women's rights litigation; however—and this may sound strange—it is wrongly placed there. This is not to suggest that the issue addressed in *Roe*, a woman's right to have an abortion performed by a competent, licensed physician in a safe, clean, clinical setting, is not central to women and their sense of well-being and control over their lives and their bodies; *it is*. But given that *Roe* was legally based on a claim of the right to privacy, not on a charge of unequal protection under the law, it is not a women's rights case in the line of *Bradwell*, *Muller*, *Reed*, and so on. In fact, in many respects, it is no more correct to call *Roe v. Wade* a women's rights case than it is to call rape a "sex crime." Both terms are misnomers for what they are supposed to be identifying. Rape is not a crime of sex but a crime of anger, disrespect, aggression, and abuse of power. True, the weapon used to accomplish this crime is a sex organ, but that does not make the crime one of sex. Sex is simply the vehicle for achieving the desired end, in this case, the active expression of hatred.

Roe, following the same line of reasoning, is not an equal protection claim (which is the claim raised in the majority of women's rights litigation), but it is a right to privacy claim. Access to a safe and legal abortion is, again, simply the vehicle used in this instance to test just where the protections of personal privacy extend.

Roe, an anonymous pregnant woman, claimed that the Texas laws restricting her right to a legal abortion to terminate her pregnancy infringed her right to privacy—a right she felt was hers under "the concept of personal 'liberty' embodied in the Fourteenth Amendment's Due Process Clause; or in personal, marital, familial, and sexual privacy said to be protected by the Bill of Rights or its penumbras" [*Roe v. Wade*, 93 S.Ct. 705, 715 (1973)]. Justice Harry A. Blackmun, writing for the Court in its seven-to-two decision, responded by looking at the history of abortion law and by exploring the scope of the murky "right to privacy."

Concluding his review of the common law position on abortion both at the time of the Constitution and throughout most of the nineteenth century, Justice Blackmun wrote that a woman then "enjoyed a substantially broader right to terminate a pregnancy than she does in most States today" [*Roe*, 1973: 720]. Seeking the cause for this shift of attitudes, Justice Blackmun cited three widely held reasons that surfaced in the late nineteenth century. The three reasons were the Victorian desire to discourage "illicit sex," the state's interest in protecting pregnant women from dangerous medical procedures, and the state's interest in protecting "prenatal life." Some of this thinking, he noted, continued right up to the time of the current case.

The right to privacy, the court majority found, "is broad enough to encompass a woman's decision whether or not to terminate her pregnancy" [*Roe*, 1973: 727]. But, Justice Blackmun continued, this right is not so absolute that she is free to choose—on her own—the when and where of her abortion. Rather, he concluded "the right of personal privacy includes the abortion decision, but . . . this right is not unqualified and must be considered against important state interests in regulation" [*Roe*, 1973: 727]. And these state interests were listed as "protection of health, medical standards, and prenatal life." [*Roe*, 1973: 728].

Thus far, there is nothing in the opinion that makes this a women's rights case save for the fact, already noted, that it involves abortion, something that only women can experience. Nothing has moved this case out of the category of a claim to a right to personal privacy. Even the discussion of the question of whether a fetus is a "person" in the eyes of the Constitution does not change this classification, for the Court simply concluded that the word *person* as used throughout the Constitution and its amendments has no "possible prenatal application" [*Roe*, 1973: 729]. The Court did acknowledge, however, that at some point a woman's right to privacy does require a balancing calculation in which her interests are weighed against those of the "potential human life." (And this weighing of women's interests against those of another group is characteristic of some women's rights cases.) Yet the Court did not rank the interests of one party—the woman or the fetus—as being absolutely dominant and the interests of the other party as being secondary. Rather, the Court found that the interests of both parties were legitimate—and valued—concerns, with each ascendant at different points in the pregnancy. Justice Blackmun concluded the decision for the Court by writing [*Roe*, 1973: 731]:

> the state does have an important and legitimate interest in preserving and protecting the health of the pregnant woman . . . and that it has still *another* important and legitimate interest in protecting the potentiality of human life. These interests are separate and distinct. Each grows in substantiality as the woman approaches term and, at a point during pregnancy, each becomes compelling.

The Court identified the first trimester as the period in which the woman's rights and her freedom to choose were "compelling." For the remaining two trimesters, however, the Court found that the state could regulate abortion procedures to ensure the "preservation and protection of maternal health."

It could be argued that in *Roe*, yet again, women's interests have been given second-class status compared to those of some other group—this time fetal interests. And it could be argued that this case, once again, portrays women as in need of state protection and assistance—they are able to make sound, rational decisions about their bodies, their lives, and the lives of their potential offspring only for a limited period of time, the first three months of the pregnancy. After that, they need help. But these views require some deep, deep digging between the lines, and the Justices, up to that date, had never been particularly subtle when seeking to limit women's rights. (Though they had been known to leave things to inference, it never took great probing to get the message. And lest it be thought that *Roe* signaled a change and that subtlety became, then, the Court's guiding principle, a look at the cases to come quickly banishes such thinking.)

The fact is that the status of women was of no real concern to the Court in deciding *Roe*, and perhaps that is perhaps where the true "women's issue" in *Roe* lies. There were no pronouncements about women's appropriate sphere, or her ability to fend for herself. There were no endorsements of stereotypical notions of women's role and status (although there is brief mention of some of the negative consequences of maternity or of additional offspring for some women, and the "continuing stigma of unwed motherhood" is noted). There were no ground-breaking announcements as to whether the Court was changing its perception of woman's role and status in society. It was as if she were merely the mechanism for raising the issue at hand and of no consequence beyond that. What it would have meant today had the opinion given more attention to the plight of women cannot be known, but the absence of that attention, along with the nature of the claim, clearly sets *Roe* apart from the history of women's rights litigation.

Ironically, although *Roe* should not be considered in the same class as other women's rights cases discussed in this book, the decision had widespread consequences for women. It gave them, albeit for a limited time, options! For at least a three-month period (and more for those women who have multiple pregnancies), a great many women would have legitimate choice. And thus, although *Roe* said little about women's status, it nevertheless altered it. The Court was accepting the notion that women were capable of making rational decisions and deserving the opportunity to carry forward their decisions in a nonstigmatizing way. It gave them credibility, dignity, and the promise of safety. The status of women, however, was in for yet more change, and this would come with very explicit pronouncements harkening their new position.

NOTE

1. Johnston, Jr., John and Knapp, Charles. 1971. Sex discrimination by law: A study in judicial perspective. *New York University Law Review*, 46 (Oct): 675-747.

7

The Dawning Continues

No written law has ever been more binding than unwritten custom supported by popular opinion.

Carrie Chapman Catt
Why We Ask for the Submission of an Amendment
Senate hearing on woman's suffrage, February 3, 1900.

Less than two years after *Reed* (and a few months after *Roe*), in the first half of 1973, the Supreme Court really did continue on its roll in expanding women's rights. The continuation came with *Frontiero v. Richardson* [93 S.Ct. 1764 (1973)], in which the Court struck down a law that allowed a difference in the payment of benefits to married male and married female members of the armed forces.

Frontiero specifically involved a federal law that allowed married male members of the armed forces to claim their wives as dependents, thereby gaining increased housing allowances and medical and dental benefits, *whether or not the wives were in fact dependent*. Under the same law, however, married female members of the armed forces could receive those benefits for their husbands *only if the husbands were in fact dependent*, with *dependency* defined as receiving at least 50 percent of his support from his spouse. Sharron Frontiero sought these benefits for herself and her husband and was told that she had to substantiate her husband's dependency. (Her husband was a full-time student and received $205 in veterans' benefits; his share of household expenses was $354.) She, in turn, claimed that the statute discriminated on the basis of sex: in order to receive the increased benefits, she was required to demonstrate her spouse's dependency on her for more than 50 percent of his support, but a male member of the services was not required to make the same demonstration to get increased benefits for his wife. She further alleged that the law discriminated against servicewomen in two ways. First, women had to demonstrate a husband's dependency; no such burden was required of men. And second, men who did not provide more than 50 percent of their wives support still received the increased benefits, but similarly situated women did not. These differences in treatment, Frontiero argued, were unconstitutionally discriminatory and violated her due process protections under the Fifth Amendment. Further, she argued that her claim should be subject to strict scrutiny because sex was a suspect class.

These were the claims that Frontiero took to the federal district court in Alabama, and it was these claims that the panel of three judges rejected. They denied her request for a permanent injunction against the enforcement of the law and also her demand for increased benefits. In the plurality opinion he authored for the Supreme Court, Justice Brennan suggested that the District Court's rationale for its decision was as follows: Since there was nothing in the statute's legislative history to indicate the purpose of the difference in treatment, it was fair to surmise that [*Frontiero v. Richardson*, 93 S.Ct. 1764, 1767-1768 (1973)]

> Congress might reasonably have concluded that, since the husband in our society is generally the "breadwinner" in the family—and the wife typically the "dependent" partner—"it would be more economical to require married female members claiming husbands to prove actual dependency than to extend the presumption of dependency to such members."

The District Court also concluded by saying that since approximately 99 percent of the armed forces was male, the law "might conceivably lead to a 'considerable saving of administrative expense and manpower'" [*Frontiero v. Richardson*, 93 S.Ct. 1764, 1768 (1973)]. Thus, the lower court upheld the law on the ground of administrative convenience, something the Supreme Court had said in *Reed* was no longer acceptable grounds for differential treatment of women and men, and the case went directly to the Supreme Court.

The *Frontiero* decision appeared early in the beginning of the run of women's rights cases that came before the Supreme Court of Chief Justice Warren Burger.[1] In this case, it is possible to see the Court beginning to form coalitions that continued, with great predictability, throughout his tenure as Chief Justice. *Frontiero* was decided in an eight-to-one vote; however, there was no majority opinion. (It is this absence of a majority opinion that makes *Frontiero* particularly dicey in the history of women's rights litigation.) Rather, there were four separate opinions. Three justices—William Douglas, Thurgood Marshall, and Byron White—concurred with the opinion of the Court authored by Justice Brennan. Justice Potter Stewart wrote his own, one-sentence, concurring opinion. Justice Blackmun and Chief Justice Burger joined Justice Lewis Powell in a separate concurring opinion. Only Justice William Rehnquist dissented, saying in a one-sentence opinion that he supported the reasons stated by the District Court.

Justice Brennan's plurality opinion picks up on *Reed* in responding to Frontiero's claims and uses an approach not seen before in a case involving women. Justice Brennan actually accepts Frontiero's claim that classifications based on sex are inherently suspect and agrees that they should be reviewed with the stricter standard of scrutiny used in Fourteenth Amendment challenges. In reading this ground-breaking decision, pay careful attention to his justification for applying the "strict scrutiny" standard.

Frontiero v. Richardson
93 S.Ct. 1764 (1973)]
Justice Brennan, plurality opinion

At the outset, [the Frontieros] contend that classifications based upon sex, like classifications based upon race, alienage, and national origin, are inherently suspect and must therefore be subjected to close judicial scrutiny. We agree and, indeed, find at least implicit support for such an approach in our unanimous decision only last Term in *Reed v. Reed*. . . .

The Court [there] noted that the Idaho statute "provides that different treatment be accorded to the applicants on the basis of their sex; it thus establishes a classification subject to scrutiny under the Equal Protection Clause" [cite omitted]. Under "traditional" equal protection analysis, a legislative classification must be sustained unless it is "patently arbitrary" and bears no rational relationship to a legitimate governmental interest.

[In *Reed*], the Court held the statutory preference for male applicants unconstitutional. In reaching this result, the Court implicitly rejected appellee's apparently rational explanation of the statutory scheme, and concluded that, by ignoring the individual qualifications of particular applicants, the challenged statute provide [sic "dissimilar treatment for men and women who are. . . similarly situated" [cite omitted)]. The Court therefore held that, even though the State's interest in achieving administrative efficiency "is not without some legitimacy," "to give a mandatory preference to members of either sex over members of the other, merely to accomplish the elimination of hearings on the merits, is to make the very kind of arbitrary legislative choice forbidden by the [Constitution]. . ." [cite omitted]. This departure from "traditional" rational-basis analysis with respect to sex-based classifications is clearly justified.

There can be no doubt that our Nation has had a long and unfortunate history of sex discrimination. Traditionally, such discrimination was rationalized by an attitude of "romantic paternalism" which, in practical effect put women, not on a pedestal, but in a cage. . . .

[The opinion here cites Justice Bradley's famous decision in *Bradwell* that man is woman's protector and defender; this is found in Chapter 5 of this book.]

As a result of notions such as these, our statute books gradually became laden with gross, sterotyped [sic] distinctions between the sexes and, indeed, throughout much of the nineteenth century the position of women in our society was, in many respects, comparable to that of blacks under the pre-Civil War slave codes. Neither slaves nor women could hold office, serve on juries, or bring suit in their own names, and married women traditionally were denied the legal capacity to hold or convey property or to serve as legal guardians of their own children [cites omitted]. And although blacks were guaranteed the right to vote in 1870, women were denied even that right—which is itself "preservative of other basic civil and political rights"—until adoption of the Nineteenth Amendment half a century later.

It is true, of course, that the position of women in America has improved markedly in recent decades. Nevertheless, it can hardly be doubted that, in part because of the high visibility of the sex characteristic, women still face pervasive, although at times more subtle, discrimination in our educational institutions, in the job market and, perhaps most conspicuously, in the political arena [cites omitted].

Moreover, since sex, like race and national origin, is an immutable characteristic determined solely by the accident of birth, the imposition of special disabilities upon the members of a particular sex because of their sex would seem to violate "the basic concept of our system that legal burdens should bear some relationship to individual responsibility. . ." [cite omitted]. And what differentiates sex from such nonsuspect statuses as intelligence or physical disability, and aligns it with the recognized suspect criteria, is that the sex characteristic frequently bears no relation to ability to perform or contribute to society. As a result, statutory distinctions between the sexes often have the effect of invidiously relegating the entire class of females to inferior legal status without regard to the actual capabilities of its individual members.

Congress itself has concluded that classifications based upon sex are inherently invidious, and this conclusion of a coequal branch of Government is not without significance to the question presently under consideration. . . .

With these considerations in mind, we can only conclude that classifications based upon sex, like classifications based upon race, alienage, or national origin, are inherently suspect, and must therefore be subjected to strict judicial scrutiny. Applying the analysis mandated by that stricter standard of review, it is clear that the statutory scheme now before us is constitutionally invalid.

The sole basis of the classification established in the challenged statutes is the sex of the individuals involved. Thus, under [these statutes] a female member of the uniformed services seeking to obtain housing and medical benefits for her spouse must prove his dependency in fact, whereas no such burden is imposed upon male members. In addition, the statutes operate so as to deny benefits to a female member, such as appellant. . . who provides less than one-half of her spouse's support, while at the same time granting such benefits to a male member who likewise provides less than one-half of his spouse's support. Thus, to this extent at least, it may fairly be said that these statutes command "dissimilar treatment for men and women who are similarly situated" [cite omitted].

Moreover, the Government concedes that the differential treatment accorded men and women under these statutes serves no purpose other than mere "administrative convenience." In essence, the Government maintains that, as an empirical matter, wives in our society frequently are dependent upon their husbands, while husbands rarely are dependent upon their wives. Thus, the Government argues that Congress might reasonably have concluded that it would be both cheaper and easier simply conclusively to presume that wives of male members are financially dependent upon their husbands, while burdening female members with the task of establishing dependency in fact.

The Government offers no concrete evidence, however, tending to support its view that such differential treatment in fact saves the Government any money. In order to satisfy the demands of strict judicial scrutiny, the Government must demonstrate, for example, that it is actually cheaper to grant increased benefits with respect to *all* male members, than it is to determine which male members are in fact entitled to such benefits and to grant increased benefits only to those members whose wives actually meet the dependency requirement. Here, however, there is substantial evidence that, if put to the test, many of the wives of male members would fail to qualify for benefits. And in light of the fact that the dependency determination with respect to the husbands of female members is presently made solely on the basis of affidavits rather than through the more costly hearing process, the Government's explanation of the statutory scheme is, to say the least, questionable.

In any case, our prior decisions make clear that, although efficacious administration of governmental programs is not without some importance, "the Constitution recognized higher values than speed and efficiency" [cite omitted]. And when we enter the realm of "strict judicial scrutiny," there can be no doubt that "administrative convenience" is not a shibboleth, the mere recitation of which dictates constitutionality [cites omitted]. On the contrary, any statutory scheme which draws a sharp line between the sexes, *solely* for the purpose of achieving adminis-

> trative convenience, necessarily commands "dissimilar treatment for men and women who are. . . similarly situated," and therefore involves the "very kind of arbitrary legislative choice forbidden by the [Constitution]. . ." [cite omitted]. We therefore conclude that, by according differential treatment to male and female members of the uniformed services for the sole purpose of achieving administrative convenience, the challenged statutes violate the Due Process Clause of the Fifth Amendment insofar as they require a female member to prove dependency of her husband.

For many, the reasoning set forth in Justice Brennan's opinion, though long in the coming, was well worth waiting for, even though not all the justices would make it as the official position of the Court. His declaration that sex was a suspect class, and that he found implicit support for this in *Reed*, was not shared by the majority of his Court brethren. With only four justices endorsing this position, and four concurring with the decision but not the position and one dissenting from the decision, there was a majority of five against declaring sex a suspect class. Nevertheless, for women's rights supporters everywhere, the fact that any Supreme Court opinion had finally endorsed the notion of sex as a suspect class—and less than two years after the Court had completely ignored Sally Reed's request to make just such a declaration—was surely a welcome sign.

According to Ginsburg (1973), who appeared as a friend of the court (*amicus curiae*) for the American Civil Liberties Union on behalf of Frontiero, the Court not only had taken a giant step beyond *Reed* but also had moved far faster than anyone had anticipated. This, however, is not that much of an earth-shaking conclusion; just consider the decades it took to make the relatively meager step taken in *Reed* and then compare that with the brief time between *Reed* and *Frontiero* to take the large step in that latter case.

What, exactly, was so astounding about *Frontiero*? In the earlier case, Ginsburg notes (and as mentioned in the discussion on *Reed*, supra), the Court simply struck down an obsolete law, one that Idaho had already repealed even before the Court handed down its decision. In *Frontiero*, however, the Court struck down a "common statutory pattern"—a pattern found in "Social Security purposes, in workmen's compensation and disability laws, and in benefit programs for federal, state and municipal employees" (Ginsburg, 1973: 3). Despite the pervasiveness of the pattern, the Court was willing to strike it down, and therein lies a fair portion of the weight and importance of this decision.

Moreover, says Ginsburg, in approaching the treatment of sex as a suspect class, the Court was in effect putting legislatures and lower courts on notice "that sex discrimination by law will no longer escape rigorous constitutional review in our nation's highest tribunal" (1973: 2). Whether *Frontiero*, and subsequent women's rights cases, did, in fact, receive this rigorous review is something to consider in your reading.

But perhaps Justice Brennan's greater break with Supreme Court tradition can be found elsewhere in his opinion. In a clearly negative and disapproving tone, Justice Brennan chastizes the Court for its past reliance on attitudes toward women that smacked of "romantic paternalism," were redolent with stereotypical notions, and served to keep women as enslaved as pre-Civil War blacks. But he does not himself appear totally immune to the influence of ancient ghosts. There is that remarkable statement that despite improvement in the lot of women, they still suffer from discrimination, "in part because of the high visibility of the sex characteristic." In reading this, it is easy to recall Montagu's warning of the double bind into which men continually put women, simultaneously valuing and devaluing them for their unique female characteristic: the ability to bear children. Thus, women are told to be feminine, yet it is the evidence of that femininity that is the cause—according to Montagu and apparently to Justice Brennan—of continued discrimination.

There is yet another ground-breaking element in Justice Brennan's opinion: He actually questioned the intentions of the government. This is diametrically opposed to the position the Court took in *Goesaert*. In that majority opinion, as noted earlier in this book, the Court rolled over and played dead, not even bothering to question the legislators' real intent in putting restrictions on women's right to be bartenders. Unlike the dissenters who questioned the legislators' motivations, the majority simply accepted as valid the assertion that there was a legitimate state purpose, despite logic to the contrary. Finally, twenty-five years later, in *Frontiero*, a plurality opinion actually challenged the federal government's thinking and behavior.

Justice Brennan's ultimate conclusions—that sex is a suspect class, that the federal statute must be reviewed under this stricter standard, and that under this standard the statute falls short—are, as just noted, a major advance. But we must remember that the declaration of sex as a suspect class was not shared by a clear majority of the Court. Justice Stewart, in his brief concurring opinion, simply cited *Reed* as his basis for finding the federal law to be invidiously discriminatory. Justice Powell and his two concurring justices (Chief Justice Burger and Justice Blackmun), were, however, explicit in rejecting the need to declare sex a suspect class.

Frontiero v. Richardson
93 S.Ct. 1764 (1973)
Justice Powell, concurring opinion

> I agree that the challenged statutes constitute an unconstitutional discrimination against servicewomen in violation of the Due Process Clause of the Fifth Amendment, but I cannot join the opinion of Mr. Justice Brennan, which would hold that all classifications based upon sex, "like classifications based upon race, alienage, and national origin," are "inherently suspect and must therefore be subjected to close scrutiny." . . . It is unnecessary for the Court in this case to characterize sex as a suspect classification, with all of the far-reaching implications of such a holding. [*Reed*], which abundantly supports our decision today, did not add sex to the narrowly limited group of classifications which are inherently suspect. In my view, we can and should

> decide this case on the authority of *Reed* and reserve for the future any expansion of its rationale.
>
> There is another, and I find compelling, reason for deferring a general categorizing of sex classifications as invoking the strictest test of judicial scrutiny. The Equal Rights Amendment, which if adopted will resolve the substance of this precise question, has been approved by the Congress and submitted for ratification by the States. If this Amendment is duly adopted, it will represent the will of the people accomplished in the manner prescribed by the Constitution. By acting prematurely and unnecessarily, as I view it, the Court has assumed a decisional responsibility at the very time when state legislatures, functioning within the traditional democratic process, are debating the proposed Amendment. It seems to me that this reaching out to pre-empt by judicial action a major political decision which is currently in process of resolution does not reflect appropriate respect for duly prescribed legislative processes.
>
> There are times when this Court, under our system, cannot avoid a constitutional decision on issues which normally should be resolved by the elected representatives of the people. But democratic institutions are weakened, and confidence in the restraint of the Court is impaired, when we appear unnecessarily to decide sensitive issues of broad social and political importance at the very time they are under consideration within the prescribed constitutional processes.

Justice Powell's opinion appears very straightforward. He rejected Justice Brennan's suggestion that the Court had declared sex a suspect class in *Reed* but said nevertheless that *Reed* was the correct precedent that enabled the Court to declare the military dependents law unconstitutional. Justice Powell's opinion is also interesting, however, because of what it asked the Court not to do and to do. First, he asked the Court not to engage in judicial interference unless absolutely necessary; in other words, let Congress do the job of legislating, he said, rather than have the Court do Congress's job. Second, he told the Court to sit back and wait to hear what the will of the people would be, to listen to "common knowledge." In this case, according to Justice Powell, the common knowledge would be the outcome of state legislatures' votes on ratifying the Equal Rights Amendment.

(If his argument were correct, ratification of the Equal Rights Amendment would have been equivalent to declaring sex a suspect class. As things have now turned out with ERA defeated, common knowledge has in effect said that the majority of justices were correct and that sex should not have been declared a suspect class.)

Despite the strong eight-to-one vote on the case, much discussion followed *Frontiero* because of the multiple and differing opinions. The focus of discussion was, naturally, whether the Court had in fact declared sex a suspect class. And the answer, gleaned from both legal opinion and history, is that it had not. With no majority opinion, there was no opinion that had the weight of holding. But the five justices who in their opinions either did not mention the issue or said it had not been addressed at the time did form a majority bloc. This majority bloc left as grist for a later mill the question of whether sex was a suspect class and, therefore, subject to strict scrutiny.

CHISELING AWAY

For two reasons, *Frontiero* is nevertheless salient in the history of women's struggle for equality. First, it is important for both its particular and general consequences. As already noted, the particular result of *Frontiero* was to strike down a law that involved a widespread pattern of discriminatory treatment of women. At the same time, the Court gave women a broader victory that was to signal a major change in the status of women in all spheres of life. Laws that separate males and females in the public realm—as opposed to the domestic—and thereby support and endorse different treatment of the sexes (as did the law challenged in *Frontiero*) perpetuate the thinking that males and females are, *in fact*, different, and continue and reinforce the devaluation of women. In striking down the law, the Court thus also began to chisel away at the widely held general assumptions of female inferiority.

Second, *Frontiero* is important because it was the first case in which at least some of the Justices supported the notion that any classification based on sex was to be closely scrutinized. And though women's rights advocates were, needless to say, disappointed that a solid Court majority had not taken this view, the issue had finally gone public in a strongly worded Supreme Court opinion. Why only some of the justices were convinced that the time had come to view sex as a suspect classification while others were not is still unclear. It might have been that the Solicitor General, who presented the government's argument against such a classification, was sufficiently persuasive, or it might have been that he was simply preaching to the choir.

In any event, the Solicitor General acknowledged that sex, like race and national origin, which were already declared suspect classifications, had "visible and immutable biological characteristics that [bear] no necessary relation to ability" (Ginsburg, 1975: 17). But, he argued, the parallels ended there; sex did not share other characteristics that were important in classifying race or national origin as suspect. He noted three important differences. First, he said, race, not sex, had "an especially disfavored status in constitutional history" (1975: 18). Second, he noted that, historically, suspect status has been applied to "disadvantaged minorities" who, because of that status are victims of subjugation by the politically powerful. Since women were not considered a minority group and were not "disabled from exerting their substantial and growing political influence" (1975: 18), sex could not qualify. And finally, he said, the legislation that affected women did not suggest that women were inferior or lacking in dignity, as was the case with laws affecting racial and ethnic minorities. Thus, he concluded, women did not need the greater protection afforded by declaring sex a suspect class.

The Solicitor General failed to realize, or chose to ignore, a significant factor. Laws that assign different standards for treating any two groups who are different only because of those "visible and immutable" *biological* characteristics that are not correlated with ability are devaluing at least one of those groups. It could be argued that there are two kinds of laws that treat groups of seemingly similar people differently (be these groups of men and women, for example, or blacks and whites): There are laws that seek to remove disadvantages or compensate one group for past disadvantages, and there are laws that seek to perpetuate current structures of disadvantage. The history of women's rights litigation has been a history of challenging laws that fall in the latter category. With *Frontiero,* however, the Court had begun at last to recognize this pattern and would continue to do so in the years to come. Nonetheless, the Court still was not ready to declare that the logical way to end this pattern of disadvantage lay in declaring sex a suspect class.

This division and, more important, the positions taken by each group were not, according to political scientist Beverly Cook (1978), an isolated occurrence. Rather, they represented an identifiable pattern. Cook reviewed the Burger Court decisions on women's rights cases from 1971 to 1977 to determine "the relative attachment of each justice to sexist precedent and the relative willingness of each to give legitimacy to new sex roles" (1978: 48). She classified cases from this period as being either those endorsing the stereotypical image of women—those cases that raised issues relating to procreation and child care—or cases challenging the stereotypical role and image of women as inferior, cases seeking to expand women's options outside the home. Cook tried to see if any patterns in judicial decision making could be discerned. She easily found some. She found that from 1971 to 1975, Chief Justice Burger and Justice Rehnquist were overwhelmingly antifeminist in their votes and opinions while Justice Marshall was consistently feminist. Justices Douglas, Stewart, Blackmun, and Powell were more supportive of women's rights in the home than out of it, while Justices Brennan and White held to the flip side, particularly supporting the expansion of women's roles outside the home. But from 1975, when Justice Douglas retired from the bench, until 1977, all the justices except Justice Stewart were consistent in their decisions, either consistently favoring women's rights or consistently voting against them.

Cook's explanation of why these easily discernible patterns arose should not be surprising, as the practice has been seen and noted before. But what might be cause for surprise is that her analysis suggests a blatancy and shamelessness with which this prejudice reveals itself. She concluded (54-55):

> The examination of the Burger Court posture since 1971 to ward female roles in American society indicates that the Justices decide cases on the basis of their personal value systems rather than by the application of neutral legal principles. . . .
>
> The analysis of judicial votes in the sex role cases decided by the Burger Court reveals the extent to which each Justice has abandoned ancient myths about woman's place. . . .
>
> The Justices rationalize their votes for one party's claim through legal formulas or traditional values, but the unarticulated psychological attitude arises from deeply rooted affections,

> sympathies, and beliefs attached to familiar institutions and roles. . . . [W]hat is important is how the Justice feels about women—women on welfare, pregnant teachers, women officers, women jurors—and their demands, in relation to how the Justice feels about the other party—industry, grade school, the military establishment, the courts—and its expectations for the female role.

Recognizing both these patterns and their explanation should reduce the likelihood of being surprised by the decisions in *Frontiero,* as well as the cases that followed during this period.

Less than one year later, in 1974, the Court was faced with a challenge that was, on its face, the flip side of *Frontiero.* The case, brought by widower Mel Kahn, challenged a Florida statute that gave an automatic $500 tax exemption to widows but not to widowers [*Kahn v. Shevin,* 94 S.Ct. 1734 (1974)]. Kahn claimed that this law violated the Equal Protection Clause of the Fourteenth Amendment. A lower Florida court agreed with him, but the state supreme court ruled against him, claiming that the law bore a reasonable relationship between its method (the automatic exemption) and its goal (overcoming in a small way the disparity in the earning power of women and men.) And so the case came to the Supreme Court, which in a six-to-three decision upheld the law's constitutionality.

Writing the majority opinion, Justice Douglas cited the "firmly entrenched" patterns in the earning differentials of women and men (and here he was referring to the entire country, not just to Florida.) As a result of these patterns, he continued, widows were usually left in far greater financial difficulty than widowers were, and in trying to make up for some of this situation, the Florida law seemed fair.

Ironically, in supporting the Florida law, Justice Douglas used the same stereotypical thinking that was used to *strike down* the law in *Frontiero.* He averred that men were typically the breadwinners in families and that if the wife died, the husband would suffer no economic loss—he would simply continue working. But if the husband died, "the widow will find herself suddenly forced into a job market with which she is unfamiliar, and in which, because of her former economic dependency, she will have fewer skills to offer" [*Kahn v. Shevin,* 94 S.Ct. 1734, 1737 (1974)]. He supported this thinking by turning not to *Frontiero* but to *Reed* as precedent, saying that the difference in the treatment of widows and widowers bore a "substantial relation to the object of the legislation" (*Ibid.*).

Justice Douglas did not ignore *Frontiero,* however, but rather suggested that the two cases were different. In *Frontiero,* he said, the difference in treatment was based solely on administrative convenience, whereas in *Kahn* the difference in treatment was "to further the state policy of cushioning the financial impact of spousal loss upon the sex for which that loss imposes a disproportionately heavy burden" [*Kahn v. Shevin,* 94 S.Ct. 1734, 1737 (1974)]. Thus, despite the fact that this determination of the consequences of spousal loss was based on stereotypical notions rejected in *Frontiero,* not on an individual assessment of the facts as was called for in *Reed,* the Court affirmed Florida's differential treatment of widows and widowers.

Before hearing what the dissenters had to say about Kahn's request, think for a moment about a point raised earlier. In the discussion following *Frontiero*, it was suggested that laws challenged under the equal protection clause of the Fourteenth Amendment are of two kinds: either perpetuating existing structures of discrimination or seeking to redress past practices of discrimination. In the Florida case, it was argued both originally by the state and subsequently in the majority opinion that the law challenged in *Kahn* falls in the latter group. But does it? Although it might help to ease to a very small extent the financial burden faced by many widows, this law certainly did not address the fundamental problem underlying the widows' situation: the lesser earning power of women. The law merely helped perpetuate the disparity, as well as the long-held notion that women cannot manage on their own but need help and support from others, be it their husbands or, as in this case, the state.

The Court's dissenters picked up on this schism between the avowed intent of the law and the actual result. Justice Brennan, joined in dissent by Justice Marshall, concluded that the Court had used the wrong standard in reaching its decision. Strict scrutiny should have been applied, he said, following the precedent of *Frontiero* in viewing sex as a suspect classification. Under that standard, the state needed to show "that the challenged legislation serves overriding or compelling interests that cannot be achieved either by a more carefully tailored legislative classification or by the use of feasible, less drastic means" [*Kahn v. Shevin*, 94 S.Ct. 1734, 1738 (1974)]. Justice Brennan did not find fault with Florida's compelling state interest: He saw the alleviation of past economic discrimination for one group of women as not only valid but also as necessary. Where he did find fault, however, was with the way Florida tried to achieve its desired end. A more narrowly constructed statute would have more accurately hit the mark, he contended, since the challenged law compensated all widows alike, whether they were financially comfortable or not.

There was one more dissenter. Justice White agreed with the other two dissenters in finding that the wrong standard had been applied. Given that sex is a suspect class, he argued, this discriminatory law required more justification than the state had provided if it were to be upheld as constitutional. If the law's goal was to alleviate current economic hardship, Justice White questioned, why did the exemption apply to women who did not need the benefit but not to men who did? Or, he continued, if the state's goal was to compensate women for past economic discrimination, then why limit the exemption to widows? He concluded that the state did not adequately explain its justification for treating women and men differently and thus the law should not stand.

It is interesting to see that in less than a year, the idea of treating sex as a suspect class not only had failed to gain adherents on the Court but, it might be argued, had also lost ground. In *Frontiero*, decided in May 1973, a plurality of four endorsed the belief that sex was a suspect class and, therefore, laws that differentiated on the basis of sex had to be reviewed with "strict scrutiny." But in *Kahn*, less than a year later, that coalition had shrunk to three. One of the supporters of the plurality decision in *Frontiero* even authored the majority opinion in *Kahn* and returned to using the more relaxed standard of a "reasonable relationship." Why? After all, as noted earlier, it is possible to see *Frontiero* and *Kahn* as simply reverse sides of the same coin: the former representing a female claiming an unfair allocation of a benefit, the latter a male claiming an unfair allocation of a benefit. The Court, however, treated them as very different situations. In *Frontiero,* the Court saw the difference in treatment as simply reflecting administrative convenience, not as a legitimate state goal; therefore, the difference in treatment was unconstitutional. In *Kahn,* however, the Court saw the difference in treatment as meeting a reasonable state goal and, because the law in question was administered through the tax system, even more leeway was given. As the Court noted, states have always been given great latitude in the construction of their tax systems.

Despite these clear differences in the judicial interpretation of these laws, it is impossible not to wonder whether the difference in outcome did not reflect both the difference in the sex of the challengers and an incomplete understanding on the part of the justices of just what sex discrimination really is. The explicit and implicit gains for women's rights achieved in *Frontiero* were weakened by the Court's decision in *Kahn;* all the stereotypes the Court seemed to dismiss when it had declared unconstitutional the law challenged by Sharron Frontiero were revived when it upheld the law challenged by Mel Kahn. In deciding against Kahn, the Court let stand the presumption of an invariable and dichotomous image of all married women as economically dependent upon their husbands and all married men as independent of their wives. It failed to recognize, as it had recognized in *Frontiero,* that there are wives who support their husbands, either in full or in part, just as there are husbands who support their wives. And it failed to recognize that when one marriage partner dies, it is not necessarily and automatically the woman who needs economic (and other) assistance.

There was yet another oversight in the Court's decision in *Kahn,* perhaps its biggest gap: It failed to recognize that sex discrimination is involved not solely in how women are treated but also in how men are treated. As pointed out repeatedly through this book, the status of women and men in society is so inextricably linked that when an image is presented about one sex—such as widows needing assistance while widowers do not—an image is created about the other sex as well—such as men are independent and women are not. That is the image of women and men that the Court was endorsing in early 1974.

NOTE

1. Warren E. Burger served on the Supreme Court from 1953 to 1969. He was Chief Justice the entire time.

8

Biology versus the Law

Fresh from brawling courts
And dusty purlieus of the law.

Sir Alfred Tennyson
In Memoriam

A mere two months after *Kahn*, the Court decided the first in a line of cases that focused squarely on an aspect of women's biological uniqueness (and, Montagu would say, one source of their special power): pregnancy. In March 1974, the Court heard arguments challenging a California disability insurance system that paid benefits to privately employed individuals who were temporarily unable to work because of disabilities <u>not</u> covered by worker's compensation [*Geduldig v. Aiello*, 94 S.Ct. 2485 (1974)]. The state's program was funded entirely by mandatory contributions deducted from the wages of participating employees, and the only way for an employee to avoid contributing to this program was voluntary participation in any one of a number of private, state-approved programs. If a participating employee suffered from a disability not covered by the worker's compensation program, s/he was eligible for compensation for a period ranging from nine days to twenty-six weeks. The disabilities covered by the program included a large number of mental and physical conditions, though not all disabling ones. There was, however, one very noticeable and specific exclusion: "certain disabilities that are attributable to pregnancy" [*Geduldig v. Aiello*, 94 S.Ct. 2485, 2487 (1974)].

The case that finally made it to the Supreme Court was different from the case as it had originated in California. Originally, there were four appellants: three with disabilities resulting from "abnormal" pregnancies (including Annette Aiello, whose name appears in the title of the case) and one, Jacqueline Jaramillo, whose disability resulted from a "normal" pregnancy. All four women met the eligibility conditions for compensation under the insurance system, except for the fact that disabilities resulting from either normal or abnormal pregnancies had been excluded from coverage. In a divided decision after hearing the case, a three-judge federal district court concluded that the pregnancy exclusion violated the equal protection clause of the Fourteenth Amendment because it lacked a rational and substantial relation to a legitimate state goal. The court then enjoined further enforcement of the provision.

But that court was unaware of what had happened just ten days before: California's supreme court had decided another case challenging the pregnancy exclusion, a case in which a woman was denied benefits for disability resulting from an ectopic pregnancy. And the California supreme court had concluded that the law's provision barred payment for disabilities resulting from "normal" pregnancies but allowed payment for disabilities resulting from "abnormal" pregnancies, such as the ectopic pregnancy.

Acting in the wake of these two not entirely consistent decisions, Dwight Geduldig, Director of the California Department of Human Resources Development and thus the person responsible for administering the insurance program, agreed to exclude from coverage only disabilities resulting from "normal" pregnancies. In addition, however, he asked the district court to reconsider its opinion in light of the state supreme court decision. The district court refused and, additionally, refused to withdraw its ban on enforcing the provision until the case had been heard by the U.S. Supreme Court. The Supreme Court agreed both to hear the case and to stay the District Court's order banning enforcement pending its own decision.

In a six-to-three decision, the Court sustained California's right to exclude from insurance benefit coverage any "disability that accompanies normal pregnancy and childbirth" [*Geduldig v. Aiello*, 94 S.Ct. 2485, 2490 (1974)].[1] Writing the majority opinion, Justice Stewart clearly structured the question before the Court as an equal protection challenge. This knowledge should prepare the reader for the steps that the Court took in reaching its decision, although perhaps not necessarily for the outcome. Pay attention to the use of the "reasonable relationship" standard in assessing California's insurance program and the rationale which that standard allows to prevail.

Geduldig v. Aiello
94 S.Ct. 2485 (1974)
Justice Stewart, for the Court

Since the program was instituted in 1946, it has been totally self-supporting, never drawing on general state revenues to finance disability or hospital benefits. The Disability Fund is wholly supported by the one percent of wages annually contributed by participating employees. At oral argument, counsel for the appellant informed us that in recent years between 90% and 103% of the revenue to the Disability Fund has been paid out in disability and hospital benefits. This history strongly suggests that the one-percent contribution rate, in addition to being easily computable, bears a close and substantial relationship to the level of benefits payable and to the disability risks insured under the program.

Over the years California has demonstrated a strong commitment not to increase the contribution rate above the one-percent level. The State has sought to provide the broadest possible disability protection that would be affordable by all employees, including those with very low incomes. Because any larger percentage or any flat dollar-amount rate of contribution would impose an increasingly regressive levy bearing most heavily upon those with the lowest incomes, the State has resisted any attempt to change the required contribution from the one-percent level. The program is thus structured, in terms of the level of benefits and the risks insured, to maintain the solvency of the Disability Fund at a one-percent annual level of contribution.

In ordering the State to pay benefits for disability accompanying normal pregnancy and delivery, the District Court acknowledged the State's contention "that coverage of these disabilities is so extraordinarily expensive that it would be impossible to maintain a program supported by employee contribution if these disabilities are included" [cite omitted]. There is considerable disagreement between the parties with respect to how great the increased costs would actually be, but they would clearly be substantial. For purposes of analysis the District Court accepted the State's estimate, which was in excess of $100 million annually, and stated: "[I]t is clear that including these disabilities would not destroy the program. The increased costs could be accommodated quite easily by making reasonable changes in the contribution rate, the maximum benefits allowable, and the other variables affecting the solvency of the program" [cite omitted].

Each of the "variables"—the benefit level deemed appropriate to compensate employee disability, the risks selected to be insured under the program, and the contribution rate chosen to maintain the solvency of the program and at the same time to permit low-income employees to participate with minimal personal sacrifice—represents a policy determination by the State. The essential issue in this case is whether the Equal Protection Clause requires such policies to be sacrificed or compromised in order to finance the payment of benefits to those whose disability is attributable to normal pregnancy and delivery.

We cannot agree that the exclusion of this disability from coverage amounts to invidious discrimination under the Equal Protection Clause. California does not discriminate with respect to the persons or groups which are eligible for disability insurance protections under the program. The classification challenged in this case relates to the asserted underinclusiveness of the set of risks that the State has selected to insure. Although California has created a program to insure most risks of employment disability, it has not chosen to insure all such risks, and this decision is reflected in the level of annual contributions exacted from participating employees. This Court has held that, consistently with the Equal Protection Clause, a State "may take one step at a time, addressing itself to the phase of the problem which seems most acute to the legislative mind. . . . The legislature may select one phase of one field and apply a remedy there, neglecting the others" [cites omitted]. Particularly with respect to social welfare programs, so long as the line drawn by the State is rationally supportable, the courts will not interpose their judgment as to the appropriate stopping point. "[T]he Equal Protection Clause does not require that a State must choose between attacking every aspect of a problem or not attacking the problem at all" [cite omitted].

The District Court suggested that moderate alterations in what it regarded as "variables" of the disability insurance program could be made to accommodate the substantial expense required to include normal pregnancy within the program's protection. The same can be said, however, with respect to the other expensive class of disabilities that are excluded from coverage—short-term disabilities. If the Equal Protection Clause were thought to compel disability payments for normal pregnancy, it is hard to perceive why it would not also compel payments for short-term disabilities suffered by participating employees.

It is evident that a totally comprehensive program would be substantially more costly than the present program and would inevitably require state subsidy, a higher rate of employee contribution, a lower scale of benefits for those suffering insured disabilities, or some combination of these measures. There is nothing in the Constitution, however, that requires the State to subordinate or compromise its legitimate interests solely to create a more comprehensive social insurance program than it already has.

The State has a legitimate interest in maintaining the self-supporting nature of its insurance program. Similarly, it has an interest in distributing the available resources in such a way as to keep benefit payments at an adequate level for disabilities that are covered, rather than to cover all disabilities inadequately. Finally, California has a legitimate concern in maintaining the contribution rate at a level that will not unduly burden participating employees, particularly low-income employees who may be most in need of the disability insurance.

> These policies provide an objective and wholly non-invidious basis for the State's decision not to create a more comprehensive insurance program than it has. There is no evidence in the record that the selection of the risks insured by the program worked to discriminate against any definable group or class in terms of the aggregate risk protection derived by that group or class from the program.[2] There is no risk from which men are protected and women are not. Likewise, there is no risk from which women are protected and men are not.

And with that, the Court overturned the district court's decision and let the California insurance program continue to exclude from coverage those disabilities resulting from "normal" pregnancies. The line of reasoning set forth in Justice Stewart's opinion is both quite extraordinary and, at the same time, nothing new in the history of women's rights litigation. The Court accepted as evidence of legitimate state interest the two economic reasons given by California for excluding normal pregnancy from the covered conditions: The State wished to keep the program self-supporting and also wanted to ensure the participation of low-income individuals by keeping the required contribution relatively low. What California did here, and what the Court endorsed, is what has been done to women many times before: The interests and needs of women were pitted against the interests and needs of another group. And women, once again, came up short. In the past, women had seen their interests subordinated to those of blacks, men, and society at large; now women's interests were being shelved in favor of low-income individuals in general. The irony here is that women make up the majority of that low-income adult population! Still, as just noted, this approach and the result were hardly unusual in the history of women's rights litigation; finding a clearly discriminatory practice not to be invidious had come to be the norm in women's rights cases.

The truly extraordinary portion of the decision is to be found in its last paragraph and its accompanying footnote, concluding that the program was not discriminatory in any way. Is this honest legal reasoning, or is this legal maneuvering to justify desired ends? Is this program really not discriminatory if it excludes from coverage something only women can experience? If, as the footnote acknowledges, only women can get pregnant, then how can it not be argued "that every legislative classification concerning pregnancy is a sex-based classification. . ."? If the basis on which a provision is defined is sex based, is that provision not sex based? And further, how can it be concluded, as Justice Stewart did, that "there is no risk from which men are protected and women are not" when, as Justice Brennan pointed out in his dissent (to follow), coverage was extended for prostate problems or for circumcision?

In reaching its decision in *Aiello*, did the Court slip back to its pre-*Reed* mentality? Were women, once again, being sacrificed? Or did *Aiello* (and *Kahn*) merely represent two small squalls in otherwise smooth sailing for women's rights in the 70s?

There was, however, a dissenting opinion in this case, one that gives some insider hints as to what might be the answers to the above questions. This opinion was authored by Justice Brennan (who had written the plurality opinion in *Frontiero* and a dissenting opinion in *Kahn*) and was endorsed by Justice Marshall (who had sided with Brennan in *Frontiero* and *Kahn*) and Justice Douglas (who had sided with Brennan in *Frontiero* but had authored the majority opinion in *Kahn*). The dissent opens by disagreeing with the Court's reliance on the looser "reasonable relationship" standard for assessing California's insurance program. Citing *Reed* and *Frontiero*, Justice Brennan argued that the strict scrutiny test should have been applied and that had this been done, the California program would not have passed muster. Then, after briefly reviewing the purpose and functioning of the program, Justice Brennan addressed what he saw as the core of the problem with the California program.

Geduldig v. Aiello
94 S.Ct. 2485 (1974)
Justice Brennan, dissenting

> . . . Finally, compensation is paid for virtually all disabling conditions without regard to cost, voluntariness, uniqueness, predictability, or "normalcy" of the disability. Thus, for example, workers are compensated for costly disabilities such as heart attacks, voluntary disabilities such as cosmetic surgery or sterilization, disabilities unique to sex or race such as prostatectomies or sickle-cell anemia, pre-existing conditions inevitably resulting in disability such as degenerative arthritis or cataracts, and "normal" disabilities such as removal of irritating wisdom teeth or other orthodontia.
>
> Despite the Code's broad goals and scope of coverage, compensation is denied for disabilities suffered in connection with a "normal" pregnancy—disabilities suffered only by women [cite omitted]. Disabilities caused by pregnancy, however, like other physically disabling conditions covered by the Codes, require medical care, often include hospitalization, anesthesia and surgical procedures, and may involve genuine risk to life. Moreover, the economic effects caused by pregnancy-related disabilities are functionally indistinguishable from the effects caused by any other disability: wages are lost due to a physical inability to work, and medical expenses are incurred for the delivery of the child and for postpartum care. In my view, by singling out for less favorable treatment a gender-linked disability peculiar to women, the State has created a double standard for disability compensation: a limitation is imposed upon the disabilities for which women workers may recover, while men receive full compensation for all disabilities suffered, including those that affect only or primarily their sex, such as prostatectomies, circumcision, hemophilia, and gout. In effect, one set of rules is applied to females and another to males. Such dissimilar

treatment of men and women, on the basis of physical characteristics inextricably linked to one sex, inevitably constitutes sex discrimination.

The same conclusion has been reached by the Equal Employment Opportunity Commission, the federal agency charged with enforcement of title VII of the Civil Rights Act of 1964, . . . which prohibits employment discrimination on the basis of sex. In guidelines issued pursuant to Title VII and designed to prohibit the disparate treatment of pregnancy disabilities in the employment context, the EEOC has declared:

> "Disabilities caused or contributed to by pregnancy, miscarriage, abortion, childbirth, and recovery therefrom are, for all job-related purposes, temporary disabilities and should be treated as such under any health or temporary disability insurance or sick leave plan available in connection with employment. Written and unwritten employment policies and practices involving matters such as the commencement and duration of leave, the availability of extensions, the accrual of seniority and other benefits and privileges, reinstatement, and payment under any health or temporary disability insurance or sick leave plan, formal or informal, shall be applied to disability due to pregnancy or childbirth on the same terms and conditions as they are applied to other temporary disabilities" [cite omitted].

In the past, when a legislative classification has turned on gender, the Court has justifiably applied a standard of judicial scrutiny more strict than that generally accorded economic or social welfare programs. . . . Yet, by its decision today, the Court appears willing to abandon that higher standard of review without satisfactorily explaining what differentiates the gender-based classification employed in this case from those found unconstitutional in *Reed* and *Frontiero*. The Court's decision threatens to return men and women to a time when "traditional" equal protection analysis sustained legislative classifications that treated differently members of a particular sex solely because of their sex [cites omitted].

I cannot join the Court's apparent retreat. I continue to adhere to my view that "classifications based upon sex, like classifications based upon race, alienage, or national origin, are inherently suspect, and must therefore be subjected to strict judicial scrutiny" [cite omitted]. When, as in this case, the State employs a legislative classification that distinguishes between beneficiaries solely by reference to gender-linked disability risks, "the Court is not . . . free to sustain the statute on the ground that it rationally promotes legitimate governmental interests; rather, such suspect classifications can be sustained only when the State bears the burden of demonstrating that the challenged legislation serves overriding or compelling interests that cannot be achieved either by a more carefully tailored legislative classification or by the use of feasible, less drastic means [cite omitted].

The State has clearly failed to meet that burden in the present case. The essence of the State's justification for excluding disabilities caused by a normal pregnancy from its disability compensation scheme is that covering such disabilities would be too costly. To be sure, as presently funded, inclusion of normal pregnancies "would be substantially more costly than the present program" [cite omitted]. The present level of benefits for insured disabilities could not be maintained without increasing the employee contribution rate, raising or lifting the yearly contribution ceiling, or securing state subsidies. But whatever role such monetary considerations may play in traditional equal protection analysis, the State's interest in preserving the fiscal integrity of its disability insurance program simply cannot render the State's use of a suspect classification constitutional. For . . . while "a State has a valid interest in preserving the fiscal integrity of its programs[,] . . . a State may not accomplish such a purpose by invidious distinctions between classes of its citizens. . . . The saving of welfare costs cannot justify an otherwise invidious classification" [cite omitted]. Thus, when a statutory classification is subject to strict judicial scrutiny, the State "must do more than show that denying (benefits to the excluded class) saves money" [cite omitted].

Moreover, California's legitimate interest in fiscal integrity could easily have been achieved through a variety of less drastic, sexually neutral means. As the District Court observed:

> "Even using (the State's) estimate of the cost of expanding the program to include pregnancy-related disabilities, however, it is clear that including these disabilities would not destroy the program. The increased costs could be accommodated quite easily by making reasonable changes in the contribution rate, the maximum benefits allowable, and the other variables affecting the solvency of the program. For example, the entire cost increase estimated by defendant could be met by requiring workers to contribute an additional amount of approximately .364 percent of their salary and increasing the maximum annual contribution to about $119" [cite omitted].

I would therefore affirm the judgment of the District Court.

It is interesting that for neither side in this case was there any question as to whether a "normal" pregnancy is a disability. Both seemed to accept as given—the majority opinion implicitly and the dissenting opinion explicitly—the fact that even a "normal" pregnancy involves some degree of disability. Where the divide lay was in the standard to be applied in judging the legitimacy of the differential designation of disabilities and, as the dissent noted, the differential designation of sex-linked disabilities.

But was that really the question? Was this really a question of a difference in *standards* or a difference in *goals*? After all, is this case any different from *Muller?* Isn't it true that here, as in *Muller*, women were being penalized for their reproductive role at the cost of their economic goals? In *Muller*, women were denied the ability to work long hours in a laundry for fear that such work would impair their ability to bear children; thus, as previously noted, their short-term and long-term economic positions were curtailed. Here in *Aiello*, women's economic well-being was being impaired (losing income if disabled as a result of a "normal" pregnancy) simply for doing what society so wanted them to do: bear children.

Thus, the question cannot help but be asked: Was the Court really concerned with protecting the self-sufficient nature of the state insurance program *and* with not overburdening low-income individuals, or was there something else involved? Was the Court, consciously or subconsciously, still willing to limit women's access to the working world and success in it? It seems such a clear consequence of *Geduldig*, some sixty years after *Muller*, that women's reproductive function continued to be used as justification for treating women workers as problematic and on that basis denying them full employment rights.

Geduldig offered an interesting window to a portion of the law's view of women. The law challenged in *Geduldig* said the following to working women: If you do not opt for parenthood, we will treat you the same as we treat males, regardless of whether the men opt for parenthood or not; however, if you wish to be a parent, then you are on your own and the state will not be required to aid you in that pursuit—unless your pregnancy is imperiled.

This case made explicit what other cases had suggested: Women are entitled to equality with males in the public sphere *only to the extent* that they arrange their lives and priorities in the way that males have traditionally arranged theirs—maintaining a full-time career pattern without time off for familial demands.

THE OTHER SIDE OF GENDER

Moving with the speed that characterized the pace of women's rights litigation once change began, the Court accepted another challenge at the start of 1975. This case, like *Kahn*, involved a man, Stephen Wiesenfeld, who challenged the provisions of a federal law that treated widows more favorably than widowers. Wiesenfeld and his wife were married in 1970; she had worked as a teacher for five years prior to the marriage and continued to do so after marriage. In fact, she was the principal source of the couple's income, as she made "considerably" more than he, and she contributed maximum social security taxes. In June 1972, however, she died in childbirth, leaving Stephen Wiesenfeld the sole parent of a newborn son. Wiesenfeld then applied for social security benefits and received them for his son but not for himself. Had he been a woman, he would have received benefits for his son *and* for himself, but as a man, he was entitled to benefits only for his son.

As a result of this denial, Wiesenfeld challenged section 402(g) of the Social Security Act which allowed benefits based on the earnings of a deceased husband and father to go to both his widow and his minor children, but benefits based on the earnings of a deceased wife and mother went only to minor children, *not* also to the widower. Wiesenfeld claimed that this practice treated males and females differently solely because of their sex and thus violated the due process clause of the Fifth Amendment.[3]

A three-judge federal district court in New Jersey agreed in outcome with Wiesenfeld. Although Wiesenfeld had suggested that the law discriminated against widowers because they were entitled to less social security benefits than widows, the federal court ruled that the differential treatment of males and females unjustifiably discriminated against female wage earners because it gave them <u>less</u> protection for their survivors than was given male wage earners for their survivors. The government (specifically embodied by Caspar Weinberger, Secretary of what was then the Department of Health, Education and Welfare) appealed to the Supreme Court.

Interestingly, in a case that in varying degrees is reminiscent of both *Frontiero* and *Kahn*, the Court decided unanimously in Wiesenfeld's favor [*Weinberger v. Wiesenfeld* [95 S.Ct. 1225 (1975)], with Justice Douglas not participating. Justice Brennan wrote the opinion for the Court, and Justice Powell authored a concurring opinion in which Chief Justice Burger joined. Justice Rehnquist authored a second concurring opinion.

After reviewing the facts of the case, Justice Brennan proceeded to address the question of the constitutionality of the challenged portion of the Social Security Act. He relied on *Frontiero* as precedent, although he suggested that the present law was even more harmful to women than the one challenged in the earlier case. But in addressing the government's claim that the law was designed to compensate women for a history of economic disadvantage, his opinion, interestingly, called upon *Kahn*. And in stating the Court's position, he wrote some of the most positive—if not, in fact,the most positive—observations on the status of women to have ever surfaced in a Supreme Court decision.

Weinberger v. Wiesenfeld
95 S.Ct. 1225 (1975)
Justice Brennan, for the Court

II

The gender-based distinction made by [Section] 402(g) is indistinguishable from that invalidated in *Frontiero v. Richardson* [cite omitted]. . . . The Court held that the statutory scheme violated the right to equal protection secured by the Fifth

Amendment. . . . "In . . . *Frontiero* the challenged (classification) based on sex (was) premised on overbroad generalizations that could not be tolerated under the Constitution. . . . (T)he assumption . . . was that female spouses of servicemen would normally be dependent upon their husbands, while male spouses of servicewomen would not" [cite omitted]. A virtually identical "archaic and overbroad" generalization, . . . "not tolerated under the Constitution" underlies the distinction drawn by [Section] 402(g), namely, that male workers' earnings are vital to the support of their families, while the earnings of female wage earners do not significantly contribute to their families' support.

[Section] 402(g) was added to the Social Security Act in 1939 as one of a large number of amendments designed to "afford more adequate protection to the family as a unit" [cite omitted]. Monthly benefits were provided to wives, children, widows, orphans, and surviving dependent parents of covered workers. However, children of covered female workers were eligible for survivors' benefits only in limited circumstances, . . . and no benefits whatever were made available to husbands or widowers on the basis of their wives' covered employment.

Underlying the 1939 scheme was the principle that "(u)nder a social-insurance plan the primary purpose is to pay benefits in accordance with the *probable needs* of the beneficiaries rather than to make payments to the estate of a deceased person regardless of whether or not he leaves dependents" [cite omitted]. . . . It was felt that "(t)he payment of these survivorship benefits and supplements for the wife of an annuitant are . . . in keeping with the principle of social insurance. . ." [cite omitted]. Thus, the framers of the Act legislated on the "then generally accepted presumption that a man is responsible for the support of his wife and children" [cite omitted].

Obviously, the notion that men are more likely than women to be the primary supporters of their spouses and children is not entirely without empirical support. . . . But such a gender-based generalization cannot suffice to justify the denigration of the efforts of women who do work and whose earnings contribute significantly to their families' support.

Section 402(g) clearly operates, as did the statutes invalidated by our judgment in *Frontiero*, to deprive women of protection for their families which men receive as a result of their employment. Indeed, the classification here is in some ways more pernicious. First, it was open to the servicewoman under the statutes invalidated in *Frontiero* to prove that her husband was in fact dependent upon her. Here, Stephen Wiesenfeld was not given the opportunity to show, as may well have been the case, that he was dependent upon his wife for his support, or that, had his wife lived, she would have remained at work while he took over care of the child. Second, in this case social security taxes were deducted from [his wife's] salary during the years in which she worked. Thus, she not only failed to receive for her family the same protection which a similarly situated male worker would have received, but she also was deprived of a portion of her own earnings in order to contribute to the fund out of which benefits would be paid to others. Since the Constitution forbids the gender-based differentiation premised upon assumptions as to dependency made in the statutes before us in *Frontiero*, the Constitution also forbids the gender-based differentiation that results in the efforts of female workers required to pay social security taxes producing less protection for their families than is produced by the efforts of men.

III

Appellant [Weinberger] seeks to avoid this conclusion with two related arguments. First, he claims that because social security benefits are not compensation for work done, Congress is not obliged to provide a covered female employee with the same benefits as it provides to a male. Second, he contends that [Section] 402(g) was "reasonably designed to offset the adverse economic situation of women by providing a widow with financial assistance to supplement or substitute for her own efforts in the marketplace, " . . . and therefore does not contravene the equal protection guarantee.

A

We do not see how the fact that social security benefits are "non-contractual" can sanction differential protection for covered employees which is solely gender based. From the outset, social security old age, survivors', and disability (OASDI) benefits have been "afforded as a matter of right, related to past participation in the productive processes of the country" [cite omitted]. It is true that social security benefits are not necessarily related directly to tax contributions, since the OASDI system is structured to provide benefits in part according to presumed need. . . . But the fact remains that the statutory right to benefits <u>is</u> directly related to years worked and amount earned by a covered employee, and not to the need of the beneficiaries directly. Since OASDI benefits do depend significantly upon the participation in the work force of a covered employee, and since only covered employees and not others are required to pay taxes toward the system, benefits must be distributed according to classifications which do not without sufficient justification differentiate among covered employees solely on the basis of sex.

B

Appellant seeks to characterize the classification here as one reasonably designed to compensate women beneficiaries as a group for the economic difficulties which still confront women who seek to support themselves and their families. The Court held in [*Kahn*] that a statute "reasonably designed to further the state policy of cushioning the financial impact of spousal loss upon the sex for whom that loss imposes a disproportionately heavy burden" can survive an equal protection attack. . . . But the mere recitation of a benign, compensatory purpose is not an automatic shield which protects against any inquiry into the actual purposes underlying a statutory scheme. Here, it is apparent both from the statutory scheme itself and from the legislative history of [Section] 402(g) that Congress' purpose in providing benefits to young widows with children was not to provide an income to women who were, because of economic discrimination, unable to provide for themselves. Rather, [Section] 402(g), linked as it is directly to responsibility for minor children, was intended to permit women to elect not to work and to devote themselves to the care of children. Since this purpose in no way is premised upon any special disadvantages of women, it cannot serve to justify a gender-based distinction which diminishes the protection afforded to women who do work.

That the purpose behind [Section] 402(g) is to provide children deprived of one parent with the opportunity for the personal attention of the other could not be more clear in the legislative history. The Advisory Council on Social Security, which developed the 1939 amendments, said explicitly that "[s]uch payments [under 402(g)] are intended as supplements to the orphans' benefits *with the purpose of enabling the widow to remain at home and care for the children*" [cite omitted; emphasis in the original]. In 1971, a new Advisory Council, considering amendments to eliminate the various gender-based distinctions in the OASDI structure, reiterated this understanding: "Present law provides benefits for the mother of young . . . children . . . if she chooses to stay home and care for the children instead of working. In the Council's judgment, it is desirable to allow a woman who is left with the care of the children the *choice* of whether to stay at home to care for the children or to go to work" [cite omitted].

Indeed, consideration was given in 1939 to extending benefits to all widows regardless of whether or not there were minor children. The proposal was rejected, apparently because it was felt that young widows without children can be expected to work, while middle-aged widows "are likely to have more savings than younger widows and many of them have children who are grown and able to help them" [cites omitted]. Thus, Congress decided *not* to provide benefits to all widows even though it was recognized that some of them would have serious problems in the job market. Instead, it provided benefits only to those women who had responsibility for minor children, because it believed that they should not be required to work.

The whole structure of survivors' benefits conforms to this articulated purpose. Widows without minor children obtain no benefits on the basis of their husband's earnings until they reach age 60 or, in certain instances of disability, age 50 [cite omitted]. Further, benefits under [Section] 402(g) cease when all children of a beneficiary are no longer eligible for children's benefits. If Congress were concerned with providing women with benefits because of economic discrimination, it would be entirely irrational to except those women who had spent many years at home rearing children, since those women are most likely to be without the skills required to succeed in the job market [cites omitted]. Similarly, the Act now provides benefits to a surviving divorced wife who is the parent of a covered employee's child, regardless of how long she was married to the deceased or of whether she or the child was dependent upon the employee for support [cite omitted]. Yet, a divorced wife who is not the mother of a child entitled to children's benefits is eligible for benefits only if she meets other eligibility requirements *and* was married to the covered employee for 20 years [cite omitted]. Once again, this distinction among women is explicable only because Congress was not concerned in [Section] 402(g) with the employment problems of women generally but with the principle that children of covered employees are entitled to the personal attention of the surviving parent if that parent chooses not to work.

Given the purpose of enabling the surviving parent to remain at home to care for a child, the gender-based distinction of [Section] 402(g) is entirely irrational. The classification discriminates among surviving children solely on the basis of the sex of the surviving parent. Even in the typical family hypothesized by the Act, in which the husband is supporting the family and the mother is caring for the children, this result makes no sense. The fact that a man is working while there is a wife at home does not mean that he would, or should be required to, continue to work if his wife dies. It is no less important for a child to be cared for by its sole surviving parent when that parent is male rather than female. And a father, no less than a mother, has a constitutionally protected right to the "companionship, care, custody, and management" of "the children he has sired and raised, (which) undeniably warrants deference and, absent a powerful countervailing interest, protection" [cite omitted]. Further, to the extent that women who work when they have sole responsibility for children encounter special problems, it would seem that men with sole responsibility for children will encounter the same child-care related problems. Stephen Wiesenfeld, for example, found that providing adequate care for his infant son impeded his ability to work, . . .

> Finally, to the extent that Congress legislated on the presumption that women as a group would choose to forgo work to care for children while men would not, the statutory structure, independent of the gender-based classification, would deny or reduce benefits to those men who conform to the presumed norm and are not hampered by their child-care responsibilities. Benefits under [Section] 402(g) decrease with increased earnings, . . . According to the appellant, "the bulk of male workers would receive no benefits in any event" [cite omitted], because they earn too much. Thus, the gender-based distinction is gratuitous; without it, the statutory scheme would only provide benefits to those men who are in fact similarly situated to the women the statute aids.
>
> Since the gender-based classification of [Section] 402(g) cannot be explained as an attempt to provide for the special problems of women, it is indistinguishable from the classification held invalid in *Frontiero*. Like the statutes there, "(b)y providing dissimilar treatment for men and women who are ... similarly situated, the challenged section violated the (Due Process) Clause" [cite omitted].

In *Wiesenfeld*, the Court, even more firmly than it had in any of its preceding decisions, discarded stereotypical assumptions about the roles of women *and* men, for it unequivocally recognized that women can, *in fact*, be the dominant—or the only—breadwinner in a family. And, on the other hand, men can, *in fact*, be—and even choose to be—the primary care giver to children. These messages were delivered clearly and explicitly, with no need to read between the lines. Thus, for the first time, the Court spoke out clearly in support of mothers and wives who worked outside the home. The Court in effect endorsed options for women: women could *choose* how to conduct their lives without worry that a choice in one arena (i.e., career) might risk harm to another arena (i.e., family). And in so doing, the Court also spoke out clearly in favor of options for men: If they chose to or needed to stay home with their children, they too could receive economic protection from the government. Thus, we see clearly in this decision in *Wiesenfeld* what has been repeatedly argued in this book: that as society broadens the roles and rights of women, implicitly or explicitly it does the same for men.

The two concurring opinions are of interest not because of their content—they are weaker in their endorsement of nontraditional roles for women and men—but because of those who wrote or endorsed them. Even though they do not do so as firmly as the majority opinion, both concurring opinions support the expansion of women's roles *outside* the home. Given Cook's assessment of the Burger Court, these concurring opinions appear to be departures from the otherwise conservative records of these three justices.

Weinberger v. Wiesenfeld
95 S.Ct. 1225 (1975)
Justice Powell, concurring

I concur in the judgment and generally in the opinion of the Court. But I would identify the impermissible discrimination effected by [Section] 402(g) somewhat more narrowly than the Court does. Social Security is designed, certainly in this context, for the protection of the *family*. Although it lacks the contractual attributes of insurance or an annuity [cite omitted], it is a contributory system and millions of wage earners depend on it to provide basic protection for their families in the event of death or disability.

Many women are the principal wage earners for their families, and they participate in the Social Security system on exactly the same basis as men. When the mother is a principal wage earner, the family may suffer as great an economic deprivation upon her death as would occur upon the death of a father wage earner. It is immaterial whether the surviving parent elects to assume primary child care responsibility rather than work, or whether other arrangements are made for child care. The statutory scheme provides benefits both to a surviving mother who remains at home and to one who works at low wages. A surviving father may have the same need for benefits as a surviving mother. The statutory scheme therefore impermissibly discriminates against a female wage earner because it provides her family less protection than it provides that of a male wage earner, even though the family needs may be identical. I find no legitimate governmental interest that supports this gender classification.

Weinberger v. Wiesenfeld
95 S.Ct. 1225 (1975)
Justice Rehnquist, concurring

Part III-B of the Court's opinion contains a thorough examination of the legislative history and statutory context which define the role and purpose of [Section] 402(g). I believe the Court's examination convincingly demonstrates that the only purpose of [Section] 402(g) is to make it possible for children of deceased contributing workers to have the personal care and attention of a surviving parent, should that parent desire to remain in the home with the child. Moreover, the Court's opinion establishes that the Government's proffered legislative purpose is so totally at odds with the context and history of [Section] 402(g) that it cannot serve as a basis for judging whether the statutory distinction between men and women rationally serves a valid legislative objective.

This being the case, I see no necessity for reaching the issue of whether the statute's purported discrimination against female workers violates the Fifth Amendment as applied in [*Frontiero*]. I would simply conclude, as does the Court in Part III-B of its opinion, that the restriction of [Section] 402(g) benefits to surviving mothers does not rationally serve any valid legislative purpose, including that for which [Section] 402(g) was obviously designed. This is so because it is irrational to distinguish between mothers and fathers when the sole question is whether a child of a deceased contributing worker should have the opportunity to receive the full-time attention of the only parent remaining to it. To my mind, that should be the end of the matter. I therefore concur in the result.

CONCLUSION

The first half of the first decade of change produced mixed messages. On the one hand, some of the stereotypical ideas about women did begin to crack: There was recognition that some women were capable of handling the world of business and that some women not only worked outside the home but earned substantial livelihoods outside the home—and even supported entirely or contributed to the support of their husbands and children. On the other hand, women continued to be penalized for their childbearing capacity and continued to be considered as a group in need of special financial assistance.

One clear development during this five-year period, however, was that society in general and the Court in particular were finally recognizing a message long known to those who had been intimately familiar and concerned with women's rights. That message, discussed repeatedly throughout this book but now phrased somewhat differently, involves a long-time misnomer: the struggle for *women's rights* really is a struggle for *equal rights for women and men*. This book traces not only the history of women's rights litigation, but also the history of litigation of the rights of both sexes, for as set forth explicitly in *Frontiero, Kahn* and *Wiesenfeld*, as women's roles and rights are rearranged, so are those of men. It is important to remember that in our society, rightly or wrongly, women and men are so integrally interrelated that pulling at one seems to necessitate pushing the other. The roles and rights of neither sex are not defined in a vacuum but rather in a shared and interactive whole. Unfortunately, to date, that whole has been viewed as a zero sum game, in which the gains of one sex can come only at the expense of the other sex.

Perhaps, however, the most important development of this period—the one causing the greatest reverberations—was not the decision in any one particular case but the cumulative weight of several. This period began with a traditional "reasonable relationship" standard for assessing the validity of equal protection claims and although the period did not end with the Court's entirely accepting the "strict scrutiny" standard sought by women's rights advocates, it appeared to many that the applied standard had, nevertheless, notably changed. As Ginsburg, who played a major role in three of the five cases of this period (acting not only as *amicus curiae* in *Frontiero* but also as counsel in *Kahn* and in *Wiesenfeld*), concludes (1975: 20):

> It appears, then, that some variant of "rational relationship" will remain the equal protection rubric invoked in gender discrimination claims by the Court's majority. *Reed* and *Frontiero* imply and *Wiesenfeld* appears to confirm, however, that the test will be applied with a "bite" it lacked before 1971.

Thus, it seemed that women had finally made some real progress. Just how much further that progress would extend was, however, still in question. But not for long.

NOTES

1. For a complete catalogue of the history of the case, as well as for the particulars of how the insurance program operated, see Justice Stewart's opinion in *Geduldig v. Aiello*, 94 S.Ct. 2485 (1974).
2. This is the footnote included in Justice Stewart's opinion:

> The dissenting opinion to the contrary, this case is thus a far cry from cases . . . involving discrimination based upon gender as such. The California insurance program does not exclude anyone from benefit eligibility because of gender but merely removes one physical condition—pregnancy—from the list of compensable disabilities. While it is true that only women can become pregnant it does not follow that every legislative classification concerning pregnancy is a sex-based classification like those considered in *Reed*, . . . and *Frontiero*, . . . Normal pregnancy is an objectively identifiable physical condition with unique characteristics. Absent a showing that distinctions involving pregnancy are mere pretexts designed to effect an invidious discrimination against the members of one sex or the other, lawmakers are constitutionally free to include or exclude pregnancy from the coverage of legislation such as this on any reasonable basis, just as with respect to any other physical condition.
>
> The lack of identity between the excluded disability and gender as such under this insurance program becomes clear upon the most cursory analysis. The program divides potential recipients into two groups—pregnant women and non-pregnant persons. While the first group is exclusively female, the second includes members of both sexes. The fiscal and actuarial benefits of the program thus accrue to members of both sexes.

3. The Supreme Court, in its subsequent decision, noted that although the Fifth Amendment does not contain an equal protection clause, it does forbid discrimination so extreme as to violate due process, and that the Court had long viewed Fifth Amendment equal protection claims in exactly the same light as Fourteenth Amendment protection claims.

9

The Bumpy Road to the Present: Two Steps Forward, One Step Backward

The law must be stable, but it must not stand still.

Roscoe Pound
Philosophy of Law

It took less than two years to see just how wise or movable the law would be for women, for by the end of 1976 the limits of their progress became manifest. In a 1976 case, the Court made clear that there were limits as to just how far it was willing to go to countenance equal protection claims based on sex. The Court was not prepared to apply the strict "suspect class" test to cases raising challenges based on sex discrimination. Rather than rising to the level of strictest scrutiny, sex discrimination cases would bump against their own "glass ceiling"; they would receive, at best, "intermediate scrutiny," a new standard to be developed in such cases, or, at worst, the "reasonable relationship" test (the old standard) that many commentators refer to as "minimal scrutiny."

DRINKING BEER AND DRIVING

At first glance, the landmark case of *Craig v. Boren* [97 S.Ct. 451 (1976)] may seem to involve a comparatively trivial issue and therefore not to be worth including in this examination of major Supreme Court cases. But that would be a superficial assessment and, ultimately, a wrong one. The case addressed the question of the age at which a person ceases to be considered a child and reaches the age of "majority" or, put less legalistically, the age of responsibility. Specifically, *Craig* questioned the state of Oklahoma's determination that the age of majority at which a person can lawfully consume "nonintoxicating" 3.2 percent beer be assessed differently for males and females. The differential determination in Oklahoma—and in every other state that varied the age of majority by sex for whatever purpose (i.e., drinking, child support, criminality)—was based on stereotypical notions about differing levels of maturity and responsibility between females and males. One of the state's specific justifications for the law was the stereotypical assumption that adolescent males were more reckless drivers than adolescent females. Thus, in order simply to see how the Court handled a classification that unquestionably relied upon stereotypical notions, *Craig* ranks high in the history of women's rights litigation.

This was not the first time the Court had been asked to evaluate the constitutionality of a law setting different ages of majority for females and males and to judge the constitutionality of a state's reliance on traditional sex stereotypes in setting these different ages. More than a year before, the Court had reviewed the case of a Utah woman objecting to a state law that allowed her ex-husband to cease making child support payments for his daughter when the daughter became eighteen—determined to be the female age of majority for this particular purpose—although he was obliged to continue making such payments for his son until the son reached age twenty-one, set as the male age of majority for this purpose [*Stanton v. Stanton*, 95 S.Ct. 1373 (1975)]. (The law also declared that either sex reached majority upon marriage, regardless of the age at the time.) Relying on *Reed* as precedent, the Court, with only Justice Rehnquist dissenting, struck down this law, saying that the state failed to show a rational basis for the distinction. And, in so doing, the Court questioned, although it did not totally discard, certain "old notions" about males and females that the Utah supreme court had relied upon in upholding the law in question. Writing for the majority, Justice Blackmun said:

> It may be true, as the Utah court observed and as is argued here, that it is the man's primary responsibility to provide a home and that it is salutary for him to have education and training before he assumes that responsibility; that girls tend to mature earlier than boys; and that females tend to marry earlier than males. . . .
>
> Notwithstanding the "old notions" to which the Utah court referred, we perceive nothing rational in the distinction drawn by [the statute], . . . A child, male or female, is still a child. No longer is the female destined solely for the home and the rearing of the family, and only the male for the marketplace and the

> world of ideas. . . . Women's activities and responsibilities are increasing and expanding. Coeducation is a fact, not a rarity. The presence of women in business, in the professions, in government and, indeed, in all walks of life where education is a desirable, if not always a necessary, antecedent is apparent and a proper subject of judicial notice. If a specified age of minority is required for the boy in order to assure him parental support while he attains his education and training, so, too, is it for the girl. To distinguish between the two on educational grounds is to be self-serving: if the female is not to be supported so long as the male, she hardly can be expected to attend school as long as he does, and bringing her education to an end earlier coincides with the role-typing society has long imposed. [*Stanton v. Stanton*, 95 S.Ct. 1373, 1378 (1975)]

Stanton gives us a clear clue as to what to expect from the Supreme Court when, more than a year later, it decides *Craig*. Or does it? As in *Stanton*, the Court struck down the challenged law, declaring it unconstitutional. But in *Craig*, the decision was seven to two, with four concurring opinions and two dissenting opinions. And the disagreement focused not so much on the fate of the law as on the standard used in judging that law. And therein lies the real and more important reason that *Craig* cannot be dismissed as ridiculous or inconsequential in the history of women's rights litigation: The Court's decision and opinions introduced a new standard for assessing equal protection challenges alleging differential treatment based on sex.

It is interesting—or ironic—to note that the case that introduced a new, and theoretically tougher, standard for review in such cases was one whose burden of complaint was that males—not females—were the ones suffering discrimination. Specifically, the challengers to the law were claiming that the Oklahoma law forbidding the sale of 3.2 percent nonintoxicating beer to females under age eighteen and males under age twenty-one was a denial of equal protection to all males between eighteen and twenty-one.[1] A three-judge federal district court in Oklahoma rejected the claim. and the case was appealed directly to the Supreme Court.

As previously noted, the Court struck down the Oklahoma law by a seven-to-two vote; Justice Brennan wrote the official Court opinion, in which Justices Marshall and White joined. Four justices—Powell, Stevens, Stewart, and Blackmun—wrote individual concurring opinions, and Justice Rehnquist and Chief Justice Burger wrote dissenting opinions. The primary point of departure prompting the multiple opinions was the issue of the standard of review to apply to this particular equal protection problem. Justice Brennan, writing for the Court, introduced the new standard, and the untutored eye and mind could easily miss the fact that this was something different from what had gone before. The other justices, in both the concurring and dissenting opinions, highlighted the difference, however, and remarked on the need, value, and legitimacy of such a standard. Thus, in reading the excerpts from the varied opinions, pay careful attention not only to what is being done but also to how it is being done.

After addressing the question of the standing of both appellants (see footnote 1), Justice Brennan turned to the question of whether the Oklahoma statute did, in fact, invidiously discriminate against males eighteen to twenty-one years. He noted that the age differential stipulated for drinking 3.2 percent beer was an exception to Oklahoma's otherwise sex-neutral definition of the age of majority. Then he moved quickly to identify the precedent the Court was using in striking down the statute as unfairly discriminatory. The precedent he turned to was *Reed*, not *Frontiero*, but it was *Reed* with added bite. This bite, evident albeit subtly, in the first paragraph below, is the initial usage of what has come to be called "intermediate scrutiny." With this as the standard, the Court asked whether the age differential in the purchase of 3.2 percent beer was warranted by any differences between males and females. Or, to adopt the terminology of the Court, is the sex-based classification an "inaccurate proxy" for some other basis for classification?

Craig v. Boren
97 S.Ct. 451 (1976)
Justice Brennan, for the Court

Analysis may appropriately begin with the reminder that *Reed* emphasized that statutory classifications that distinguish between males and females are "subject to scrutiny under the Equal Protection Clause" [cite omitted]. To withstand constitutional challenge, previous cases establish that classifications by gender must serve important governmental objectives and must be substantially related to achievement of those objectives. . . . Decisions following *Reed* similarly have rejected administrative ease and convenience as sufficiently important objectives to justify gender-based classifications. . . .

[*Reed*] has also provided the underpinning for decisions that have invalidated statutes employing gender as an inaccurate proxy for other, more germane bases of classification. . . . In light of the weak congruence between gender and the characteristic or trait that gender purported to represent, it was necessary that the legislatures choose either to realign their substantive laws in a gender-neutral fashion, or to adopt procedures for identifying those instances where the sex-centered generalization actually comported with fact. . . .

. . . We turn then to the question whether, under *Reed,* the difference between males and females with respect to the purchase of 3.2% beer warrants the differential in age drawn by the Oklahoma statute. We conclude that it does not.

The District Court recognized that *Reed v. Reed* was controlling. In applying the teachings of that case, the court found the requisite important governmental objective in the traffic-safety goal proffered by the Oklahoma Attorney General. It then concluded that the statistics introduced by the appellees established that the gender-based distinction was substantially related to achievement of that goal.

We accept for purposes of discussion the District Court's identification of the objective underlying [the statute] as the enhancement of traffic safety. Clearly, the protection of public health and safety represents an important function of state and local governments. However, appellees' statistics in our view cannot support the conclusion that the gender-based distinction closely serves to achieve that objective and therefore the distinction cannot under *Reed* withstand equal protection challenge.

The appellees introduced a variety of statistical surveys. First, an analysis of arrest statistics for 1973 demonstrated that 18-20-year-old male arrests for "driving under the influence" and "drunkenness" substantially exceeded female arrests for that same age period. Similarly, youths aged 17-21 were found to be overrepresented among those killed or injured in traffic accidents, with males again numerically exceeding females in this regard. Third, a random roadside survey in Oklahoma City revealed that young males were more inclined to drive and drink beer than were their female counterparts. Fourth, Federal Bureau of Investigation nationwide statistics exhibited a notable increase in arrests for "driving under the influence." Finally, statistical evidence gathered in other jurisdictions, particularly Minnesota and Michigan, was offered to corroborate Oklahoma's experience by indicating the pervasiveness of youthful participation in motor vehicle accidents following the imbibing of alcohol. Conceding that "the case is not free from doubt" [cite omitted], the District Court nonetheless concluded that this statistical showing substantiated "a rational basis for the legislative judgment underlying the challenged classification" [cite omitted].

Even were this statistical evidence accepted as accurate, it nevertheless offers only a weak answer to the equal protection question presented here. The most focused and relevant of the statistical surveys, arrests of 18-20 year olds for alcohol-related driving offenses, exemplifies the ultimate unpersuasiveness of this evidentiary record. Viewed in terms of the correlation between sex and the actual activity that Oklahoma seeks to regulate—driving while under the influence of alcohol—the statistics broadly establish that .18% of females and 2% of males in that age group were arrested for that offense. While such a disparity is not trivial in a statistical sense, it hardly can form the basis for employment of a gender line as a classifying device. Certainly if maleness is to serve as a proxy for drinking and driving, a correlation of 2% must be considered an unduly tenuous "fit." Indeed, prior cases have consistently rejected the use of sex as a decisionmaking [sic] factor even though the statutes in question certainly rested on far more predictive empirical relationships than this.

Moreover, the statistics exhibit a variety of other shortcomings that seriously impugn their value to equal protection analysis. Setting aside the obvious methodological problems, the surveys do not adequately justify the salient features of Oklahoma's gender-based traffic-safety law. None purports to measure the use and dangerousness of 3.2% beer as opposed to alcohol generally, a detail that is of particular importance since, in light of its low alcohol level, Oklahoma apparently considers the 3.2% beverage to be "nonintoxicating" [cite omitted]. Moreover, many of the studies, while graphically documenting the unfortunate increase in driving while under the influence of alcohol, make no effort to relate their findings. Indeed, the only survey that explicitly centered its attention upon young drivers and their use of beer—albeit apparently not of the diluted 3.2% variety—reached results that hardly can be viewed as impressive in justifying either a gender or age classification.

There is no reason to belabor this line of analysis. It is unrealistic to expect either members of the judiciary or state officials to be well versed in the rigors of experimental or statistical technique. But this merely illustrates that proving broad sociological propositions by statistics is a dubious business, and one that inevitably is in tension with the normative philosophy that underlies the Equal Protection Clause. Suffice to say that the showing offered by the appellees does not satisfy us that sex represents a legitimate, accurate proxy for the regulation of drinking and driving. In fact, when it is further recognized that Oklahoma's statute prohibits only the selling of 3.2% beer to young males and not their drinking the beverage once acquired (even after purchase by their 18-20-year-old female companions), the relationship between gender and traffic safety becomes far too tenuous to satisfy *Reed's* requirement that the gender-based difference be substantially related to achievement of the statutory objective.

We hold, therefore, that under *Reed,* Oklahoma's 3.2% beer statute invidiously discriminates against males 18-20 years of age.

Appellees argue, however, that [the statute] enforce[s] state policies concerning the sale and distribution of alcohol and by force of the Twenty-first Amendment should therefore be held to withstand the equal protection challenge.... Our view is, and we hold, that the Twenty-first Amendment does not save the invidious gender-based discrimination from invalidation as a denial of equal protection of the laws in violation of the Fourteenth Amendment....

[B]oth federal and state courts uniformly have declared the unconstitutionality of gender lines that restrain the activities of customers of state-regulated liquor establishments irrespective of the operation of the Twenty-first Amendment [cites omitted]. Even when state officials have posited sociological or empirical justifications for these gender-based differentiations, the courts have struck down discriminations aimed at an entire class under the guise of alcohol regulation. In fact, social science studies that have uncovered quantifiable differences in drinking tendencies dividing along both racial and ethnic lines strongly suggest the need for application of the Equal Protection Clause in preventing discriminatory treatment that almost certainly would be perceived as invidious. In sum, the principles embodied in the Equal Protection Clause are not to be rendered inapplicable by statistically measured but loose-fitting generalities concerning the drinking tendencies of aggregate groups. We thus hold that the operation of the Twenty-first Amendment does not alter the application of equal protection standards that otherwise govern this case.

We conclude that the gender-based differential contained in [this statute] constitutes a denial of the equal protection of the laws to males aged 18-20 and reverse the judgement of the District Court.

Given that *Craig* did introduce a new, third standard of review for sex discrimination cases, it is important to look at the justices' own debate on the validity and wisdom of introducing this third tier in the scrutiny hierarchy. What follows are excerpts from two of the concurring opinions and the two dissenting opinions. This latter group should be read for what it has to say on both the third tier and the constitutionality of the Oklahoma law.

Craig v. Boren
97 S.Ct. 451 (1976)
Justice Powell, concurring

I join the opinion of the court as I am in general agreement with it. I do have reservations as to some of the discussion concerning the appropriate standard for equal protection analysis and the relevance of the statistical evidence. Accordingly, I add this concurring statement.

With respect to the equal protection standard, I agree that [*Reed*] is the most relevant precedent. But I find it unnecessary, in deciding this case, to read that decision as broadly as some of the Court's language may imply. *Reed* and subsequent cases involving gender-based classifications make clear that the Court subjects such classifications to a more critical examination than is normally applied when "fundamental" constitutional rights and "suspect classes" are not present.

I view this as a relatively easy case. No one questions the legitimacy or importance of the asserted governmental objective: the promotion of highway safety. The decision of the case turns on whether the state legislature, by the classification it has chosen, had adopted a means that bears a "fair and substantial relation" to this objective [cites omitted].

It seems to me that the statistics offered by appellees and relied upon by the District Court do tend generally to support the view that young men drive more, possibly are inclined to drink more, and—for various reasons—are involved in more accidents than young women. Even so, I am not persuaded that these facts and the inferences fairly drawn from them justify this classification based on a three-year age differential between the sexes, and especially one that it so easily circumvented as to be virtually meaningless. Putting it differently, this gender-based classification does not bear a fair and substantial relation to the object of the legislation.

Justice Stevens, concurring

There is only one Equal Protection Clause. It requires every State to govern impartially. It does not direct the courts to apply one standard of review in some cases and a different standard in other cases. Whatever criticism may be leveled at a judicial opinion implying that there are at least three such standards applies with the same force to a double standard.

I am inclined to believe that what has become known as the two-tiered analysis of equal protection claims does not describe a completely logical method of deciding cases, but rather is a method the Court has employed to explain decisions that actually apply a single standard in a reasonably consistent fashion. I also suspect that a careful explanation of the reasons motivating particular decisions may contribute more to an identification of that standard than an attempt to articulate it in all-encompassing terms. It may therefore be appropriate for me to state the principal reasons which persuaded me to join the Court's opinion.

In this case, the classification is not as obnoxious as some the Court has condemned, nor as inoffensive as some the Court has accepted. It is objectionable because it is based on an accident of birth, because it is a mere remnant of the now almost universally rejected tradition of discriminating against males in this age bracket, and because, to the extent it reflects any physical difference between males and females, it is actually perverse. The question then is whether the traffic safety justification put forward by the State is sufficient to make an otherwise offensive classification acceptable.

The classification is not totally irrational. For the evidence does indicate that there are more males than females in this age bracket who drive and also more who drink. Nevertheless, there are several reasons why I regard the justification as unacceptable. It is difficult to believe that the statute was actually intended to cope with the problem of traffic safety, since it has only a minimal effect on access to a not very intoxicating beverage and does not prohibit its consumption. Moreover, the empirical data submitted by the State accentuate the unfairness of treating all 18-21-year-old males as inferior to their female counterparts. The legislation imposes a restraint on 100% of the males in the class allegedly because about 2% of them have probably violated one or more laws relating to the consumption of alcoholic beverages. It is unlikely that this law will have a significant deterrent effect either on that 2% or on the law-abiding 98%. But even assuming some such slight benefit, it does not seem to me that an insult to all of the young men of the State can be justified by visiting the sins of the 2% on the 98%.

Chief Justice Burger, dissenting

I am in general agreement with Mr. Justice Rehnquist's dissent, but even at the risk of compounding the obvious confusion created by those voting to reverse the District Court, I will add a few words. . . .

. . . Though today's decision does not go so far as to make gender-based classifications "suspect," it makes gender a disfavored classification. Without an independent constitutional basis supporting the right asserted or disfavoring the classification adopted, I can justify no substantive constitutional protection other than the normal . . . protection afforded by the Equal Protection Clause.

Justice Rehnquist, dissenting

The Court's disposition of this case is objectionable on two grounds. First is its conclusion that *men* challenging a gender-based statute which treats them less favorably than women may invoke a more stringent standard of judicial review than pertains to most other types of classifications. Second is the Court's enunciation of this standard, without citation to any source, as being that "classifications by gender must serve *important* governmental objectives and must be *substantially* related to achievement of those objectives" [cite omitted; emphasis in the original]. The only redeeming feature of the Court's opinion, to my mind, is that it apparently signals a retreat by those who joined the plurality opinion in [*Frontiero*], from their view that sex is a "suspect" classification for purposes of equal protection analysis. I think the Oklahoma statute challenged here need pass only the "rational basis" equal protection analysis. . . , and I believe that it is constitutional under that analysis.

In [*Frontiero*], the opinion for the plurality sets forth the reasons of four Justices for concluding that sex should be regarded as a suspect classification for purposes of equal protection analysis. These reasons center on our Nation's "long and unfortunate history of sex discrimination" [cite omitted], which has been reflected in a whole range of restrictions on the legal rights of women, . . . Noting that the pervasive and persistent nature of the discrimination experienced by women is in part the result of their ready identifiability, the plurality rested its invocation of strict scrutiny largely upon the fact that "statutory distinctions between the sexes often have the effect of invidiously relegating the entire class of females to inferior legal status without regard to the actual capabilities of its individual members" [cite omitted].

Subsequent to *Frontiero*, the Court has declined to hold that sex is a suspect class, . . . and no such holding is imported by the Court's resolution of this case. However, the Court's application here of an elevated or "intermediate" level scrutiny, like that invoked in cases dealing with discrimination against females, raises the question of why the statute here should be treated any differently from countless legislative classifications unrelated to sex which have been upheld under a minimum rationality standard [cites omitted].

Most obviously unavailable to support any kind of special scrutiny in this case, is a history or pattern of past discrimination, such as was relied on by the plurality in *Frontiero* to support its invocation of strict scrutiny. There is no suggestion in the Court's opinion that males in this age group are in any way peculiarly disadvantaged, subject to systematic discriminatory treatment, or otherwise in need of special solicitude from the courts.

The Court does not discuss the nature of the right involved, and there is no reason to believe that it sees the purchase of 3.2% beer as implicating any important interest, let alone one that is "fundamental" in the constitutional sense of invoking strict scrutiny. Indeed, the Court's accurate observation that the statute affects the selling but not the drinking of 3.2% beer, . . . further emphasizes the limited effect that it has on even those persons in the age group involved. There is, in sum, nothing about the statutory classification involved here to suggest that it affects an interest, or works against a group, which can claim under the Equal Protection Clause that it is entitled to special judicial protection.

It is true that a number of our opinions contain broadly phrased dicta implying that the same test should be applied to all classifications based on sex, whether affecting females or males. . . . However, before today, no decision of this Court has applied an elevated level of scrutiny to invalidate a statutory discrimination harmful to males, except where the statute impaired an important personal interest protected by the Constitution. There being no such interest here, and there being no plausible argument that this is a discrimination against females, the Court's reliance on our previous sex-discrimination cases is ill-founded. It treats gender classification as a talisman which—

without regard to the rights involved or the persons affected—calls into effect a heavier burden of judicial review.

The Court's conclusion that a law which treats males less favorably than females "must serve important governmental objectives and must be substantially related to achievement of those objectives" apparently comes out of thin air. The Equal Protection Clause contains no such language, and none of our previous cases adopt that standard. I would think we have had enough difficulty with the two standards of review which our cases have recognized—the norm of "rational basis," and the "compelling state interest" required where a "suspect classification" is involved—so as to counsel weightily against the insertion of still another "standard" between those two. How is this Court to divine what objectives are important? How is it to determine whether a particular law is "substantially" related to the achievement of such objective, rather than related in some other way to its achievement? Both of the phrases used are so diaphanous and elastic as to invite subjective judicial preferences or prejudices relating to particular types of legislation, masquerading as judgements whether such legislation is directed at "important" objectives or, whether the relationship to those objectives is "substantial" enough.

I would have thought that if this Court were to leave anything to decision by the popularly elected branches of the Government, where no constitutional claim other than that of equal protection is invoked, it would be the decision as to what governmental objectives to be achieved by law are "important," and which are not. As for the second part of the Court's new test, the Judicial Branch is probably in no worse position than the Legislative or Executive Branches to determine if there is *any* rational relationship between a classification and the purpose which it might be thought to serve. But the introduction of the adverb "substantially" requires courts to make subjective judgments as to operational effects, for which neither their expertise nor their access to data fits them. And even if we manage to avoid both confusion and the mirroring of our own preferences in the development of this new doctrine, the thousands of judges in other courts who must interpret the Equal Protection Clause may not be so fortunate. . . .

Quite apart from these alleged methodological deficiencies in the statistical evidence, the Court appears to hold that that evidence, on its face, fails to support the distinction drawn in the statute. The Court notes that only 2% of males (as against .18% of females) in the age group were arrested for drunk driving, and that this very low figure establishes "an unduly tenuous fit" between maleness and drunk driving in the 18 to 20-year-old group. On this point the Court misconceives the nature of the equal protection inquiry.

The rationality of a statutory classification for equal protection purposes does not depend upon the statistical "fit" between the class and the trait sought to be singled out. It turns on whether there may be a sufficiently higher incidence of the trait within the included class than in the excluded class to justify different treatment. Therefore the present equal protection challenge to this gender-based discrimination poses only the question whether the incidence of drunk driving among young men is sufficiently greater than among young women to justify differential treatment. Notwithstanding the Court's critique of the statistical evidence, that evidence suggests clear differences between the drinking and driving habits of young men and women. Those differences are grounds enough for the State reasonably to conclude that young males pose by far the greater drunk-driving hazard, both in terms of sheer numbers and in terms of hazard on a per-driver basis. The gender-based difference in treatment is this case is therefore not irrational.

The Court's argument that a 2% correlation between maleness and drunk driving is constitutionally insufficient therefore does not pose an equal protection issue concerning discrimination between males and females. The clearest demonstration of this is the fact that the precise argument made by the Court would be equally applicable to a flat bar on such purchases by *anyone*, male or female, in the 18-20 age group; in fact it would apply a *fortiori* in that case given the even more "tenuous fit" between drunk-driving arrests and femaleness. The statistics indicate that about 1% of the age group population as a whole is arrested. What the Court's argument is relevant to is not equal protection, but due process—whether there are enough persons in the category who drive while drunk to justify a bar against purchases by all members of the group. . . .

The Oklahoma Legislature could have believed that 18-20-year-old males drive substantially more, and tend more often to be intoxicated than their female counterparts; that they prefer beer and admit to drinking and driving at a higher rate than females; and that they suffer traffic injuries out of proportion to the part they make up of the population. Under the appropriate rational-basis test for equal protection, it is neither irrational nor arbitrary to bar them from making purchases of 3.2% beer, which purchases might in many cases be made by a young man who immediately returns to his vehicle with the beverage in his possession. The record does not give any good indication of the true proportion of males in the age group who drink and drive (except that it is no doubt greater than the 2% who are arrested), but whatever it may be I cannot see that the mere purchase right involved could conceivably raise a due process question. There being no violation of either equal protection or due process, the statute should accordingly be upheld.

Although the outcome of *Craig* may lead many to say that men, not women, were the beneficiaries of the decision, that would be a totally erroneous conclusion. Two clear products of this decision went beyond the immediate consequence for Oklahoma's young male beer drinkers. The first effect is obvious: the introduction of the new "intermediate standard" of review requiring that in equal protection challenges, the government be able to show that sex-based classifications be *substantially* related to meeting *important* government objectives; otherwise a statute built on such a classification will fall. This clearly applied to both women and men. Nowhere does the standard say that it is to be used only when men are alleging harm; it can be applied when either sex feels the object of invidious discrimination. The benefit of this standard for an individual (or individuals) of either sex alleging such discrimination is to make it harder for the government to justify differential treatment.

The second product of *Craig* was the rejection, yet again but adding more weight each time it happened, of the practice of legislating on the basis of stereotypical notions of what males and females do or do not do. By implication, this rejection accepts the realization of just how confining and controlling—and just how unfair—stereotyping is for all members of any group, in this case males and females. Both women and men benefit from the Court's rejecting the notion that males and females can and should be put into their own respective gender-colored pigeonholes. And not even the special cachet of a state's right to police the sale and distribution of alcohol was strong enough to overcome either the new standard or the realization of the harm that comes with legislation by stereotypes.

TO WHOSE ADVANTAGE?

The introduction of a new standard thought to be to women's advantage raises an important question. Does it, in fact, really work out to women's advantage? Or to anyone's advantage? True, "intermediate scrutiny" places more of a burden on government than did "minimal scrutiny," thereby making it harder to justify sex-based classifications. Obviously, however, "strict scrutiny" would be a greater burden on government. And though it is harder for laws to pass constitutional muster under "intermediate scrutiny" than "minimal scrutiny," it is not as hard as it would be under "strict scrutiny."

So the question remains: Did women win with *Craig*, or were they severely harmed? Has the ability to fall back on "intermediate scrutiny" acted over the years as a helpful proxy (for the justices) to avoid confronting the politically and legally tricky issue of declaring sex a suspect class? And thus, have women once again been held back and closed out?

In the years that followed *Craig*, there was much discussion and debate on the appropriateness and consequences of the new standard. A new standard had indeed been introduced, but it was not clear in the aftermath of *Craig*, nor is it still, just what that new standard *really* means. Paul Weidner, a political scientist, noted that in the three years following *Craig*, the Court decided seven sex discrimination cases citing *Craig* as precedent;

however, he added, the Justices "remained deeply divided over the rationale for the decisions" (Weidner, 1980: 888). And when Weidner looked at the voting patterns of the Justices (á la Cook's analysis of the Burger Court's voting patterns in the early 1970s, discussed earlier), he found distinct patterns (898-899).

Justice Rehnquist, Chief Justice Burger and, to a slightly lesser degree, Justice Stewart were "extremely deferential" to (read "relied on") minimal scrutiny in judging sex discrimination cases. At the other end of the continuum, Justices Brennan and Marshall seemed the most ready to apply "strict scrutiny even though they may no longer verbalize it in traditional terms" (Weidner, 898). Weidner grouped Justice White with Justices Brennan and Marshall, labeling him, however, as not quite so firm in this approach as the other two. None of the remaining three justices—Justices Blackmun, Powell, and Stevens—was a supporter of declaring sex a suspect class; Weidner identified them as the swing group, "responsible for the degree to which gender-based discriminations are subject to an intermediate standard of review" (899). Thus, though *Craig* changed things, the degree to which it did so is not clear. As Weidner notes (897):

> In 1976, in *Craig*, the Court appeared to endorse a more stringent test for gender classifications, and it was generally believed that this intermediate standard of review at least made gender a "near-suspect" classification. However, it is still an open question whether the *Craig* formulation represented a significant doctrinal change or was a mere verbal distinction. (1980:897)

That open question still remains in many people's minds. And it is one that each reader will have to answer for herself or himself.

The Court, however, did not have to wait long before another opportunity arose to try out the new standard. In two 1977 cases, the first two of the seven surveyed by Weidner, a majority of the Court used *Craig* as precedent. In one case, the Court threw out a procedure that discriminated against men and in the other upheld a system that in effect discriminated in favor of women.

In the first case, *Califano v. Goldfarb*, 97 S.Ct. 1021 (1977), the Court declared invalid a provision of the Social Security Act allowing a widow to receive benefits regardless of whether she had or had not been dependent on her husband while a widower was eligible only if he had been dependent on his wife for at least half of his support. Both in content and outcome, this case is clearly reminiscent of *Frontiero*.

In the second case, *Califano v. Webster*, 97 S.Ct. 1192 (1977), the Court upheld another provision of the Social Security Act that established the method for calculating old-age insurance benefits. This method provided that in computing the "average monthly wage" on which benefits were based, female wage earners could exclude three more of their low-earning years than male earners could. The result of the method was to give a woman a higher benefit than a man with a comparable work history.

Thus, as will become even more evident over time, *Craig* did not become the precedent for a steady course of striking down laws built upon sex-based classifications. Nevertheless, there may be a modicum of logic in what did result. The two cases support Weidner's analysis: The Court struck down such classifications when they were based solely on stereotypic thinking but upheld them when they were designed to redress women's historically inferior economic position (Weidner, 897-898).

TITLE VII AND WOMEN'S RIGHTS

The Supreme Court had more to consider in 1977 than the chance to test "minimal scrutiny"; it also got its first women's rights challenge under Title VII of the Civil Rights Act of 1964. Before looking at this most interesting case, it is wise to review Title VII, "Equal Employment Opportunity" (42 U.S.C. 2000d-6). Essentially, Title VII is very straightforward. It states that it is unlawful for any employer of more than fifteen workers to discriminate on the basis of race, color, religion, national origin, or sex in *any area* of employment (i.e., hiring, firing, compensation, benefits, promotion, etc.). In essence, it could be said that Title VII does for employment rights what the Equal Protection Clause does for other areas of life, making it illegal to use "arbitrary and artificial" factors in employment practices if such usage would result in invidious discrimination.

There is, however, one important exception to this prohibition, and that is a "bona fide occupational qualification," or BFOQ. A BFOQ allows for hiring or promoting on the basis of sex (or some of the other identified characteristics) if it can be shown that such a discriminatory practice is reasonably related to the requirements of the job for which a person is being hired. Thus, a movie director looking for a leading woman is not required to include a few actors in her search; she can screen only actresses and not be in violation of Title VII.

The case of *Dothard v. Rawlinson*, 97 S.Ct. 2720 (1977), challenged an Alabama law that set minimum height (5′2") and weight (120 pounds) requirements for the job of "correctional counselor" (more commonly known as a prison guard). While the suit was pending, the Alabama Board of Corrections adopted an additional regulation stipulating that in male maximum security facilities, guard positions requiring close physical proximity to inmates could be filled only by males. This further restricted women's access to guard positions: Those women who could meet the general height and weight requirements were still ineligible to compete for about 75 percent of the state's available guard positions.

Dianne Rawlinson, a twenty-two-year-old college graduate who had majored in correctional psychology, applied for but was denied employment as a guard because she failed to meet the height and weight requirements. She filed suit in a federal district court on behalf of herself and similarly situated females, claiming that since women generally have a harder time than men in meeting minimum weight and height requirements, the weight and height restrictions, as well as the sex restrictions on maximum security sites, were violations of Title VII and a denial of her Fourteenth Amendment right of equal protection. (A cofiler challenged the higher height and weight requirements for state troopers—at least 5′9" and 160 pounds.) The three-judge district court agreed with Rawlinson, saying that the requirements created an arbitrary barrier to equal employment and were thus forbidden under Title VII. The state appealed directly to the Supreme Court, claiming that the requirements, far from being arbitrary were a valid occupational qualification.

Thus, more than one hundred years after *Bradwell*, almost seventy years after *Muller*, and almost thirty years after *Goesaert*, the Court was, in essence, hearing these cases all over again, addressing the same issue all over again—that of women denied access to employment opportunities solely because of their sex. There was one slight difference, however. In the earlier cases, sex was being used as a proxy to preserve employment opportunities for men. In Rawlinson, height and weight requirements were being used as veiled proxy for sex, and then sex again was used to preserve job opportunities for men. Despite the one hundred-year time span, all of the laws under challenge were examples of vehicles leading to legal job segregation; the law was being used to say, "Only males need apply." In the nineteenth century, those males were lawyers, then bakers, then bartenders; now in the last half of the twentieth century, the males were correctional guards and law enforcement officers. For women, the implications of the Alabama law, seventy years after *Muller*, were exactly the same as those stemming from *Muller*: fewer job opportunities, limited or no possibility for advancement, and, as the bottom line, lower income.

Had women indeed made any progress in the course of the preceding one hundred years, since a century later the same war raged on the battlefield of the Court? Despite victory in some individual battles, women were still struggling for the same basic right: The right to have their competency and abilities considered and judged as individual workers rather than as members of a large group that was, far too often, stereotypically assessed.

But, in fact, there may have been some invidious change. Legislators, and as a consequence laws, may have become more subtle in their efforts to exclude women. The nature of Rawlinson's claim, which is unlike any other encountered thus far, points this up. Rawlinson did not allege, as had the previously cited cases, that the law set out intentionally to discriminate against women. Rather, she claimed that the height and weight requirements, while "facially neutral" (an important phrase and concept to consider—that something is on its face neutral and nondiscriminatory), actually worked in practice to disqualify women disproportionately, thereby discriminating against them. Since most men exceed Alabama's minimum height and weight requirements and fewer women meet or exceed them, using them for hiring screened out far more women than men. Thus, she argued, the law *as worded* did not purposefully exclude women, but the law *in its application* did. (No less damaging in effect, there is, however, a difference in fact and, in the eyes of the law, between purposeful, intentional discrimination and that which results unintentionally.)

It was this claim, along with the charge of explicit sex discrimination in the provision regulating the hiring of guards in maximum security prisons, that reached the Supreme Court. Justice Stewart wrote the decision for the Court, in which the Court agreed eight to one to strike down the height and weight requirements but voted six to three to uphold the sex restriction for maximum security guards. Justice Stewart was joined by Justices Powell and Stevens, and Justice Rehnquist authored a concurring opinion that agreed with the result but not the rationale, in which he was joined by Chief Justice Burger and Justice Blackmun. Justice Marshall, joined by Justice Brennan, wrote an opinion agreeing with the decision to invalidate the height and weight requirements but arguing that the court should also have thrown out the restriction on employing women in male maximum security prisons. Finally, Justice White simply dissented, declaring that Rawlinson had failed to developed a *prima facie* case of discrimination (see below).

Moving straight to the heart of the issue at hand, Justice Stewart's decision noted that in cases claiming that a "facially neutral" statute actually did discriminate against one group, a claimant must establish a *prima facie* case of discrimination by showing "that the facially neutral standards in question select applicants for hire in a significantly discriminatory pattern" (*Dothard*, 1977: 2726-2727). Once this has been done, an employer has the opportunity to protect the constitutionality of the statute by showing that the standard is, *in fact*, related to the job at hand. But the claimant can still win the case by showing how other factors could be used in the selection process to achieve the same desired end legitimately, without the discriminatory effect. Having outlined what, in the abstract, needed to be done, Justice Stewart then explored the case at hand to see whether, in fact, Rawlinson had mounted a solid *prima facie* case of discrimination.

Dothard v. Rawlinson
97 S.Ct. 2720 (1977)
Justice Stewart, for the Court

. . . Although women 14 years of age or older compose 52.75% of the Alabama population and 36.89% of its total labor force, they hold only 12.9% of its correctional counselor positions. In considering the effect of the minimum height and weight standards on this disparity in [the] rate of hiring between the sexes, the District Court found that the 5′2" requirement would operate to exclude 33.29% of the women in the United States between the ages of 18-79, while excluding only 1.28% of men between the same ages. The 120-pound weight restriction would exclude 22.29% of the women and 2.35% of the men in this age group. When the height and weight restrictions are combined, Alabama's statutory standards would exclude 41.13% of the female population while excluding less than 1% of the male population. Accordingly, the District Court found that Rawlinson had made out a *prima facie* case of unlawful sex discrimination.

The appellants argue that a showing of disproportionate impact on women based on generalized national statistics should not suffice to establish a *prima facie* case. They point in particular to Rawlinson's failure to adduce comparative statistics concerning actual applicants for correctional counselor positions in Alabama. There is no requirement, however, that a statistical showing of disproportionate impact must always be based on analysis of the characteristics of actual applicants [cite omitted]. The application process might itself not adequately reflect the actual potential applicant pool, since otherwise qualified people might be discouraged from applying because of a self-recognized inability to meet the very standards challenged as being discriminatory. . . . A potential applicant could easily determine her height and weight and conclude that to make an application would be futile. Moreover, reliance on general population demographic data was not misplaced where there was no reason to suppose that physical height and weight characteristics of Alabama men and women differ markedly from those of the national population.

For these reasons, we cannot say that the District Court was wrong in holding that the statutory height and weight standards had a discriminatory impact on women applicants. The plaintiffs in a case such as this are not required to exhaust every possible source of evidence, if the evidence actually presented on its face conspicuously demonstrates a job requirement's grossly discriminatory impact. If the employer discerns fallacies or deficiencies in the data offered by the plaintiff, he is free to adduce countervailing evidence of his own. In this case no such effort was made.

We turn, therefore, to the appellants' argument that they have rebutted the *prima facie* case of discrimination by showing that the height and weight requirements are job related. These requirements, they say, have a relationship to strength, a sufficient but unspecified amount of which is essential to effective job performance as a correctional counselor. In the District Court, however, the appellants produced no evidence correlating the height and weight requirements with the requisite amount of strength thought essential to good job performance. Indeed, they failed to offer evidence of any kind in specific justification of the statutory standards.

If the job-related quality that the appellants identify is bona fide, their purpose could be achieved by adopting and validating a test for applicants that measures strength directly. Such a test, fairly administered, would fully satisfy the standards of Title VII because it would be one that "measure(s) the person for the job and not the person in the abstract" [cite omitted]. But nothing in the present record even approaches such a measurement.

For the reasons we have discussed, the District Court was not in error in holding that Title VII of the Civil Rights Act of 1964, as amended, prohibits application of the statutory height and weight requirements to Rawlinson and the class she represents.

Unlike the statutory height and weight requirements, Regulation 204 explicitly discriminates against women on the basis of their sex. In defense of this overt discrimination, the appellants rely on [Title VII, Section 703], which permits sex-based discrimination "in those certain instances where. . . sex. . . is a bona fide occupational qualification reasonably necessary to the normal operation of that particular business or enterprise."

The District Court rejected the bona-fide-occupational-qualification (bfoq) defense, relying on the virtually uniform view of the federal courts that 703(e) provides only the narrowest of exceptions to the general rule requiring equality of employment opportunities. This view has been variously formulated. . . . But whatever the verbal formulation, the federal courts have agreed that it is impermissible under Title VII to refuse to hire an individual woman or man on the basis of stereotyped characterizations of the sexes, and the District Court in the present case held in effect that Regulation 204 is based on just such stereotypical assumptions.

We are persuaded—by the restrictive language of 703(e), the relevant legislative history, and the consistent interpretation of the Equal Employment Opportunity Commission—that the bfoq exception was in fact meant to be an extremely narrow exception to the general prohibition of discrimination on the basis of sex. In the particular factual circumstances of this case, however, we conclude that the District Court erred in rejecting the State's contention that Regulation 204 falls within the narrow ambit of the bfoq exception.

The environment in Alabama's penitentiaries is a peculiarly inhospitable one for human beings of whatever sex. Indeed, a Federal District Court has held that the conditions of confinement in the prisons of the State, characterized by "rampant violence" and a "jungle atmosphere," are constitutionally intolerable [cite omitted]. The record in the present case shows that because of inadequate staff and facilities, no attempt is made in the four maximum-security male penitentiaries to classify or segregate inmates according to their offense or level of dangerousness—a procedure that, according to expert testimony, is essential to effective penological administration. Consequently, the estimated 20% of the male prisoners who are sex offenders are scattered throughout the penitentiaries' dormitory facilities.

In this environment of violence and disorganization, it would be an oversimplification to characterize Regulation 204 as an exercise in "romantic paternalism" [cite omitted]. In the usual case, the argument that a particular job is too dangerous for women may appropriately be met by the rejoinder that it is the purpose of Title VII to allow the individual woman to make that choice for herself. More is at stake in this case, however, than an individual woman's decision to weigh and accept the risks of employment in a "contact" position in a maximum-security male prison.

The essence of a correctional counselor's job is to maintain prison security. A woman's relative ability to maintain order in a male, maximum-security, unclassified penitentiary of the type

> Alabama now runs could be directly reduced by her womanhood. There is a basis in fact for expecting that sex offenders who have criminally assaulted women in the past would be moved to do so again if access to women were established within the prison. There would also be a real risk that other inmates, deprived of a normal heterosexual environment, would assault women guards because they were women. In a prison system where violence is the order of the day, where inmate access to guards is facilitated by dormitory living arrangements, where every institution is understaffed, and where a substantial portion of the inmate population is composed of sex offenders mixed at random with other prisoners, there are few visible deterrents to inmate assaults on women custodians.
>
> Appellee Rauwlinson's [sic] own expert testified that dormitory housing for aggressive inmates poses a greater security problem than single-cell lockups, and further testified that it would be unwise to use women as guards in a prison where even 10% of the inmates had been convicted of sex crimes and were not segregated from the other prisoners. The likelihood that inmates would assault a woman because she was a woman would pose a real threat not only to the victim of the assault but also to the basic control of the penitentiary and protection of its inmates and the other security personnel. The employee's very womanhood would thus directly undermine her capacity to provide the security that is the essence of a correctional counselor's responsibility.
>
> There was substantial testimony from experts on both sides of this litigation that the use of women as guards in "contact" positions under the existing conditions in Alabama maximum-security male penitentiaries would pose a substantial security problem, directly linked to the sex of the prison guard. On the basis of that evidence, we conclude that the District Court was in error in ruling that being male is not a bona fide occupational qualification for the job of correctional counselor in a "contact" position in an Alabama male maximum-security penitentiary.

In actuality, as can be seen from the preceding excerpts, *Dothard* was a comparatively simple and straightforward decision; nevertheless, it had widespread impact because it struck down a major guarantor of occupational segregation. For decades, height and weight requirements had been a central part of the selection criteria for police officers, prison guards, and fire fighters. These were the very jobs often chosen by lower-class men seeking to improve their position in society, jobs sought specifically because they offered both a decent salary and job security. Minimum height and weight requirements closed off to women this particular route to economic advancement and job security. Yet with apparent ease and very little fussing, the Court slew this time-honored dragon.

Although the question may be simply another exercise in Monday-morning quarterbacking, it must nonetheless be asked: If the battle in the end proved to be so easily won, why did it take so long for the challenge to be brought? The answer lies in Justice Stewart's explanation as to why it was not necessary, and in fact might have been misleading, to use actual comparative statistics of applicants to develop a *prima facie* case rather than the national statistics Rawlinson used. As Justice Stewart said, women who might be interested in applying for such a job would not bother to apply if they knew they could not meet the height and/or weight requirements. This would seem simply "common sense." How many of us have at some point in our lives decided not to try for something, even though we thought we were up to the task, because we did not meet a key *stipulated* requirement? We simply think: Why bother? But how many of us have ever thought instead: Why don't I challenge the need for this particular requirement?

Now think about this question in light of the political, economic, and social status of women at the time of *Dothard*. All of us, either consciously or unconsciously, are to some degree limited by what we are told we can or cannot do. Some of us challenge those stipulations, some of us do not. When we do, we are sometimes successful, sometimes not. But before we challenge, we consider carefully whom and what we are challenging and the implications of that challenge. Female or male, few of us lightly challenge the law or tradition. For a woman of Rawlinson's time or earlier—a woman raised with society's stereotypical notions of female obedience, subservience, conformity, timidity, and acceptance—the thought of challenging the law or tradition was a highly risky and even terrifying undertaking. Thus, *Dothard* highlights the catch-22 in women's relationship with the law: challenging the law can set women free, but since we all, women and men, normally think of the law as a relatively constant vehicle of constraint (Don't steal. Don't run a red light. Don't smoke where it is prohibited.), we do not often think of using that same vehicle (i.e., the law) as a way to free ourselves from constraints In short, the law can set us free as well as restrain us, but before we can attempt to use it to free ourselves, we must first see and recognize it as unjustly restraining us.

Dothard had its limitations, however. After all, it let stand the explicit use of sex to deny women access to contact positions in male maximum security prisons. And it did so by saying the rule was designed to meet a legitimate state worry but was not an exercise in "romantic paternalism," the phrase used in *Frontiero*. Certainly, there is nothing romantic about maximum security prisons, but there was unquestionably paternalism in both Alabama's rule and the Court's reasoning. In this part of its decision, the Court was taking many steps backward. First, by expressing its concern over the proximity of sex offenders to female guards, the Stewart opinion implicitly supported the notion that sex crimes are crimes about sex rather than crimes of violence. Few, if any, experts would endorse the Court's view on that. The Court also said that it feared for the safety of women guards in general, the implication here being that the Court saw female guards as females first and authority figures second. The Court reached this compassionate, but paternalistic, conclusion despite the fact that no evidence was presented to show that any *trained* female corrections officers had ever been attacked. (Two females actually had been attacked, but there was no evidence showing that they had been attacked *because they were female.* Moreover, neither one was a trained guard; one was a clerical worker and the other a visiting student.)

Thus, the Court appeared to be allowing exactly what it had said in *Craig* should not happen: it legislated for 100 percent of the group based on its fear for "2 percent." In so doing, the Court took more steps backward, returning to the days of making decisions for women rather than letting women weigh the options themselves. The Court decided categorically that Alabama's maximum security prisons were too dangerous for women guards (although not for male guards), not that a woman interested in becoming a guard should be allowed to decide for herself (as it permitted men to do). The Court thus returned to the days of penalizing women in order to protect some other group, in this case would-be male guards. And the Court did so without any evidence as to whether what it foresaw would actually happen if women were allowed in as guards (i.e., the calm and security of the institutions would be threatened by their presence and inability to handle the job).[2] The Court simply decided on its own instincts that in order to keep the institutions stable and to secure the well-being of inmates and male guards, women's access to these jobs had to be denied.

This leads to yet another backward step: By upholding this restriction, the Court effectively restricted women's access to advancement in the prison hierarchy. In many, if not all U.S. prison systems, promotion has historically depended upon having had two types of experience: having worked in a position providing inmate contact and having worked in larger institutions, which were almost always the male institutions and usually maximum security institutions. Without this background, promotional opportunities were generally limited to moving within a specific institution or type of institution; moving to systemwide positions was almost impossible. The Court's decision here further curtailed women's earning power.

For its final step backward, the Court reintroduced its reliance on stereotypical notions. In viewing women guards as more likely to be victims of assault by inmates and in refusing to allow each individual woman to assess for herself and decide for herself whether she wanted to expose herself to the risks involved in a given job, the Court reverted to generalizing about women as a group, precluding the possibility of looking at the individual characteristics of each member. And that, in essence, is stereotyping. In *Dothard,* therefore, women gained a major victory in their struggle for progress, but at the same time a number of battles they thought they had won were unexpectedly reopened.[3]

All this is what the majority of the Court did. But opinions by other justices added to the legacy of *Dothard.* And, it could be argued, some of the progress stemming from Justice Stewart's opinion was clearly undermined by parts of these other opinions. Despite the fact that these opinions lacked the weight of the official Court opinion, they nonetheless exposed a split in the Court's thinking. For example, the concurring opinion written by Justice Rehnquist, which was joined by Justice Blackmun and Chief Justice Burger, agreed with the Court's conclusion that the height and weight restrictions should be rejected but that the sex restrictions for maximum security guard positions was a legitimate occupational qualification. Where the Rehnquist opinion split with the Court, however, was in its rationale.

Essentially, Justice Rehnquist indicated that he had no problem philosophically with the idea that strength was necessary for the job of prison guard and that height and weight were valid indicators of strength. He said he had voted to reject the height and weight requirements on the ground that Alabama had not presented its case convincingly enough. In other words, he reached a decision on legal rather than philosophical grounds. He faulted Alabama for failing to rebut the statistical evidence presented by Rawlinson and for failing to argue that the appearance of physical strength was just as necessary for the job of corrections guard as actual strength. He maintained that Alabama, as the appellant, had not carried out the necessary burden of showing a job-related reason for the height and weight qualifications [*Dothard v. Rawlinson*, 97 S.Ct. 2720, 2732, (1977)]:

> Appellants argued only the job-relatedness of actual physical strength; they did not urge that an equally job-related qualification for prison guards is the *appearance* of strength. As the Court notes, the primary job of correctional counselor in Alabama prisons "is to maintain security and control of the inmates. . . " [cite omitted], a function that I at least would imagine is aided by the psychological impact on prisoners of the presence of tall and heavy guards. If the appearance of strength had been urged upon the District Court here as a reason for the height and weight minima, I think that the District Court would surely have been entitled to reach a different result than it did. For, even if not perfectly correlated, I would think that Title VII would not preclude a State from saying that anyone under 5'2" or 120 pounds, no matter how strong in fact, does not have sufficient appearance of strength to be a prison guard.
>
> . . . As appellants did not even present the "appearance of strength" contention to the District Court as an asserted job-related reason for the qualification requirements, I agree that their burden was not met. The District Court's holding thus did not deal with the question of whether such an assertion could or did rebut appellee Rawlinson's *prima facie* case.

Justice Rehnquist makes it clear that he does not find fault with the restrictions but rather with the legal argument—or lack thereof. This passage, in which he marked out the path for another possible legislative attempt to impose height and weight requirements, also contained a damning implication. Along with his colleagues who endorsed the Court's opinion in this case, he reaffirmed the validity of stereotypical thinking—but his endorsement was painted with a much broader brush than the sexual stereotyping of his colleagues. By suggesting that an appearance of strength could, if properly argued, be sustained as a job-related requirement, he reinforced the fallacy that one can presume to know someone's true characteristics solely on the basis of appearance. In effect, he validated the notion that one can indeed tell a book by its cover. No better example of this fallacy could be found than in playing out Justice Rehnquist's reliance on such stereotyping. *If* effective execution of the job of prison guard requires that a person *in fact* be strong—another stereotype that he relies upon despite evidence to the contrary—then hiring simply on the basis of the *appearance* of strength (as indicated by height and weight), and not on the basis of a demonstration of *actual* strength, merely sets the person up for failure. Such a hiring policy would also create great risk for that individual, his fellow guards, other workers and inmates. This image of a corrections officer ignores the fact that officers are to keep order and gain respect by being *authority* figures, not by using physical force. This, however, is something that Justice Marshall, with Justice Brennan agreeing, points out in his opinion, concurring in part with the majority judgment and dissenting in part.

Justice Marshall agreed with the Court's opinion in striking down the height and weight requirements and with the Court's interpretation that a bona fide occupational qualification must be "narrowly construed." He disagreed, however, with the Court's decision that applying that principle to validate a sex restriction on maximum security guard positions was constitutional. Justice Marshall acknowledged the correctness of the Court's position that it was a woman's right to decide for herself, rather than have the state decide in a blanket disqualification of all women, whether a job was too dangerous for her and whether she could adequately protect herself. But when the Court said that intolerable conditions in the Alabama penitentiaries made permissible the sex restriction on work as a maximum security prison guard, Justice Marshall broke with his brethren.

Dothard v. Rawlinson
97 S.Ct. 2720, (1977)
Justice Marshall, dissenting

> What would otherwise be considered unlawful discrimination against women is justified by the Court, however, on the basis of the "barbaric and inhumane" conditions in Alabama prisons, conditions so bad that state officials have conceded that they violate the Constitution. . . . To me, this analysis sounds distressingly like saying two wrongs make a right. It is refuted by the plain words of 703(e). The statute requires that a bfoq be "reasonably necessary to the normal operation of that particular business or enterprise." But no governmental "business" may operate "normally" in violation of the Constitution. Every action of government is constrained by constitutional limitations. While those limits may be violated more frequently than we would wish, no one disputes that the "normal operation" of all government functions takes place within them. A prison system operating in blatant violation of the Eighth Amendment is an exception that should be remedied with all possible speed, . . . In the meantime, the existence of such violations should not be legitimatized by calling them "normal." Nor should the Court accept them as justifying conduct that would otherwise violate a statute intended to remedy age-old discrimination.

The Court's error in statutory construction is less objectionable, however, than the attitude it displays toward women. Though the Court recognizes that possible harm to women guards is an unacceptable reason for disqualifying women, it relies instead on an equally speculative threat to prison discipline supposedly generated by the sexuality of female guards. There is simply no evidence in the record to show that women guards would create any danger to security in Alabama prisons significantly greater than that which already exists. All of the dangers—with one exception discussed below—are inherent in a prison setting, whatever the gender of the guards.

The Court first sees women guards as a threat to security because "there are few visible deterrents to inmate assaults on women custodians" [cite omitted]. In fact, any prison guard is constantly subject to the threat of attack by inmates, and "invisible" deterrents are the guard's only real protection. No prison guard relies primarily on his or her ability to ward off an inmate attack to maintain order. Guards are typically unarmed and sheer numbers of inmates could overcome the normal complement. Rather, like all other law enforcement officers, prison guards must rely primarily on the moral authority of their office and the threat of future punishment for miscreants. As one expert testified below, common sense, fairness, and mental and emotional stability are the qualities a guard needs to cope with the dangers of the job. . . . Well qualified and properly trained women, no less than men, have these psychological weapons at their disposal.

The particular severity of discipline problems in the Alabama maximum-security prisons is also no justification for the discrimination sanctioned by the Court. . . . If male guards face an impossible situation, it is difficult to see how women could make the problem worse, unless one relies on precisely the type of generalized bias against women that the Court agrees Title VII was intended to outlaw. For example, much of the testimony of appellant's witnesses ignores individual differences among members of each sex and reads like "ancient canards about the proper role of women" [cite omitted]. The witnesses claimed that women guards are not strict disciplinarians; that they are physically less capable of protecting themselves and subduing unruly inmates; that inmates take advantage of them as they did their mothers, while male guards are strong father figures who easily maintain discipline, and so on. Yet the record shows that the presence of women guards has not led to a single incident amounting to a serious breach of security in any Alabama institution. And, in any event, "(g)uards rarely enter the cell blocks and dormitories" [cite omitted], where the danger of inmate attacks is the greatest.

It appears that the real disqualifying factor in the Court's view is "[t]he employee's very womanhood." The Court refers to the large number of sex offenders in Alabama prisons, and to "[t]he likelihood that inmates would assault a woman because she was a woman." With all respect, this rationale regrettably perpetuates one of the most insidious of the old myths about women—that women, wittingly or not, are seductive sexual objects. The effect of the decision, made I am sure with the best of intentions, is to punish women because their very presence might provoke sexual assaults. It is women who are made to pay the price in lost job opportunities for the threat of depraved conduct by prison inmates. Once again, "[t]he pedestal upon which women have been placed has. . . , upon closer inspection, been revealed as a cage [cite omitted]. It is particularly ironic that the cage is erected here in response to feared misbehavior by imprisoned criminals.

The Court points to no evidence in the record to support the asserted "likelihood that inmates would assault a woman because she was a woman" [cite omitted]. Perhaps the Court relies upon common sense, or "innate recognition." . . . But the danger in this emotionally laden context is that common sense will be used to mask the "romantic paternalism" and persisting discriminatory attitudes that the Court properly eschews [cite omitted]. To me, the only matter of innate recognition is that the incidence of sexually motivated attacks on guards will be minute compared to the "likelihood that inmates will assault" a guard because he or she is a guard.

The proper response to inevitable attacks on both female and male guards is not to limit the employment opportunities of law-abiding women who wish to contribute to their community, but to take swift and sure punitive action against the inmate offenders. Presumably, one of the goals of the Alabama prison system is the eradication of inmates' antisocial behavior patterns so that prisoners will be able to live one day in free society. Sex offenders can begin this process by learning to relate to women guards in a socially acceptable manner. To deprive women of job opportunities because of the threatened behavior of convicted criminals is to turn our social priorities upside down.

Although I do not countenance the sex discrimination condoned by the majority, it is fortunate that the Court's decision is carefully limited to the facts before it. I trust the lower courts will recognize that the decision was impelled by the shockingly inhuman conditions in Alabama prisons, and thus that the "extremely narrow [bfoq] exception" recognized here [cite omitted], will not be allowed "to swallow the rule" against sex discrimination. . . . Expansion of today's decision beyond its narrow factual basis would erect a serious roadblock to economic equality for women.

Justice Marshall's opinion, from a true champion of women's rights, blasts stereotypic thinking. He admonishes the Court for the stereotypical and damaging image of women it has purveyed and for the economic prison to which it has confined her. In his closing sentence, he raises the specter of the question asked earlier: How do *Dothard* and *Muller* differ in their consequences for women? The answer: not at all.

OLD PRACTICES: NEW CHALLENGES

Although *Dothard* challenged an old issue dressed in modern garb, two cases the Court decided in 1979 were anything but a reincarnation of old concerns.[4] Like *Dothard*, each challenged a long-standing practice of behavior. And as with *Dothard*, there has to be more than a little bit of wonder as to why the challenge to these practices was so long in coming. The answer may be a combination of the inhibiting power of the law, as discussed earlier in relation to *Dothard*, and the slowness with which society changes.

The first of the two 1979 cases to come before the Court, *Orr v. Orr*, 440 U.S. 268, (1979), was brought, perversely, for the wrong reason. It challenged another Alabama law but, once again, a law that was not unique to Alabama. This law required husbands, upon divorce, to pay alimony but made no such demands upon wives. William Orr challenged this law only after Lillian Orr, his ex-wife, filed contempt charges against him, more than two years after the divorce was granted because he was in arrears in his alimony payments. His challenge was not fueled by a sense of injustice that husbands were required to pay but that even well-to-do wives were not. If he had felt that, it would seem logical that he would have filed his case immediately following the alimony decree. Nor was his challenge fueled by a claim that he was the deserving recipient of post-marriage support; he made no such claim. Rather, his challenge was prompted by the simple desire, for whatever reason, not to pay the alimony. It is interesting that in the vast majority of cases in which men have been the ones to challenge discriminatory practices, the issues involved have been explicitly and directly tied to the wallet—either seeking greater benefits or seeking to avoid paying them to others. When women have been the challengers, however, the issues have involved a far broader range of concerns—some being direct efforts to obtain more income but far more being assaults on barriers to opportunities and options (though some of these, of course, would have involved subsequent access to more income). There may not be a "right" or "wrong" reason for challenging a discriminatory practice, but somehow a simple desire to avoid paying money, especially when it might involve harm to children as failure to pay alimony could involve, does not seem a "right" reason. One can argue that challenges to discriminatory practices should rest on loftier behavior than the simple desire to avoid paying money. On the other hand, if the goal is the elimination of discriminatory laws and behavior, ought we to concern ourselves with the nature of the catalyst for change?

In any event, William Orr's challenge did result in the invalidation of a sex-based classification that put the burden of paying alimony only on husbands and not also on wives. He claimed that he should not be required to pay alimony if similarly situated wives could not be so ordered. After an unsuccessful journey through the Alabama state courts, he took his equal protection claim to the U.S. Supreme Court. And the Court, in a six-to-three decision, declared the challenged practice unconstitutional.

Justice Brennan wrote the opinion for the Court and was joined by Justices Marshall, Stewart, and White. Justices Blackmun and Stevens each wrote brief concurring opinions, and Chief Justice Burger and Justices Rehnquist and Powell dissented.

After disposing of several legal questions about Orr's standing to bring the case,[5] Justice Brennan addressed the question before the Court: Was the sex-based alimony law constitutional? Relying on *Craig* as precedent (although willing to suggest that even under *Reed* this law could not stand), Justice Brennan provided the Court's rationale for declaring the law invalid and for rejecting the notion that it met "important governmental objectives."

Orr v. Orr
99 S.Ct. 1102 (1979)
Justice Brennan, for the Court

> [Mr. Orr] views the Alabama alimony statutes as effectively announcing the State's preference for an allocation of family responsibilities under which the wife plays a dependent role,... We agree, . . . that prior cases settle that this purpose cannot sustain the statutes. . . . If the statute is to survive constitutional attack, therefore, it must be validated on some other basis.
>
> The opinion of the [Alabama Court] suggests other purposes that the statute may serve. Its opinion states that the Alabama statutes were "designed" for "the wife of a broken marriage who needs financial assistance" [cite omitted]. This may be read as asserting either of two legislative objectives. One is a legislative purpose to provide help for needy spouses, using sex as a proxy for need. The other is a goal of compensating women for past discrimination during marriage, which assertedly has left them unprepared to fend for themselves in the working world following divorce. We concede, of course, that assisting needy spouses is a legitimate and important governmental objective. We have also recognized "reduction of the disparity in economic condition between men and women caused by the long history of discrimination against women... as... an important governmental objective" [cite omitted]. It only remains, therefore, to determine whether the classification at issue here is "substantially related to achievement of those objectives" [cite omitted].
>
> Ordinarily, we would begin the analysis of the "needy spouse" objective by considering whether sex is a sufficiently "accurate proxy" [cite omitted], for dependency. . . . Similarly, we would initially approach the "compensation" rationale by

asking whether women had in fact been significantly discriminated against in the sphere to which the statute applied a sex-based classification, . . .

But in this case, even if sex were a reliable proxy for need, and even if the institution of marriage did discriminate against women, these factors still would "not adequately justify the salient features of" Alabama's statutory scheme [cite omitted]. Under the statute, individualized hearings at which the parties' relative financial circumstances are considered already occur [cites omitted]. There is no reason, therefore, to use sex as a proxy for need. Needy males could be helped along with needy females with little if any additional burden on the State. In such circumstances, not even an administrative-convenience rationale exists to justify operating by generalization or proxy. Similarly, since individualized hearings can determine which women were in fact discriminated against vis-á-vis their husbands, as well as which family units defied the stereotype and left the husband dependent on the wife, Alabama's alleged compensatory purpose may be effectuated without placing burdens solely on husbands. Progress toward fulfilling such a purpose would not be hampered, and it would cost the State nothing more, if it were to treat men and women equally by making alimony burdens independent of sex. "Thus, the gender-based distinction is gratuitous; without it, the statutory scheme would only provide benefits to those men who are in fact similarly situated to the women the statute aids" [cite omitted], and the effort to help those women would not in any way be compromised.

Moreover, use of a gender classification actually produces perverse results in this case. As compared to a gender-neutral law placing alimony obligations on the spouse able to pay, the present Alabama statutes give an advantage only to the financially secure wife whose husband is in need. Although such a wife might have to pay alimony under a gender-neutral statute, the present statutes exempt her from that obligation. Thus, "[t]he [wives] who benefit from the disparate treatment are those who were nondependent on their husbands" [cite omitted]. They are precisely those who are not "needy spouses" and who are "least likely to have been victims of discrimination," . . . by the institution of marriage. A gender-based classification which, as compared to a gender-neutral one, generates additional benefits only for those it has no reason to prefer cannot survive equal protection scrutiny.

Legislative classifications which distribute benefits and burdens on the basis of gender carry the inherent risk of reinforcing stereotypes about the "proper place" of women and their need for special protections [cite omitted]. Thus, even statutes purportedly designed to compensate for and ameliorate the effects of past discrimination must be carefully tailored. Where, as here,

> the State's compensatory and ameliorative purposes are as well served by a gender-neutral classification as one that gender classifies and therefore carries with it the baggage of sexual stereotypes, the State cannot be permitted to classify on the bases of sex. And this is doubly so where the choice made by the State appears to redound—if only indirectly—to the benefit of those without need for special solicitude.

And with that decision, the Court struck down the practice, heretofore followed religiously in state after state—of making divorced or separated husbands only the payer and former wives only the payee. In so doing, the Court deposed the commonly held stereotypes that automatically placed women in the home and in an inferior economic position. The Court was recognizing that its traditional classification of women was not always consistent with reality. Although perhaps not obvious at first glance, this decision of the Court remained consistent with the post-*Craig* pattern identified by Weidner: It invalidated a law that was based solely on stereotypical notions. Despite the state's claim that this sex-based law was necessary in order to redress women's past economic disadvantage, the Court recognized it correctly as a stereotypically based law that contributed no more toward redressing women's economic problems than would a sex-neutral law. With this decision, the Court continued solidifying the path it started with *Frontiero* and broadened with *Kahn*—the recognition that a man can be the economically dependent partner in a marriage, either by choice or by necessity, and that a man can need the economic assistance of his present or former wife. And, as has previously been pointed out, in noting this, the Court also recognized the flip side as well: Some women, either by choice or by necessity, form the economic base of a family and, therefore, may need to give economic assistance to their former or present husbands. By requiring laws to take this picture of reality into account, the Court helped redraw for the nation the image of women and marriage in America. No longer would there be an automatic assumption about the roles women and men would play before, during and, if need be, after marriage.

The dissenting opinions in *Orr* differ from those in previous cases. Here, the dissenters do not attack the majority for the conclusion it reached but rather attack it for reaching any conclusion at all. No dissenter—Justice Powell who authored his own dissent nor Justice Rehnquist, who authored another dissent in which Chief Justice Burger joined—faulted the majority directly for its rejection of sexual stereotypes or for voiding the Alabama alimony statute. Rather, they attack the majority for too quickly assuming that the Court had any jurisdiction in the case; they see the case clearly as a states' rights issue in which the Supreme Court is interfering prematurely and, therefore, perhaps unnecessarily.

There is also in Justice Rehnquist's opinion a suggestion of displeasure with the Court's ultimate decision because he accuses the Court of being too "eager" to strike down the alimony law and therefore too "casual" in its belief in the Court's jurisdiction to hear the case. In his attack and in his choice of words, one can hear a disgruntled justice, unhappy with the outcome, charging his brethren with putting political interests ahead of sound legal reasoning. In *Dothard*, he had found himself endorsing an outcome he did not like politically but that he believed had at least been arrived at via sound legal reasoning.

Nevertheless, in this case, the dissents did not detract from the strength of the Court's explicit and implicit pronouncements on the status of the sexes in America, 1979.

VETERANS' PREFERENCE

Several months after *Orr*, the Court decided the constitutionality of another widely accepted practice whose effect was to discriminate against women in their access to jobs. This case, however, was tinged with a double sorrow: The discriminatory practice under attack was predicated upon still another exercise in discrimination, one that, ironically, was not to be challenged for yet another two years.

The case involved Helen Feeney's challenge to the constitutionality of a Massachusetts law giving veterans lifetime preference in hiring or promotion for certain state jobs. The law provided that veterans who qualified for classified state civil service positions—approximately 60 percent of the public sector jobs in the state—*must* be considered for appointment or promotion ahead of any qualifying nonveterans. A veteran was defined as "any person, male or female, including a nurse, who was honorably discharged from the United States Armed Forces after at least ninety days of active service, at least one day of which was during 'wartime'" [*Personnel Administrator of Massachusetts v. Feeney*, 99 S.Ct. 2282, 2287 (1979)]. According to the figures available at the time that Feeney began her litigation in 1975, "98% of the veterans in Massachusetts were male; only 1.8% were female" [*Personnel Administrator of Massachusetts v. Feeney*, 99 S.Ct. 2282, 2291 (1979)]. Moreover, at the time of Feeney's challenge, becoming a veteran was, to a great extent, interwoven with being subject to the draft, and only males were so subject. Feeney's challenge threw into relief, although it did not raise, the question of the constitutionality of the draft.

Feeney was a twelve-year veteran of state employment who sought promotion to a better job. Of two civil service exams that she took for promotion, she scored second on one and third on the other. Despite this, on one final applicants list she was ranked sixth, trailing five male veterans, and on the second list she was ranked thirteenth, coming after twelve male veterans, all but one of whom scored lower than she on the test.[6] Frustrated by her inability to get promotion because she was "consistently eclipsed by veterans" [*Personnel Administrator of Massachusetts v. Feeney*, 99 S.Ct. 2282, 2288 (1979)], Feeney brought suit before a three-judge federal district court, alleging that the Massachusetts statute discriminated against women and, therefore, was in violation of the Equal Protection Clause.

Two of the three district court judges who heard her case agreed with her, concluding that the law had a strong negative impact on employment opportunities for women. The judges acknowledged that the goals of the law—to give thanks and support to the country's defenders—were both legitimate and worthy, and that the law was not intentionally discriminatory. They argued, nonetheless, that the exclusionary consequences for women were so devastating that the state must find another way to achieve its goals, one that did not also have such negative consequences.

The Attorney General of Massachusetts appealed the ruling to the U.S. Supreme Court, which initially remanded the case to the district court for further action. The Court wanted the district court to reconsider its ruling in light of an earlier Supreme Court decision looking at another seemingly neutral law that, nonetheless, resulted in racial discrimination. In that case [*Washington v. Davis*, 96 S.Ct. 2040, (1976)], the Court had held that "a neutral law does not violate the Equal Protection Clause solely because it results in a racially disproportionate impact. . ." [*Personnel Administrator of Massachusetts v. Feeney*, 99 S.Ct. 2282, 2286 (1979)]. To be declared invalid, the Court had held there that discrimination must be the intent of the statute, not a mere consequence.

The district court took another look at the case, including the decision the Supreme Court had asked it to consider, but then, still in a two-to-one decision, it again declared the law invalid. The majority declared that the veterans' preference was "inherently nonneutral because it favors a class from which women have traditionally been excluded, and that the consequences [of the law] for the employment opportunities of women were too inevitable to have been 'unintended" [*Personnel Administrator of Massachusetts v. Feeney*, 99 S.Ct. 2282, 2286 (1979)]. Still dissatisfied with this outcome, the state attorney general once again appealed to the Supreme Court. This time the Court agreed to hear the case and determine whether, in fact, the Massachusetts mandatory lifetime hiring preference for veterans discriminated against women and thus violated the Equal Protection Clause. The Court's earlier action ordering the lower court to take the *Davis* decision into account should have prepared everyone for a decision upholding the Massachusetts' veterans' preference law, and that is indeed what the Court held. Nonetheless, the reasoning upon which the Court relied exposes a facet of the Equal Protection Clause not yet covered in this book.

The Court vote was seven to two, with only Justices Marshall and Brennan dissenting. Writing for the majority in *Personnel Administrator of Massachusetts v. Feeney*, 99 S.Ct. 2282 (1979),[7] Justice Stewart acknowledged a long national history of preferential treatment for veterans, with the federal government and most state governments giving them some degree of hiring preference. The opinion termed the challenged Massachusetts law one of the most "generous" in the country in its allowance of an "absolute lifetime" preference and went on to review the history of the law, its application and its rationale: "to reward veterans for the sacrifice of military service, to ease the transition from military to civilian life, to encourage patriotic service, and to attract loyal and well-disciplined people to civil service" [*Personnel Administrator of Massachusetts v. Feeney*, 99 S.Ct. 2282, 2289 (1979)].

Justice Stewart declared that the sole question before the Court was this: Had Massachusetts, "in granting an absolute lifetime preference to veterans, . . . discriminated against women in violation of the Equal Protection Clause of the Fourteenth Amendment" [*Personnel Administrator of Massachusetts v. Feeney*, 99 S.Ct. 2282, 2292 (1979)]? His answer reveals, just as did answers from the Court in the late 1800s, much about how the Court saw women's rights and privileges. Women learned that in the eyes of a majority of the Supreme Court, even the Equal Protection Clause is not absolute and that it, too, can be abridged for a compelling state goal.

Personnel Administrator of Massachusetts v. Feeney
99 S.Ct. 2282 (1979)
Justice Stewart, for the Court

The equal protection guarantee of the Fourteenth Amendment does not take from the States all power of classification [cite omitted]. Most laws classify, and many affect certain groups unevenly, even though the law itself treats them no differently from all other members of the class described by the law. When the basic classification is rationally based, uneven effects upon particular groups within a class are ordinarily of no constitutional concern [cite omitted]. The calculus of effects, the manner in which a particular law reverberates in a society, is a legislative and not a judicial responsibility [cite omitted]. In assessing an equal protection challenge, a court is called upon only to measure the basic validity of the legislative classification [cite omitted]. When some other independent right is not at stake, . . . and when there is "no reason to infer antipathy" [cite omitted], it is presumed that "even improvident decisions will eventually be rectified by the democratic process. . ." [cite omitted].

Certain classifications, however, in themselves supply a reason to infer antipathy. Race is a paradigm. A racial classification, regardless of purported motivation, is presumptively invalid and can be upheld only upon an extraordinary justification [cite omitted]. This rule applies as well to a classification that is ostensibly neutral but is an obvious pretext for racial discrimination [cite omitted]. But, . . . even if a neutral law has a disproportionately adverse effect upon a racial minority, it is unconstitutional under the Equal Protection Clause only if that impact can be traced to a discriminatory purpose.

Classifications based upon gender, not unlike those based upon race, have traditionally been the touchstone for pervasive and often subtle discrimination [cite omitted]. This Court's recent cases teach that such classifications must bear a close and substantial relationship to important governmental objectives [cite omitted], and are in many settings unconstitutional [cites omitted]. Although public employment is not a constitutional right [cite omitted], and the States have wide discretion in framing employee qualifications [cite omitted], these precedents dictate that any state law overtly or covertly designed to prefer males over females in public employment would require an exceedingly persuasive justification to withstand a constitutional challenge under the Equal Protection Clause of the Fourteenth Amendment.

[We recognize] that when a neutral law has a disparate impact upon a group that has historically been the victim of discrimination, an unconstitutional purpose may still be at work. But those cases signaled no departure from the settled rule that the Fourteenth Amendment guarantees equal laws, not equal results. *Davis* upheld a job-related employment test that white people passed in proportionately greater numbers than Negroes, for there had been no showing that racial discrimination entered into the establishment or formulation of the test. [Another case] upheld a zoning board decision that tended to perpetuate racially segregated housing patterns, since apart from its effect, the board's decision was shown to be nothing more than an application of a constitutionally neutral zoning policy. Those principles apply with equal force to a case involving alleged gender discrimination.

When a statute gender-neutral on its face is challenged on the ground that its effects upon women are disproportionately adverse, a twofold inquiry is thus appropriate. The first question is whether the statutory classification is indeed neutral in the sense that it is not gender-based. If the classification itself, covert [or] overt, is not based upon gender, the second question is whether the adverse effect reflects invidious gender-based discrimination. . . .

The question whether [the Massachusetts statute] establishes a classification that is overtly or covertly based upon gender must first be considered. The appellee has conceded that [the statute] is neutral on its face. She has also acknowledged that state hiring preferences for veterans are not *per se* invalid, for she has limited her challenge to the absolute lifetime preference. . . . The District Court made two central findings that are relevant here: first, [the statute] serves legitimate and worthy purposes; second, that the absolute preference was not established for the purpose of discriminating against women. The appellee has thus acknowledged and the District Court has thus found that the distinction between veterans and nonveterans. . . is not a pretext for gender discrimination. The appellee's concession and the District Court's finding are clearly correct.

. . . there can be but one answer to the question whether this veteran preference excludes significant numbers of women from preferred state jobs because they are women or because they are nonveterans. Apart from the facts that the definition of "veterans" in the statute has always been neutral as to gender and that Massachusetts has consistently defined veteran status in a way that has been inclusive of women who have served in the military, this is not a law that can plausibly be explained only as a gender-based classification. Indeed, it is not a law that can rationally be explained on that ground. Veteran status is not uniquely male. Although few women benefit from the preference the nonveteran class is not substantially all female. To the contrary, significant numbers of nonveterans are men, and all nonveterans—male as well as female—are placed at a disadvantage. Too many men are affected by [this statute] to permit the inference that the statute is but a pretext for preferring men over women.

Moreover, as the District Court implicitly found, the purposes of the statute provide the surest explanation for its impact. Just as there are cases in which impact alone can unmask an invidious classification [cite omitted], there are others, in which—not withstanding impact—the legitimate noninvidious purposes of a law cannot be missed. This is one. The distinction made by [this statute] is, as it seems to be, quite simply between veterans and nonveterans, not between men and women.

The . . . question, then, is whether the appellee has shown that a gender-based discriminatory purpose has, at least in some measure, shaped the Massachusetts veterans' preference legislation. . . . she points to two basic factors which in her view distinguish [this statute] from the neutral rules at issue in [*Davis*] . . . . The first is the nature of the preference, which is said to be demonstrably gender-biased in the sense that it favors a status reserved under federal military policy primarily to men. The second concerns the impact of the absolute lifetime preference upon the employment opportunities of women, an impact claimed to be too inevitable to have been unintended. The appellee contends that these factors, coupled with the fact that the preference itself has little if any relevance to actual job performance, more than suffice to prove the discriminatory intent required to establish a constitutional violation.

The contention that this veterans' preference is "inherently nonneutral" or "gender-biased" presumes that the State, by favoring veterans, intentionally incorporated into its public employment policies the panoply of sex-based and assertedly discriminatory federal laws that have prevented all but a handful of women from becoming veterans. There are two serious difficulties with this argument. First, it is wholly at odds with the District Court's central finding that Massachusetts has not offered a preference to veterans for the purpose of discriminating against women. Second, it cannot be reconciled with the assumption made by both the appellee and the District Court that a more limiting hiring preference for veterans could be sustained. Taken together, these difficulties are fatal.

To the extent that the status of veteran is one that few women have been enabled to achieve, every hiring preference for veterans, however, modest or extreme, is inherently gender-biased. If Massachusetts by offering such a preference can be said intentionally to have incorporated into its state employment policies the historical gender-based federal military personnel practices, the degree of the preference could or should make no constitutional difference. Invidious discrimination does not become less so because the discrimination accomplished is of a lesser magnitude. Discriminatory intent is simply not amenable to calibration. It either is a factor that has influenced the legislative choice or it is not. The District Court's conclusion that the absolute veterans' preference was not originally enacted or subsequently reaffirmed for the purpose of giving an advantage to males as such necessarily compels the conclusion that the State is intended [Sic] nothing more than to prefer "veterans." Given this finding, simple logic suggests that an intent to exclude women from significant public jobs was not at work in this law. To reason that it was, by describing the preference as "inherently nonneutral" or "gender-biased," is merely to restate the fact of impact, not to answer the question of intent.

To be sure, this case is unusual in that it involves a law that by design is not neutral. The law overtly prefers veterans as such. As opposed to the written test at issue in *Davis*, it does not purport to define a job-related characteristic. To the contrary, it confers upon a specifically described group—perceived to be particularly deserving—a competitive headstart. But the District Court found, and the appellee has not disputed, that this legislative choice was legitimate. The basic distinction between veterans and nonveterans, having been found not gender-based, and the goals of the preference having been found worthy, [the statute] must be analyzed as is any other neutral law that casts a greater burden upon women as a group than upon men as a group. The enlistment policies of the Armed Services may well have discrimination on the basis of sex [cite omitted]. But the history of discrimination against women in the military is not on trial in this case.

The appellee's ultimate argument rests upon the presumption, common to the criminal and civil law, that a person intends the natural and foreseeable consequences of his [Sic] voluntary actions. Her position was well stated in the concurring opinion in the District Court:

> "Conceding . . . that the goal here was to benefit the veteran, there is no reason to absolve the legislature from awareness that the means chosen to achieve this goal would freeze women out of all those state jobs actively sought by men. To be sure, the legislature did not wish to harm women. But the cutting-off of women's opportunities was an inevitable concomitant of the chosen scheme—as inevitable as the proposition that if tails is up, heads must be down. Where a law's consequences are *that* [emphasis in the original] inevitable, can they meaningfully be described as unintended?" [cite omitted]

> This rhetorical question implies that a negative answer is obvious, but it is not. The decision to grant a preference to veterans was of course "intentional." So, necessarily, did an adverse impact upon nonveterans follow from that decision. And it cannot seriously be argued that the Legislature of Massachusetts could have been unaware that most veterans are men. It would thus be disingenuous to say that the adverse consequences of this legislation for women were unintended, in the sense that they were not volitional or in the sense that they were not foreseeable.
>
> "Discriminatory purpose," however, implies more than intent as volition or intent as awareness of consequences [cite omitted]. It implies that the decisionmaker, in this case a state legislature, selected or reaffirmed a particular course of action at least in part "because of," not merely "in spite of," its adverse effects upon an identifiable group. Yet nothing in the record demonstrates that this preference for veterans was originally devised or subsequently re-enacted because it would accomplish the collateral goal of keeping women in a stereotypic and predefined place in the Massachusetts Civil Service.
>
> To the contrary, the statutory history shows that the benefit of the preference was consistently offered to "any person" who was a veteran. That benefit has been extended to women under a very broad statutory definition of the term veteran. The preference formula itself, which is the focal point of this challenge, was first adopted—so it appears from this record—out of a perceived need to help a small group of older Civil War veterans. It has since been reaffirmed and extended only to cover new veterans. When the totality of legislative actions establishing and extending the Massachusetts veterans' preference are considered [cite omitted], the law remains what it purports to be: a preference for veterans of either sex over nonveterans of either sex, not for men over women.

And thus relying upon the distinction between a law that without question intends to discriminate and a law that discriminates as an unintended consequence, the Court upheld Massachusetts' hiring preference for veterans. In analyzing this decision, we, too, could differentiate along similar lines, balancing the undeniably likely consequences of this resulting decision against the undeniably likely consequences of an opposite decision. This Court, obviously, thought it had followed sound legal reasoning in reaching its decision; it believed not only that it was possible to differentiate between a law that discriminated with intent and one that discriminated merely as an unfortunate consequence, and that the latter did not violate the constitutional notion of equal protection but the former did.

Moreover, in finding that the Massachusetts legislature could not have intended to damage women, Justice Stewart suggested—in what could easily be judged to be a pejorative and paternalistic tone—that the legislature had in fact leaned over backward in favor of women by extending the benefit of veteran status to women "under a very broad statutory definition of the term veteran" [*Personnel Administrator of Massachusetts v. Feeney*, 99 S.Ct. 2282, 2296 (1979)].

The long history of discrimination against women is one the Court has only recently begun to acknowledge and even on occasion to try to redress. With this in mind, consider whether it is sound legal—and social and political—reasoning to ignore a law's unmistakable discriminatory impact on women simply because the discrimination was not the law's design? Given that long history of discrimination, is it sound legal, social, and political reasoning to condone behavior that *appears* not to be motivated by maliciousness yet nevertheless has the same devastating impact, to use the words of the lower court in *Feeney*, as behavior motivated by maliciousness?

There seemed to be a great willingness on the part of the Court to accept wolves in sheep's clothing, despite the fact that both the disguised wolf and the undisguised wolf are capable of equal damage. And, in fact, it could be easily argued that the disguised wolf is even more dangerous because it can wreak havoc undetected and even implicitly endorsed. In the case of veterans' preference, the wolf was exposed but nevertheless embraced.

The potential havoc may be better understood by recognizing the following: With the exception of the particulars, *Feeney* was no different from *Bradwell*, *Muller*, *Goesaert*, or *Rawlinson*. The Court in *Bradwell* said that states may set their own requirements for eligibility for the bar. In *Feeney*, more than one hundred years later, the Court rephrased this only slightly, noting that states have "wide discretion in framing employee qualifications" [*Personnel Administrator of Massachusetts v. Feeney*, 99 S.Ct. 2282, 2293 (1979)]. In both instances, the laws worked to restrict women's access to jobs far more than they restricted men's access. For that matter, *Feeney* echoes all the other employment access cases discussed thus far in this book—*Muller*, *Goesaert*, and *Rawlinson*. In all those challenges, laws had worked to restrict women's access to jobs and income, leaving more opportunities open to men. With the exception of *Rawlinson*, all of those laws were upheld as constitutional, regardless of whether the law was determined to be facially neutral or not.

In this entire litany of cases, the majority seems to accept unquestioningly (though the minority does not, as will be seen) a concept that really deserves to be questioned. An earlier question in this volume asked whether there could be such a thing as benign discrimination; now the question of whether there really can be such a thing as a facially neutral law must be asked. Can a law whose admitted consequence is disproportionate discrimination against one group really be said to be "facially neutral"? If on the face of things, the law is still recognized as carrying a discriminatory *impact*, though not necessarily a discriminatory *design*, where is the neutrality?

There is, however, a way to understand the Court's willingness to accept the existence of a facially neutral law under these particular circumstances. The Court recognized that perhaps veterans' preference, in general, might be inherently biased, given that the opportunity to become a veteran is not widely available to women (despite Massachusetts' efforts to include women in its definition of veteran by specifically including nurses). The Court in this instance remained true to its long-held practice, often noted here, of deciding a case on the narrowest possible grounds. It merely acknowledged that the inability of women to achieve the status of veteran might be the result of discriminatory recruiting and drafting practices on the part of the military. But the Court deftly avoided confronting that reality of that causal link by simply saying the latter question was not presently before the Court. And by refusing to address the validity of that larger question, the Court could continue to view the Massachusetts law as "facially neutral." It would not, however, be much longer before the Court would be confronted squarely with that larger question.

The *Feeney* decision illuminated the dark areas still clouding women's path in the courts, not the least of which was that the majority of justices were still not ready to give discriminatory practices challenged by women a rigorous level of review. An even more important disclosure was the uncertain scope of the Equal Protection Clause, thought by many to give absolute job protection. *Feeney* told women that the Equal Protection Clause was not as all-embracing or as egalitarian as had been thought—or hoped. It would protect equality for men and women when a law was clearly designed to produce a discriminatory effect, but it would not protect them when inequalities resulted unintentionally.

Feeney also exemplifies the way women are often doubly damned by discriminatory laws. In this case, women were first denied equal access to the armed forces, something many would label "benign discrimination." Second, women were denied equal access to the job market, not because they were unqualified but because they were unable to achieve the preferred status of veteran.

Two justices in *Feeney* were not, however, so willing to accept what their brethren accepted. In a dissenting opinion in which Justice Brennan joined, Justice Marshall argued that the fact that a state wanted to provide advantages to one group did not rule out the possibility that it might simultaneously want to disadvantage another group. The dissenters saw Massachusetts' law as demonstrating "purposeful gender-based discrimination" that bore "no substantial relationship to a legitimate governmental objective" [*Personnel Administrator of Massachusetts v. Feeney*, 99 S.Ct. 2282, 2297 (1979)] and was, therefore, in violation of the Equal Protection Clause. Justice Marshall went on to note that in the past, when faced with assessing facially neutral laws, the Court had "considered the degree, inevitability, and foreseeability of any disproportionate impact as well as the alternatives reasonably available" [*Personnel Administrator of Massachusetts v. Feeney*, 99 S.Ct. 2282, 2298 (1979)]. And then Justice Marshall proceeded to apply that consideration to *Feeney*.

Personnel Administrator of Massachusetts v. Feeney
99 S.Ct. 2282 (1979)
Justice Marshall, dissenting

In the instant case, the impact of the Massachusetts statute on women is undisputed. Any veteran with a passing grade on the civil service exam must be placed ahead of a nonveteran, regardless of their respective scores. The District Court found that, as a practical matter, this preference supplants test results as the determinant of upper level civil service appointments [cite omitted]. Because less than 2% of the women in Massachusetts are veterans, the absolute-preference formula has rendered desirable state civil service employment an almost exclusively male prerogative [cite omitted].

As the District Court recognized, this consequence follows foreseeably, indeed inexorably, from the long history of policies severely limiting women's participation in the military. Although neutral in form, the statute is anything but neutral in application. It inescapably reserves a major sector of public employment to "an already established class which, as a matter of historical fact, is 98% male" [cite omitted]. Where the foreseeable impact of a facially neutral policy is so disproportionate, the burden should rest on the State to establish that sex-based considerations played no part in the choice of the particular legislative scheme. . . .

Clearly, that burden was not sustained here. The legislative history of the statute reflects the Commonwealth's patent appreciation of the impact the preference system would have on women, and an equally evident desire to mitigate that impact only with respect to certain traditionally female occupations. Until 1971, the statute and implementing civil service regulations exempted from operation of the preference any job requisitions "especially calling for women" [cite omitted]. In practice, this exemption, coupled with the absolute preference for veterans, has created a gender-based civil service hierarchy, with women occupying low-grade clerical and secretarial jobs and men holding more responsible and remunerative positions [cite omitted].

Thus, for over 70 years, the Commonwealth has maintained, as an integral part of its veterans' preference system, an exemption relegating female civil service applicants to occupations traditionally filled by women. Such a statutory scheme both reflects and perpetuates precisely the kind of archaic assumptions about women's roles which we have previously held invalid [cites omitted]. Particularly when viewed against the range of less discriminatory alternatives available to assist veterans, Massachusetts' choice of a formula that so severely restricts public employment opportunities for women cannot reasonably be thought gender-neutral [cite omitted]. The Court's conclusion to the contrary—that "nothing in the record" evinces a "collateral goal of keeping women in a stereotypic and predefined place in the Massachusetts Civil Service" [cite omitted]—displays a singularly myopic view of the facts. . . .

To survive challenge under the Equal Protection Clause, statutes reflecting gender-based discrimination must be substantially related to the achievement of important governmental objectives [cites omitted]. [Massachusetts] here advance[s] three interests in support of the absolute-preference system: (1) assist-

> ing veterans in their readjustment to civilian life; (2) encouraging military enlistment; and (3) rewarding those who have served their country [cite omitted]. Although each of those goals is unquestionably legitimate, the "mere recitation of a benign, compensatory purpose" cannot of itself insulate legislative classifications from constitutional scrutiny [cite omitted]. And in this case, the Commonwealth has failed to establish a sufficient relationship between it [Sic] objective and the means chosen to effectuate them.
>
> [In reviewing how well the statute met each of the State's three claims, Justice Marshall called the statute an unnecessarily broad way to help veterans return to civilian life. As for the second purpose of encouraging enlistment, he again questioned whether the Massachusetts law was really the best way to achieve that goal.]
>
> Finally, the Commonwealth's third interest, rewarding veterans, does not "adequately justify the salient features" of this preference system [cites omitted]. Where a particular statutory scheme visits substantial hardship on a class long subject to discrimination, the legislation cannot be sustained unless "carefully tuned to alternative considerations" [cites omitted]. Here, there are a wide variety of less discriminatory means by which Massachusetts could effect its compensatory purposes. . . . Unlike [alternative practices], the costs of which are distributed across the taxpaying public generally, the Massachusetts statute exacts a substantial price from a discrete group of individuals who have long been subject to employment discrimination, and who, "because of circumstances totally beyond their control, have (had) little if any chance of becoming members of the preferred class" [cite omitted].

Thus, Justices Marshall and Brennan reached the conclusion that the Massachusetts law was in violation of the Constitution and that the lower court, not the Supreme Court, had made the correct decision. But the difference in outcome that divides the majority and minority seems to indicate a very real difference in approach as well. Justices Marshall and Brennan, in the tradition of those early Supreme Court dissenters who were willing to challenge not only discriminatory practices but also their fellow justices, seem more willing to tackle the hard questions head on, thereby challenging some long-standing practices. Not satisfied with accepting the notion of a facially neutral law, these justices looked beyond the framework. Was it really possible, they asked, that a law that actually put a handicap on women could be regarded as neutral, no matter what the claims of its sponsors? Viewing the patently obvious consequence of the law—which not only precluded job opportunities for women but also limited what opportunities were available to traditional female jobs (read "low-paying and low-status jobs"), these justices refused to categorize the law as facially neutral. In effect, to use the language of a later day, these justices recognized that the Massachusetts law served to keep the pink collar firmly buttoned in Massachusetts.

Feeney was a clear blow to women's struggle for equal rights. Yet the second half of the 1970s was not all defeat. In the area of employment rights, the Court was not kind to women. But in the area of women's personal lives—in cases such as *Craig*, *Stanton*, and *Orr*—the Court was more progressive, consistently lifting the burden of having to live in accordance with laws reflecting stereotypical expectations of what girls and women might and might not do. (In so doing, the Court was equally kind to males, freeing them, too, from having to live according to stereotypical expectations.) Coming after decades of an unwillingness, or inability, to recognize the fallacies and harm in such notions, the Court's turnabout here forms a decided victory in women's struggle for their rights. This victory would, however, prove to be tenuous as the start of the 1980s brought a return to some highly stereotypical thinking.

NOTES

1. There were two appellants in *Craig*. Craig, at the time the suit was originally filed, was a male under the age of twenty-one; by the time the case reached the Supreme Court, he had turned twenty-one. Because he had been representing only himself, not all males between the ages of eighteen and twenty-one, the Court said he lacked standing and declared his claim moot. The second appellant, Whitener, was a female, a licensed vendor both at the time the case was originally filed and when it reached the Supreme Court. The state questioned her standing in filing a claim of a denial of equal protection to males eighteen to twenty-one since she herself did not fall into that group. The Court, however, affirmed her standing, saying that the state had never challenged her standing before the case reached the Supreme Court but had all along acted on the assumption that her claim was legitimate. The Court further held that her injuries—loss of revenue or the possibility of losing her license if she violated the law—gave her standing.

2. In fact, the Court had received an *amicus* brief from the state of California outlining its success in using female guards in all-male institutions.

3. It is true that the ruling on the sex restriction for maximum security guard positions applied only for Alabama and other states with institutions in as much disarray as Alabama's. At the time of Rawlinson's case, Alabama's penal system was vastly overcrowded, plagued by a high level of violence, and operating under conditions that were intolerable in the eyes of the district court. Thus, this decision did not apply to states whose penal systems were operating under acceptable conditions.

4. In fact, in 1979 the Court heard a third sex discrimination case that is not discussed here. *Caban v. Mohammed*, 99 S.Ct. 1760 (1979), had a much narrower scope of influence than the other women's rights cases discussed here, and since not every case can be covered in depth in this book, the case is here relegated to a footnote. The case involved Abdiel Caban's challenge

of a New York state law that allowed an unwed mother to prevent the adoption of her child simply by denying consent but did not give that same right to the unwed father, even when he had been actively involved with the children, as in Caban's case. The Court, in a five-to-four decision, declared the statute unconstitutional as a violation of the Fourteenth Amendment's Equal Protection Clause.

5. For the full text of the discussion on both the issue of Orr's standing and the Court's jurisdiction in this case, see *Orr v. Orr*, 99 S.Ct. 1102, 1107-1111 (1979).

6. For Justice Stewart's complete text on both the history of the Massachusetts law and on Helen Feeney's employment history, see *Personnel Administrator of Massachusetts v. Feeney*, 99 S.Ct. 2282, 2286-2292 (1979).

7. Justice Stevens, joined by Justice White, concurred in the majority opinion but added one clarification of his own. For this opinion, see *Personnel Administrator of Massachusetts v. Feeney*, 99 S.Ct. 2282, 2297 (1979).

10

The Seesaw Continues

The majestic egalitarianism of the law, which forbids rich and poor alike to sleep under bridges, to beg in the streets, and to steal bread.

Anatole France
Le Lys Rouge

The first half of 1981 produced three Supreme Court decisions that affected the direction of the course of women's rights, a direction not altogether positive. The decisions in the first and last of the three cases resorted to stereotypical conceptualizations of sex roles, thereby undermining both the philosophical and true gains women had made in the late seventies. The middle case, although aiding more than might have been expected but much less than had been hoped, declined to tackle head-on the validity of the concept of "comparable worth." In all three cases, clear indications of dissent and dissatisfaction appeared among the justices themselves, indicating anything but agreement as to what was and should be the role of women as the country moved closer to the twenty-first century.

STATUTORY RAPE

Like a number of its more recent predecessors, the first 1981 decision addressed another long-standing and widely followed practice. This time, however, a criminal statute was under challenge, one that dealt directly, rather than by proxy, with the issues of women's sexuality and women's right to control their own bodies and sexuality. The case, *Michael M. v. Superior Court of Sonoma County*, 101 S.Ct. 1200 (1981), challenged California's statutory rape law, a law similar to one in most states' criminal statutes. As with many of the cases reaching the Court in the second half of the 1970s, it must be asked here why the challenge to this type of law was so long in coming. Unlike those cases, however, that demonstrated the Court's willingness to depart to some degree from, if not let go of, stereotypical notions of the sexes, *Michael M.* is striking in its archaic adherence to those same formulations. What is even more striking is that this case is so recent, coming after the birth of the youngest readers of this book!

To aid in understanding *Michael M.*, it is important to understand the difference between rape and statutory rape. Rape, at the time of *Michael M.*, was generally understood to be a man's carnal knowledge of a woman not his wife, forcibly, and against her will. Statutory rape, on the other hand, is defined in most jurisdictions as a male's carnal knowledge of a female who is under the age of consent, the precise determination of that age varying from state to state. Some states specify minimum ages before male perpetrators can be held liable. Some also make an issue of whether consent was given or not; in those states, if consent was given, there is no statutory rape even if the female is under age. States that do not concern themselves with whether or not consent was given but simply define statutory rape as carnal knowledge of an underage female would seem to be operating on the assumption that females under the age of consent lack the mental capacity to give informed consent. This assumes that the young females understand neither the physiological nature of the act to which they are consenting nor the social consequences of engaging in that act. (The correlate of this, of course, is that males, regardless of how young they are, do understand both.)

At the time of *Michael M.*, California defined statutory rape as a male's having sexual intercourse with a female who was under the age of eighteen and not his wife. Moreover, even if both parties consented, only the male could be held criminally liable. Michael, who at the time of the incident was seventeen and one-half years old, was charged with the statutory rape of Sharon, a sixteen and one-half year-old female. Around midnight one evening, Sharon and her sister were waiting at a bus stop when Michael and some friends joined them. Sharon and Michael left the group and began kissing. When Sharon refused Michael's further advances, he hit her in the face; she then gave in and had intercourse with him.

Michael was arrested for statutory rape, but prior to the start of his trial, he challenged the law as unconstitutional, alleging that it discriminated on the basis of sex in failing to hold females equally guilty and was, therefore, in violation of both the California state constitution and the federal constitution.

Denied consideration of his claim by two lower state courts, Michael appealed to the California supreme court, which agreed that the statutory rape law discriminated on the basis of sex in that it stipulated that only males could be liable and that females could only be victims. But when the state supreme court then subjected the law to strict scrutiny, the standard it chose to use in reviewing this law, it determined that the discriminatory practice met a compelling state interest and that, therefore, the statute was constitutional. Noting that the difference in treatment of the males and females reflected "not. . . mere social convention but. . . the immutable physiological fact that it is the female exclusively who can become pregnant" [*Michael M. v. Superior Court of Sonoma County*, 101 S.Ct. 1200, 1203 (1981)], the court acknowledged as valid the State's "compelling interest in preventing pregnancies" (Ibid.). The state had enumerated that compelling interest by pointing to the "'tragic human costs of illegitimate teenage pregnancies,' including the large number of teenage abortions, the increased medical risk associated with teenage pregnancies, and the social consequences of teenage childbearing" (Ibid.). And then the state supreme court concluded that "[b]ecause males alone can 'physiologically cause the result which the law properly seeks to avoid,' . . . the gender classification was readily justified as a means of identifying offender and victim" (Ibid.).

Obviously not content with this decision, Michael M. appealed his case to the U.S. Supreme Court, which, in a five-to-four decision, upheld the California supreme court's decision, and most, though not all, of its judgment. With this outcome in mind, reflect now for a moment on the facts and merits of this case. Is it reasonable or just that only males be held liable to prosecution for statutory rape in cases in which the underage female consents? Is Michael M., like William Orr, challenging the law for self-protection or because of a principled belief that there is an injustice in the challenged law that needs to be redressed? Does it matter what his motive is? In noting that "males alone" cause the result the California law sought to prevent, did California's court accurately analyze the reality of the situation? And, in a more general vein, is this a law that "deserved" to be challenged and, if so, along the lines Michael M. followed? Remember these questions in reading the opinions from the case.

As previously noted, the Supreme Court upheld California's supreme court decision. Justice Rehnquist wrote the opinion, a plurality opinion joined by Chief Justice Burger and Justices Stewart and Powell. Justices Blackmun and Stevens wrote a separate concurring opinion, and Justices Brennan, Marshall, and White wrote one dissent and Justice Stevens another. Although the dissenting opinions are the more telling commentary on the tensions of the times as they related to changing views on sex role stereotypes, Justice Rehnquist's plurality opinion for the Court obviously cannot be ignored. It noted that although the Court agreed with the lower court's outcome, it did not agree with that court's decision to apply the strict scrutiny standard.[1] The U.S. Supreme Court chose rather to rely upon less rigorous levels of scrutiny, the intermediate standard outlined in *Craig* and *Reed*.

Justice Rehnquist recalled that the Court had previously held that a law resting upon a sex classification might stand, even though discriminatory, so long as the result was not *invidious* discrimination and that the difference in treatment reflected the reality that men and women are not always similarly situated. And citing *Wiesenfeld,* in which the Court endorsed a government's right to "provide for the special problems of women" [*Michael M. v. Superior Court of Sonoma County,* 101 S.Ct. 1200, 1204 (1981)], the opinion clearly identified pregnancy as one of those special situations unique to women, thereby making women and men not similarly situated in this case.

Thus, having told the exact direction in which the Court was going to travel, Justice Rehnquist charts the course. Having selected the minimum rational relation test with the attendant closer review established in *Craig,* Justice Rehnquist looked to see if the law served and met a legitimate state goal. Acknowledging that the goal of the statute, originally passed in 1850, was not clear, he accepted California's identification of that goal as preventing teenage pregnancies. In so doing, Justice Rehnquist brushed aside as unimportant whatever the original goal might have been, and accepted the state's contention that a clear, *present* goal of the statute was to prevent teenage pregnancies.

Before turning to Justice Rehnquist's opinion, it is important to reflect on his seemingly casual dismissal of the original intent of the law. Think back for a moment on the number of times in other cases that the justices valiantly sought to discern the original intent of a law. Think of the *Slaughter-House Cases* or of *Bradwell* or of *Feeney,* to mention but a few examples. Yet here the Court seemed unconcerned with the original intent of a law enacted in 1850, despite the fact that the position of women in 1850, and therefore the concerns a legislature might then have had, was vastly different than women's position in 1978, when Michael was charged with the statutory rape of Sharon.

In 1850 women were still viewed as the property of some man, her husband or her father. Fathers were concerned with protecting their property rights in their young daughters and seeing that those daughters were not sullied goods, unable to fare well on the marriage market. In 1850, were the state legislators really worried about skyrocketing rates of teenage pregnancy as they were in 1978? There is nothing to suggest this. Therefore, it is wise, in reading the excerpt that follows, to question just what issue the Court was addressing in *Michael M.* Whom or what was the Court concerned with protecting: young females? illegitimate children? state outlays for welfare mothers? What?

Michael M. v. Superior Court of Sonoma County
101 S.Ct. 1200 (1981)
Justice Rehnquist, for the Court

We are satisfied not only that the prevention of illegitimate pregnancy is at least one of the "purposes" of the statute, but also that the State has a strong interest in preventing such pregnancy. At the risk of stating the obvious, teenage pregnancies, which have increased dramatically over the last two decades, have significant social, medical, and economic consequences for both the mother and her child, and the State. Of particular concern to the State is that approximately half of all teenage pregnancies end in abortion. And of those children who are born, their illegitimacy makes them likely candidates to become wards of the State.

We need not be medical doctors to discern that young men and young women are not similarly situated with respect to the problems and risks of sexual intercourse. Only women may become pregnant, and they suffer disproportionately the profound physical, emotional and psychological consequences of sexual activity. The statute at issue here protects women from sexual intercourse at an age when those consequences are particularly severe.

The question thus boils down to whether a State may attack the problem of sexual intercourse and teenage pregnancy directly by prohibiting a male from having sexual intercourse with a minor female. We hold that such a statute is sufficiently related to the State's objectives to pass constitutional muster.

Because virtually all of the significant harmful and inescapably identifiable consequences of teenage pregnancy fall on the young female, a legislature acts well within its authority when it elects to punish only the participant who, by nature, suffers few of the consequences of his conduct. It is hardly unreasonable for a legislature acting to protect minor females to exclude them from punishment. Moreover, the risk of pregnancy itself constitutes a substantial deterrence to young females. No similar natural sanctions deter males. A criminal sanction imposed solely on males thus serves to roughly "equalize" the deterrents on the sexes.

We are unable to accept [Michael M.'s] contention that the statute is impermissibly underinclusive and must, in order to pass judicial scrutiny, be *broadened* [emphasis in the original] so as to hold the female as criminally liable as the male. It is argued that this statute is not *necessary* [emphasis in the original] to deter teenage pregnancy because a gender-neutral statute, where both male and female would be subject to prosecution, would serve that goal equally well. The relevant inquiry, however, is not whether the statute is drawn as precisely as it might have been, but whether the line chosen by the California Legislature is within constitutional limitations [cite omitted].

In any event, we cannot say that a gender-neutral statute would be as effective as the statute California has chosen to enact. The State persuasively contends that a gender-neutral statute would frustrate its interest in effective enforcement. Its view is that a female is surely less likely to report violations of the statute if she herself would be subject to criminal prosecution. In an area already fraught with prosecutorial difficulties, we decline to hold that the Equal Protection Clause requires a

> legislature to enact a statute so broad that it may well be incapable of enforcement. . . .
>
> There remains only [Michael M.'s] contention that the statute is unconstitutional as it applied to him because he, like Sharon, was under 18 at the time of sexual intercourse. [Michael M.] argues that the statute is flawed because it presumes that as between two persons under 18, the male is the culpable aggressor. We find [his] contentions unpersuasive. Contrary to his assertions, the statute does not rest on the assumption that males are generally the aggressors. It is instead an attempt by a legislature to prevent illegitimate teenage pregnancy by providing an additional deterrent for men. The age of the man is irrelevant since young men are as capable as older men of inflicting the harm sought to be prevented.
>
> In upholding the California statute we also recognize that this is not a case where a statute is being challenged on the grounds that it "invidiously discriminates" against females. To the contrary, the statute places a burden on males which is not shared by females. But we find nothing to suggest that men, because of past discrimination or peculiar disadvantages, are in need of the special solicitude of the courts. Nor is this a case where the gender classification is made "solely for. . . administrative convenience" [cite omitted]. As we have held, the statute instead reasonably reflects the fact that the consequences of sexual intercourse and pregnancy fall more heavily on the female than on the male.

One must really look carefully at the validity of the Court's logic. First, is it logical to expect, as Justice Rehnquist believed, that the threat of criminal charges against a male will protect females from sexual intercourse? Second, where is the logic in concluding that the threat of pregnancy deters females from having sexual intercourse, while at the same time accepting as a legitimate state goal the need to stem the rise in teenage pregnancy? If the goal is really to try to deter teenage pregnancy, would it not be more logical to place a double deterrent on the female: the threat of both pregnancy *and* criminal sanction? Third, is the threat of pregnancy equal to the threat of criminal sanction? And fourth, if the state was concerned with preventing pregnancy, then why not hold culpable only those males who in fact impregnate the females?

Flaws in logic aside, it is impossible not to be struck by the paternalistic tone and content of this opinion. Justice Rehnquist explicitly categorizes the legislature's action as "protecting" females, as evidenced by its desire not to punish them. (This practice of not punishing females, or punishing them more leniently, is often pointed to as a tangible example of paternalism. Legislators and judges adhering to stereotypical images of women as timid, meek, sweet, and easily lead astray feel less a need to bring the heavy hand of the law down upon them.) Yet despite the stated desire to "protect" young females, neither California nor the Court expresses anywhere a concern that in statutory rape, the girl's body is being used not in accordance with her own wishes but those of the man. Where is the protection there?

And so, again, a woman's ability to become pregnant is being used to stigmatize her. Once again, this exclusive female attribute becomes the rationale for allowing a state's paternalistic practice of intervening "on a female's behalf." This reversion raises, once more, the question asked so frequently in these pages: Is this approach really in her behalf? Does it really aid her or does it continue to bind her in the position of the weaker and inferior sex? In its opinion, the Court relied upon the stereotypical image of a female as naive, irrational, and unable to think and judge for herself—and the stereotypical image of a male as exactly the opposite. Thus, she is presumed not to be responsible for the consequences of her behavior—in this case, sexual intercourse—while he is assumed to be responsible not only for his but for hers as well. And this even when there is a mere difference of one year in their ages!

By endorsing the notion that because men suffer least from the consequence of statutory rape, they are being punished for the rape while women are not, is not the Court at the same time endorsing the notion that men are less responsible for their offspring, whether those offspring are legitimate or not? And thus is not the Court, after having begun finally to free its decision making from stereotypical notions, returning to support yet another facet of traditional sex role stereotypes—that women nurture but men do not?

The Court's dissenters, however, continued their attempts begun in the late seventies to try to thwart legislation built upon or endorsing a stereotypical positioning of men and women. Both dissenting opinions, the one authored by Justice Brennan and joined by Justices Marshall and White and that authored by Justice Stevens, maintained that only a sex-neutral law would be constitutional. They attacked those stereotypical assumptions with few words but nonetheless conveyed a potent message, even though it comes in opinions lacking the weight of legal precedent. These justices made clear that they saw such notions as arcane and as an invalid basis for legislating.

Justice Brennan's dissent lamented the fact that the plurality decision paid too much attention to the value of meeting the state's goal of reducing teenage pregnancy and too little to the question of whether "the sex-based discrimination in the California statute is *substantially* [emphasis in the original] related to the achievement of that goal" [*Michael M. v. Superior Court of Sonoma County*, 101 S.Ct. 1200, 1214 (1981)]. It is the state's responsibility, he asserted, to prove that relationship, adding that this cannot be done without the state's "showing that a gender-neutral statute would be a less effective means of achieving that goal" [*Michael M. v. Superior Court of Sonoma County*, 101 S.Ct. 1200, 1215 (1981)]. To meet this burden, California would have to prove (Ibid.)

> that there are fewer teenage pregnancies under its gender-based statutory rape law than there would be if the law were gender neutral. To meet this burden, the State must show that because its statutory rape law punished only males, and not females, it

> more effectively deters minor females from having sexual intercourse.

The Brennan opinion then went on to fault California for not producing such evidence and for not attempting to substantiate its claim that a gender-neutral law would be more difficult to enforce and would generate problems of its own. (This despite the fact, the opinion noted, that at least thirty-seven states had sex-neutral statutory rape laws at the time.) Finally, Justice Brennan responded to California's claim that the important government goal met by this statute was the prevention of teenage pregnancy. On the contrary, he said [*Michael M. v. Superior Court of Sonoma County*, 101 S.Ct. 1200, 1217-1218 (1981)]:

> Until very recently, no California court or commentator had suggested that the purpose of California's statutory rape law was to protect young women from the risk of pregnancy. Indeed, the historical development of [the statute] demonstrates that the law was initially enacted on the premise that young women, in contrast to young men, were to be deemed legally incapable of consenting to an act of sexual intercourse. Because their chastity was considered particularly precious, those young women were felt to be uniquely in need of the State's protection. In contrast, young men were assumed to be capable of making such decisions for themselves; the law therefore did not offer them any special protection.
>
> It is perhaps because the gender classification in California's statutory rape law was initially designed to further these outmoded sexual stereotypes, rather than to reduce the incidence of teenage pregnancy, that the State has been unable to demonstrate a substantial relationship between the classification and its newly asserted goal.

It is Justice Steven's dissent, however, that is more interesting, presenting strong implied criticism of the thinking of the justices who contributed to the majority vote. He challenged their acceptance of both the assumed deterrent effect of a statutory rape law and the differential assumption of responsibility given to males and females in that situation.

Michael M. v. Superior Court of Sonoma County
101 S.Ct. 1200 (1981)
Justice Stevens, dissenting

> Local custom and belief—rather than statutory laws of venerable but doubtful ancestry—will determine the volume of sexual activity among unmarried teenagers. The empirical evidence cited by the plurality demonstrates the futility of the notion that a statutory prohibition will significantly affect the volume of that activity or provide a meaningful solution to the problems created by it. . . .

The question in this case is whether the difference between males and females justifies this statutory discrimination based entirely on sex.

. . . I think the plurality is quite correct in making the assumption that the joint act that this law seeks to prohibit creates a greater risk of harm for the female than for the male. But the plurality surely cannot believe that the risk of pregnancy confronted by the female—any more than the risk of venereal disease confronted by males as well as females—has provided an effective deterrent to voluntary female participation in the risk-creating conduct. Yet the plurality's decision seems to rest on the assumption that the California Legislature acted on the basis of that rather fanciful notion.

In my judgment, the fact that a class of persons is especially vulnerable to a risk that a statue is designed to avoid is a reason for making the statute applicable to that class. The argument that a special need for protection provides a rational explanation for an exemption is one I simply do not comprehend.

In this case, the fact that a female confronts a greater risk of harm than a male is a reason for applying the prohibition to her—not a reason for granting her a license to use her own judgment on whether or not to assume the risk. Surely, if we examine the problem from the point of view of society's interest in preventing the risk-creating conduct from occurring at all, it is irrational to exempt 50% of the potential violators. And, if we view the government's interest as that of a *parens patriae* seeking to protect its subjects from harming themselves, the discrimination is actually perverse. Would a rational parent making rules for the conduct of twin children of opposite sex simultaneously forbid the son and authorize the daughter to engage in conduct that is especially harmful to the daughter? That is the effect of this statutory classification.

If pregnancy or some other special harm is suffered by one of the two participants in the prohibited act, that special harm no doubt would constitute a legitimate mitigating factor in deciding what, if any, punishment might be appropriate in a given case. But from the standpoint of fashioning a general preventive rule—or, indeed, in determining appropriate punishment when neither party in fact has suffered any special harm—I regard a total exemption for the members of the more endangered class as utterly irrational.

In my opinion, the only acceptable justification for a general rule requiring disparate treatment of the two participants in a joint act must be a legislative judgment that one is more guilty than the other. The risk-creating conduct that this statute is designed to prevent requires the participation of two persons—one male and one female. In many situations it is probably true that one is the aggressor and the other is either an unwilling, or at least a less willing, participant in the joint act. If a statute

> authorized punishment of only one participant and required the prosecutor to prove that participant had been the aggressor, I assume that the discrimination would be valid. Although the question is less clear, I also assume, for the purpose of deciding this case, that it would be permissible to punish only the male participant, if one element of the offense were proof that he had been the aggressor, or at least in some respects the more responsible participant in the joint act. The statute at issue in this case, however, requires no such proof. The question raised by this statute is whether the State, consistently with the Federal Constitution, may always punish the male and never the female when they are equally responsible or when the female is the more responsible of the two.
>
> It would seem to me that an impartial lawmaker could give only one answer to that question. The fact that the California Legislature has decided to apply its prohibition only to the male may reflect a legislative judgment that in the typical case the male is actually the more guilty party. Any such judgment must, in turn, assume that the decision to engage in the risk-creating conduct is always—or at least typically—a male decision. If that assumption is valid, the statutory classification should also be valid. But what is the support for the assumption? It is not contained in the record of this case or in any legislative history or scholarly study that has been called to our attention. I think it is supported to some extent by traditional attitudes toward male-female relationships. But the possibility that such a habitual attitude may reflect nothing more than an irrational prejudice makes it an insufficient justification for discriminatory treatment that is otherwise blatantly unfair. For, as I read this statute, it requires that one, and only one, of two equally guilty wrongdoers be stigmatized by a criminal conviction. . . .
>
> A rule that authorizes punishment of only one of two equally guilty wrongdoers violates the essence of the constitutional requirement that the sovereign must govern impartially.

Because Justice Stevens recognized that a female may be a coaggress or, if not in fact the sole aggressor, in a statutory rape scenario, he saw California's law as unconstitutional. Some might claim that his opinion is antifemale, but those people might want to explore that conclusion further. It is true that Justice Stevens advocates equal punishment for the male and female participants, and thus is not going along with the Court's decision to permit California to treat the female more leniently. Yet which is the true profemale stance: the paternalistic position of the Court plurality or the egalitarian position of Justice Stevens? Who is really antifemale: those who say, "There, there, we will think for you and protect you because you aren't quite ready to think for yourself," or those who say, "You are responsible for the consequences of your actions"?

Justice Stevens was willing to point out the fallacious end to which stereotypes can lead, and it was he who strongly kept alive criticism of the Court's reliance on such thinking. His statement is more than mere criticism, however, for although it lacks the weight of an official Court holding, it nevertheless notified the country at large that at least one Supreme Court justice believed in continuing the practice of striking down as invalid laws that relied upon stereotypical constructions of sex roles. His opinion also showed that at least one justice recognized that the world in which such stereotypes originated was not the world of the United States of America, 1981.

Opinions of dissenters call into relief the question of just what shapes the basis for judicial decision making. In the majority of the cases covered here, at least one justice questions the legal validity of a fellow justice's opinion. It is possible to make here a generalized version of the question raised by Justice Rehnquist in his dissenting opinion in *Orr*: Are justices making decisions that they arrive at by unbiased legal reasoning, or are they making decisions they consider "politically correct" (and perhaps "socially correct" as well), regardless of the availability of valid legal support for that decision?

Michael M. must thus be viewed as a major setback in women's struggle for equal rights and self-determination. Following a series of decisions in which the Court consistently decried reliance on gender and sex stereotypes in making laws affecting the personal lives of individuals, the sudden return to such reliance in *Michael M.* becomes all the more striking and damaging. The damage arises from the fact that after having moved away from such assumptions, the Court now called them up anew to again confine females to their role as child bearer and to reintroduce the notion of the legitimacy of and necessity of legislative and judicial protection of females. The Court took from women, yet again, the assumption that they are able to control their own bodies and lives to the same degree that men can.

EQUAL PAY FOR EQUAL WORK

The second women's rights case of 1981 (*County of Washington v. Gunther*, 101 S.Ct. 2242) started initially in the lower courts as an "equal pay" challenge under Title VII, and although this was not the issue that finally went to the Supreme Court, it is appropriate to explain here what "equal pay" and "comparable worth" are all about. A most controversial notion both then and now, the concept of equal pay says that regardless of their sex, employees who work at tasks of equal or comparable skill and importance to an organization should be paid the same wages or salary, even though the jobs do not demand exactly the same type of labor. For example, men who worked as "janitors" or "grounds keepers," jobs and titles generally reserved for men, were historically paid more than women who worked as "cleaning women," although the nature of those jobs and their relative importance in an organizational hierarchy were the same.

In the 1981 case of *Gunther*, female guards working in the female portion of the jail in Washington County, Oregon, alleged that they received lower salaries than the male guards working in the male section of the jail. (Specifically, as of February 1, 1973, monthly salaries for female guards ranged from $525 to $668 while the range for males was $701 to $940 [*County of Washington v. Gunther*, 101 S.Ct. 2242, 2245 (1981)].) The women claimed that the pay differential was due not to a difference in work, which was essentially the same in both sections of the jail, but to the difference in the sex of the guards. They also pointed to the fact that the county set the women's salary, though not the men's, lower than salaries found in the county's own survey of other job markets.

The U.S. District Court in Oregon, however, determined that the female guards "devoted much of their time to less valuable clerical duties" [*County of Washington v. Gunther*, 101 S.Ct. 2242, 2245 (1981)], and, thus, the jobs were not really comparable. The Ninth U. S. Circuit Court affirmed that decision, and the women guards did not appeal this judgment to the Supreme Court.

Thus, the validity of the notion of comparable worth was not heard by the Supreme Court (and the Court made it clear, as will be seen below, that the question that ultimately came before it was not a question of comparable worth).

It was another aspect of the original case that the Supreme Court did consider. The women who brought the case, four guards who had been discharged when their jobs were eliminated because the county closed the female portion of the jail, also had alleged that Washington County engaged in "intentional sex discrimination" by setting a pay differential in guards' salaries, and that this violated Title VII of the Civil Rights Act. The district court dismissed this claim without hearing evidence, saying it could not be brought under Title VII because the case did not meet the criteria of being a comparable worth case. The court of appeals, however, disagreed and ordered the lower court to hear the case as a Title VII challenge and judge accordingly. The county then appealed this ruling to the Supreme Court, which in a five-to-four decision upheld the court of appeals judgment.

But the Court, perhaps wisely avoiding the controversy surrounding the broad issue of equal pay for equal work, stuck to good Court tradition and immediately targeted "the narrowness of the question" [*County of Washington v. Gunther*, 101 S.Ct. 2242, 2246 (1981)] before it. Writing for the five-man majority (being joined by Justices Marshall, Stevens, White, and Blackmun), Justice Brennan framed the question before the Court not as one of comparable worth, but as the following: Could a claim of intentional sex discrimination in determining salaries be heard under the last sentence of Title VII? This was the claim that the district court had originally denied and that the court of appeals had upheld.

As one of the many situations it covers, Title VII prohibits sex discrimination in the determination of compensation. The last sentence of Title VII, commonly called the Bennett Amendment after its Senate sponsor, states that

> It shall not be an unlawful employment practice under this subchapter for any employer to differentiate upon the basis of sex in determining the amount of the wages or compensation paid or to be paid to employees of such employer if such differentiation is authored by the [Equal Pay Act].

The Equal Pay Act, in turn, barred discrimination on the basis of pay in the determination of wages for equal work, unless a difference in pay reflected "(i) a seniority system; (ii) a merit system; (iii) a system which measures earnings by quantity or quality of production; or (iv) a differential based on any other factor other than sex."

In appealing the circuit court decision to the Supreme Court, Washington County argued that the Bennett Amendment disallowed wage discrimination claims that were not also the result of equal work claims, as defined in the Equal Pay Act. Under this act, equal work means performing under "similar working conditions" jobs that require "equal skill, effort, and responsibility" [*County of Washington v. Gunther*, 101 S.Ct. 2242, 2247 (1981)]. The female guards argued that the Bennett Amendment merely incorporated the four exceptions enumerated in the Equal Pay Act into Title VII, and thus claims of intentional sex discrimination could indeed be heard under Title VII. As the court of appeals had done, the Supreme Court accepted the women's interpretation and understanding, although not without admitting room for ambiguity. The Court reached this conclusion after a careful review of the legislative history of the Bennett Amendment, including the sponsor's statement as to the goal of his amendment.

The value of this decision for women whose salaries might be suffering the effects of sex discrimination may, until this point, be lost. But the enormity of the implications of this decision for women can be seen in the following passage of Justice Brennan's decision, where he explains why the Court could not accept Washington County's interpretation of the purpose of the Bennett Amendment [*County of Washington v. Gunther*, 101 S.Ct. 2242, 2252-2253 (1981)].

> Under [Washington County's] reading of the Bennett Amendment, only those sex-based wage discrimination claims that satisfy the "equal work" standard of the Equal Pay Act could be brought under Title VII. In practical terms, this means that a woman who is discriminatorily underpaid could obtain no relief—no matter how egregious the discrimination might be—unless her employer also employed a man in an equal job in the same establishment, at a higher rate of pay. Thus, if an employer hired a woman for a unique position in the company and then admitted that her salary would have been higher had she been male, the woman would be unable to obtain legal redress under [Washington County's] interpretation. Similarly, if an employer used a transparently sex-biased system for wage determination, women holding jobs not equal to those held by men would be denied the right to prove that the system is a pretext for discrimination. Moreover, . . . if the employer required its female work-

> ers to pay more into its pension program than male workers were required to pay, the only women who could bring a Title VII action under [Washington County's] interpretation would be those who could establish that a man performed equal work: a female auditor thus might have a cause of action while a female secretary might not. Congress surely did not intend the Bennett Amendment to insulate such blatantly discriminatory practices from judicial redress under Title VII. . . .
>
> [Washington County's] reading is thus flatly inconsistent with our past interpretations of Title VII as "prohibit[ing] all practices in whatever form which create inequality in employment opportunity due to discrimination on the basis of race, religion, sex, or national origin" [cite omitted]. "In forbidding employers to discriminate against individuals because of their sex, Congress intended to strike at the *entire spectrum* [emphasis in the original] of disparate treatment of men and women resulting from sex stereotypes."

By rejecting Washington County's argument, the Court lessened the enormity of the task facing women who wished to challenge a sex-based discriminatory salary system. This is not to suggest that the task suddenly became insignificant; it remained an extremely difficult one. Had Washington County's position prevailed, however, women would have had to establish not only the fact that they were doing equal work to men *but also* the fact that they were receiving lower wages than those same men solely because they were female. Had the Court accepted this position, the women guards would not have been allowed, ultimately, to present their evidence of sex discrimination to the district court, having already lost their claim of doing comparable work as male guards.

Thus, the Court did not require women to establish that they were doing equal work. It required them only to show that their salary reflected a sex bias on the part of their employers, and this made it easier for women to attempt to redress their long-standing inferior position. Perhaps it could be said that the Court restored to women's economic potential a little of what had taken away in *Feeney*. For example, although they might not necessarily compete equally with male veterans to obtain a job, women could at least, if they had a job, challenge pay differentials between themselves and a male veteran. Even though the Court legitimately sidestepped the question of comparable worth, something women's rights advocates saw (and still see) as a crucial building block on the path to women's strong economic standing, the Court nevertheless did add other blocks to that path.

There is an interesting parallel, however, between this Oregon case and its predecessor more than seventy years earlier. In *Muller*, a woman's earning power was determined solely on the basis of her sex, and that power was set at less than a man's. *Gunther* echoed this determination. Simply because of their sex, female guards were deemed to be worth less than male guards (since society measures worth in terms of pay). Thus, seventy years later, the yardstick had not changed. What had changed, however, was the willingness of the law and the Court to condone that practice. In 1908, the

Court, relying on stereotypes, accepted this discriminatory treatment of women as valid. In 1981, the Court declared that claims of sex discrimination in the determination of wages must be fully documented and carefully evaluated.

Not all the justices were happy with this decision, however. Justice Rehnquist, authoring the dissent joined by Chief Justice Burger and Justices Stewart and Powell, argued that Washington County's interpretation was correct and "that there can be no Title VII claim of sex-based wage discrimination without proof of 'equal work'" [*County of Washington v. Gunther*, 101 S.Ct. 2242, 2254 (1981)]. But declaring the ruling "so narrowly written as to be meaningless" [*County of Washington v. Gunther*, 101 S.Ct. 2242, 2255 (1981)], he appeared more displeased with the Court's rationale in reaching its decision than with the outcome. Not for the first time, Justice Rehnquist admonished the Court (Ibid.):

> The Court is obviously more interested in the consequences of its decision than in discerning the intention of Congress. In reaching its desired result, the Court conveniently and persistently ignores relevant legislative history and instead relies wholly on what it believes Congress *should* [emphasis in the original] have established.

Justice Rehnquist then reviewed the legislative histories of the Equal Pay Act, Title VII, and the Bennett Amendment, and concluded that "governmental intervention to equalize wage differentials was to be undertaken only within one circumstance: when men's and women's jobs were identical or nearly so, hence unarguably of equal worth" [*County of Washington v. Gunther*, 101 S.Ct. 2242, 2257 (1981)].[2] Justice Rehnquist offered this in support of his stance that for women to make a wage discrimination case, they must be able to show that the work they are doing is "equal" to the work the men are doing, not simply "comparable."

And though he admitted to ambiguity in the language of the Bennett Amendment, he concluded that "the most plausible interpretation of the Amendment is that it incorporates the substantive standard of the Equal Pay Act—the equal pay for equal work standard—into Title VII" [*County of Washington v. Gunther*, 101 S.Ct. 2242, 2259 (1981)]. Expressing his relief that the Court did not extend its opinion to include situations involving comparable work, Justice Rehnquist nevertheless concluded by chastising the Court for placing "upon Title VII a 'gloss of its own choosing.'" [*County of Washington v. Gunther*, 101 S.Ct. 2242, 2266 (1981)].

Two important observations may be made about Justice Rehnquist's opinion. In the first place, three other justices supported it, meaning that the majority opinion had carried by only one vote. Although a majority is all that is legally necessary to establish a legal precedent, much more may in fact be needed to begin changing the hearts and minds of the public. Second, what the four dissenters endorsed was a very strong and clear statement that they believed that a claim of sex-based salary discrimination *must* be tied to a claim of *equal* work. Title VII, they contended, certainly could not be extended to cases merely claiming comparable worth.

The contrast between the majority and dissenting opinions is striking, and it is a contrast not just in outcome, but also in intensity. In outcome, the difference is apparent: The majority opinion—fortunately for women the one that counts—calmly opened the door a bit more for redressing past wrongs; the minority opinion sought to keep that door firmly closed. And the minority, the justices who did not want that door moved, voiced their position with much vehemence; in their language and in their detailed coverage of legislative history, one can detect a certain fear. The minority circled the camp a few too many times for combating only a simple and nonthreatening enemy.

So what is it that was feared? An onslaught on the courts by women asserting claims of sex-based wage discrimination? A consequent rising economic power base for women, with a concomitant rise in their political and social power base? To adapt a phrase from Shakespeare, the minority opinion "doth protest too much."

WOMEN AND THE DRAFT

In the third women's rights case of early 1981, decided just twenty-two days after *Gunther*, Justice Rehnquist had neither to protest nor to admonish his colleagues. He authored the majority opinion that answered the question left unaddressed in *Feeney*: Was the military draft discriminatory on the basis of sex? In this case, unlike *Gunther* but very much as with *Michael M.*, the Court looked head on at stereotypical notions of the sex roles of women and men.

In *Rostker v. Goldberg*, 101 S.Ct. 2646 (1981), the justices were asked to determine whether the military draft, which required only males to register, was in violation of the Due Process Clause of the Fifth Amendment. As with other cases challenging long-standing practices that appeared to be discriminatory, one questions why this challenge did not come sooner. There are two possible responses, which may not answer the question but at least may shed some light. First, the draft is an intermittent phenomenon, something a president can choose to activate or discontinue. Thus, its impact—discriminatory or otherwise—is not continually felt. Second, the constitutionality of a sex-based draft had been challenged previously. In fact, the 1981 case was a reincarnation of that first case.

The evolution of that earlier case, as Justice Rehnquist outlined it in his opinion, began in 1971, the later days of the Vietnam War. In 1971, several males facing induction into the military challenged, on several grounds, the Military Selective Service Act (MSSA). (The MSSA is the vehicle by which the government generates a pool of military inductees.) By 1974, several of the claims had been disposed of, and the one remaining claim—that the Selective Service Act discriminated on the basis of sex because only males could be drafted—was stalled for technical reasons in the federal district court for the eastern district of Pennsylvania. There it remained until early 1980 when, in response to the Soviet invasion of Afghanistan, President Carter asked Congress to reactivate the draft.

He also requested that the Selective Service Act simultaneously be amended to allow both women and men to be drafted, and, since the draft had been inactive, he asked Congress to allocate the necessary funds. Congress refused to amend the law to allow women to register for the draft and allocated only enough money to register males. With the draft scheduled to begin on July 21, 1980, the district court on July 1 turned the old stalled case into a class action suit, the class consisting of all males then registered or eligible for registration for the draft. Seventeen days later, the district court, citing *Craig* as precedent, found that the draft did in fact violate the Fifth Amendment. What is interesting, in light of the Supreme Court's subsequent decision, is that the district court, in reaching its judgment, relied upon evidence heard by Congress that "military opinion, backed by extensive study, is that the availability of women registrants would materially increase flexibility, not hamper it" [*Rostker v. Goldberg*, 101 S.Ct. 2646, 2651 (1981)]. Bernard Rostker, the Director of Selective Service, filed an appeal with the Supreme Court.

The speed with which this case then moved bespeaks the importance of the issue. Inactive for years, the case had a Supreme Court decision in just over a year. After all, to the extent that a nation is defined by its military strength, the question of how that strength will be selected and staffed is crucial. One could conclude, therefore, that the extent to which women are allowed to help in that crucial role in good part defines women's position in a nation. *Rostker* would show that that position was not, in the United States in 1981, a valued one.

A six-to-three decision supported the constitutionality of the draft. The majority consisted of Chief Justice Burger and Justices Blackmun, Powell, Rehnquist, Stevens, and Stewart. Justice White wrote one dissenting opinion, in which Justice Brennan joined, and Justice Marshall wrote a second dissent, in which Justice Brennan again joined.

Writing for the majority, Justice Rehnquist acknowledged that whenever the Court reviews an act of Congress, it must do so with great deference and that extra care may be required when that act of Congress pertains to the military since Congress is allowed to act with great latitude in military matters. But, he also pointed out, even in military matters Congress must act within the restraints of the Constitution.

With this as background, he turned to the task of assessing the validity of the claim that the Military Selective Service Act violated the Due Process Clause of the Fifth Amendment. Referring to the Court's previous interpretations in *Reed, Craig,* and *Michael M.* as to what constituted a legitimate government purpose, Justice Rehnquist concluded that there was no question but that the job of "raising and supporting armies is an 'important governmental interest'" [*Rostker v. Goldberg*, 101 S.Ct. 2646, 2654 (1981)]. And noting that Congress, after looking at two alternatives for meeting that interest—a sex-based draft and a sex-neutral draft—had chosen the former, he framed the task before the Court as the following (Ibid.):

> "[w]hen that decision is challenged on equal protection grounds, the question a court must decide is not which alternative it would have chosen, had it been the primary decisionmaker, but

> whether that chosen by Congress denies equal protection of the laws."

His phrasing of this question is telling. It tells that the Court had reached its decision by looking only at the constitutionality of the path chosen by Congress but had not undertaken its own independent review of the relative constitutional merits of the two alternatives. This language implicitly criticizes the lower court for undertaking its own review of the evidence offered in support of each alternative.

And then Justice Rehnquist offered another telling insight, one that sheds light on the *Rostker* decision and prior ones as well. He said that [*Rostker v. Goldberg*, 101 S.Ct. 2646, 2655 (1981)]

> This case is quite different from several of the gender-based discrimination cases we have considered in that, despite [Goldberg et al.'s] assertions, Congress did not act "unthinkingly" or "reflexively and not for any considered reason" [cite omitted]. The question of registering women for the draft not only received considerable national attention and was the subject of wide-ranging public debate, but also was extensively considered by Congress in hearings, floor debate, and in committee. Hearings held by both Houses of Congress in response to the President's request for authorization to register women adduced extensive testimony and evidence concerning the issue.

Thus, the Court's finding is clear: Congress reached its determination of what was best for the country after a comprehensive and careful review of the issues, not as the result of judgments based on stereotypical thinking.

In concluding that Congress had engaged in this careful and comprehensive review, the Court freed itself from having to make a comprehensive review of its own on the validity of stereotypical notions of the suitability of women for combat positions. And yet, in the end, these stereotypical notions were the thrust of the issue left before the Court. The Court had accepted Congress' position that "any future draft . . . would be characterized by a need for combat troops" [*Rostker v. Goldberg*, 101 S.Ct. 2646, 2657 (1981)]. Since the military establishment had historically barred women from combat, and even President Carter in his request to make the draft sex neutral had said he was not suggesting a change in the combat restriction for women, the Court said it "must examine [the] constitutional claim concerning registration with these combat restrictions firmly in mind" [*Rostker v. Goldberg*, 101 S.Ct. 2646, 2658 (1981)]. Thus, it reviewed the constitutionality of the claim against an all-male draft but not the validity of the combat restriction on which the claim ultimately rested.

And here, ironically, is a clear parallel between *Rostker* and *Feeney*. *Rostker* addressed, finally, the constitutionality of the sex-based draft that increased the potential damage for women identified in Helen Feeney's challenge of veterans' preference. At the time of *Feeney*, the Court had acknowledged the relevance of a sex-based draft but had not, understandably, assessed its constitutionality. Now, in *Rostker*, the Court assessed the constitutionality of the draft but not the constitutional validity of its reliance on stereotypical assumptions about women's suitability for combat. Instead, as in *Feeney*, the Court implicitly accepted those assumptions as valid. It pointed to Congress' acceptance of them in voting for a sex-based—rather than a sex-neutral—draft as the best way to meet a compelling governmental interest.

Here is how Justice Rehnquist described the actions of Congress and the Court's reasons for upholding the law as constitutional.

Rostker v. Goldberg
101 S.Ct. 2646 (1981)
Justice Rehnquist, for the Court

The District Court stressed that the military need for women was irrelevant to the issue of their registration. As that court put it: "Congress could not constitutionally require registration under the MSSA of only black citizens or only white citizens, or single out any political or religious group simply because those groups contain sufficient persons to fill the needs of the Selective Service System [cite omitted]. The reasoning is beside the point. The reason women are exempt from registration is not because military needs can be met by drafting men. This is not a case of Congress arbitrarily choosing to burden one of two similarly situated groups, such as would be the case with an all-black or all-white, or an all-Catholic or all-Lutheran, or an all-Republican or all-Democratic registration. Men and women, because of the combat restrictions on women, are simply not similarly situated for purposes of a draft or registration for a draft.

Congress' decision to authorize the registration of only men, therefore, does not violate the Due Process Clause. The exemption of women from registration is not only sufficiently but also closely related to Congress' purpose in authorizing registration [cite omitted]. The fact that congress [sic] and the Executive have decided that women should not serve in combat fully justifies Congress in not authorizing their registration, since the purpose of registration is to develop a pool of potential combat troops. . . . "[T]he gender classification is not invidious, but rather realistically reflects the fact that the sexes are not similarly situated" in this case [cite omitted]. The Constitution requires that Congress treat similarly situated persons similarly, not that it engage in gestures of superficial equality.

In holding the MSSA constitutionally invalid the District Court relied heavily on the President's decision to seek authority to register women and the testimony of members of the Executive Branch and the military in support of that decision [cite omitted]. As stated by the administration's witnesses before Congress, however, the President's "decision to ask for authority to register women is based on equity" [cite omitted]. This was also the basis for the testimony by military officials [cite omitted]. The Senate Report, evaluating the testimony before the Committee, recognized that "(t)he argument for registration and induction of women. . . is not based on military necessity, but on consideration of equity" [cite omitted]. Congress was certainly entitled, in the exercise of its constitutional powers to raise and regulate armies and navies, to focus on the question of military need rather than "equity." As Senator Nunn of the Senate Armed Services Committee put it:

> "Our committee went into very great detail. We found that there was no military necessity cited by any witnesses for the registration of females.
>
> "The main point that those who favored the registration of females made was that they were in favor of this because of the equality issue, which is, of course, a legitimate view. But as far as military necessity, and that is what we are primarily, I hope, considering in the overall registration bill, there is no military necessity for this" [cite omitted].

. . . Although the military experts who testified in favor of registering women uniformly opposed the actual drafting of women [cite omitted], there was testimony that in the event of a draft of 650,000 the military could absorb some 80,000 female inductees [cite omitted]. The 80,0000 would be used to fill noncombat positions, freeing men to go to the front. In relying on this testimony in striking down the MSSA, the District Court palpably exceeded its authority when it ignored Congress' considered response to this line of reasoning.

In the first place, assuming that a small number of women could be drafted for noncombat roles, Congress simply did not consider it worth the added burdens of including women in draft and registration plans. "It has been suggested that all women be registered, but only a handful actually be inducted in an emergency. The Committee finds this a confused and ultimately unsatisfactory solution" [Senate report, cite omitted]. As the Senate Committee recognized a year before, "training would be needlessly burdened by women recruits who could not be used in combat" [cite omitted]. ("Other administrative problems such as housing and different treatment with regard to dependency, hardship and physical standards would also exist.") It is not for this Court to dismiss such problems as insignificant in the context of military preparedness and the exigencies of a future mobilization.

Congress also concluded that whatever the need for women for noncombat roles during mobilization, whether 80,000 or less, it could be met by volunteers. . . .

Most significantly, Congress determined that staffing non-combat positions with women during mobilization would be positively detrimental to the important goal of military flexibility.

> "[T]here are other military reasons that preclude very large numbers of women from serving. Military flexibility requires that a commander be able to move units or ships quickly. . . . In peace and war, significant rotation of personnel is necessary. We should not divide the military into two groups—one in permanent combat and one in permanent support. Large numbers of non-combat positions must be available to which combat troops can return for duty before being redeployed" [Senate report, cite omitted]. . . . In sum, Congress carefully evaluated the testimony that 80,000 women conscripts could be usefully employed in the event of a draft and rejected it in the permissible exercise of its constitutional responsibility.

And with a final chastising of the district court for not being sufficiently deferential to the decisions of Congress, the Court upheld the constitutionality of the sex-based draft.

Rostker may be a decision that readers find very hard to assess objectively; they may instead resort to a quick thumbs-up or thumbs-down verdict based on either gut reaction, unexamined tradition, or both. The stereotypical image of women as unfit for and incapable of combat—or, more important, the mirror image of men as the *only ones* fit for and capable of combat (thereby affirming their machismo)—is one of the most deeply entrenched images in our culture. Thus, of all the sex-based laws that have been challenged so far, the challenge to the draft may be the hardest to dissect objectively. To do so necessitates serious questioning of the validity of the long-held dichotomous, either-or image of men and women. Yet *Rostker*, like all the preceding cases, must be scrutinized to see whether the Court, in the words of Justice Rehnquist, had not put its own gloss on the issue.

By citing and agreeing with Congress' assessment that there was no military need for a sex-neutral draft because there was no military room for women in combat positions, the Court summarily dismissed the possibility that women could in fact make contributions in combat—something women would prove themselves quite capable of doing a mere ten years later in the Gulf War. In its dismissal, the Court contradicted what it had said in *Rawlinson* should not be done: It categorically dismissed an entire group of people from a position on the basis of a proxy criterion, instead of measuring each individual applicant's ability to do the job, in this case to take part in combat. In *Rawlinson*, the Court had said that a woman's ability to be a correctional guard should be individually assessed and that a woman should not be categorically dismissed for failing to meet the proxy criterion of a certain height and weight. In *Rostker,* the Court said that instead of assessing each woman's ability to take part in combat, it was acceptable to dismiss all women from the draft categorically because they failed to meet the proxy criterion of being male. (Recall that Justice Rehnquist concurred in *Rawlinson,* despite not liking the outcome, because he did like the legal reasoning.) Constant pointing to an absence of "military necessity" for registering females automatically dismissed the contributions that women could make in combat if allowed while automatically endorsing the contributions that only males could make. That, as has been noted before, is how stereotypical thinking works.

This dismissal is consistent with a broader pejorative tone evident in both Congress' and the Court's conclusion that if women were allowed to participate in the draft, they would only be in the military's way. The whole expressed concern with equity, which the Court rightly dismissed as "gestures of superficial equality," appears to be a paternalistic nod in women's direction. The saddest component of this figurative pat on women's heads is that it underscored the fact that all who expressed support for the "equity concern"—members of the Court, Congress, and the Executive branch—did not understand that the women's rights struggle sought not superficialities or tokenism or appeasement but a chance for full and equal participation—in peace or in war.

As noted above, there were two dissenting opinions, and the opinion by Justice Marshall, joined in part by Justice Brennan, was a ringing one.[3] On three major points, however, Justice Marshall agreed with the majority. The first point was that the Court was not being asked to rule on the constitutionality of the practice of barring women from combat. The second point was that the review standard established in Craig was the correct precedent (although he did not believe that the majority, in its analysis in *Rostker,* actually adhered to that standard). And the third point was that the government's need to raise a military force was indeed a compelling state interest.

Suggesting, however, that the majority deferred too much to congressional judgments in this case, Justice Marshall charted his own course, often sounding like Justice Rehnquist had in earlier decisions in criticizing the legal prowess of the justices on the other side of the issue.

Rostker v. Goldberg
101 S.Ct. 2646 (1981)
Justice Marshall, dissenting

The Court today places its imprimatur on one of the most potent remaining public expressions of "ancient canards about the proper role of women" [cite omitted]. It upholds a statute that requires males but not females to register for the draft, and which thereby categorically excludes women from a fundamental civic obligation.

... before we can sustain the MSSA, the Government must demonstrate that the gender-based classification it employs bears "a close and substantial relationship to (the achievement of) important governmental objectives" [cite omitted].

.... In my judgment, there simply is no basis for concluding in this case that excluding women from registration is substantially related to the achievement of a concededly important governmental interest in maintaining an effective defense.

The Government does not defend the exclusion of women from registration on the ground that preventing women from serving in the military is substantially related to the effectiveness of the Armed Forces. Indeed, the successful experience of women serving in all branches of the Armed Services would belie any such claim. . . .

According to the Senate Report, "(t)he policy precluding the use of women in combat is . . . the most important reason for not including the women in a registration system" [cite omitted]. . . . [S]ince the combat restrictions on women have already been accomplished through statutes and policies that remain in force whether or not women are required to register or to be drafted, including women in registration and draft plans will not result in their being assigned to combat roles. Thus, even assuming that precluding the use of women in combat is an important governmental interest in its own right, there can be no suggestion that the exclusion of women from registration and a draft is substantially related to the achievement of this goal. . . .

. . . The Court essentially reasons that the gender classification employed by the MSSA is constitutionally permissible because nondiscrimination is not necessary to achieve the purpose of registration to prepare for a draft of combat troops. In other words, the majority concludes that women may be excluded from registration because they will not be needed in the event of a draft.

This analysis, however, focuses on the wrong question. The relevant inquiry under the [*Craig*] test is not whether a *gender-neutral* [emphasis in the original] classification would substantially advance important governmental interests. Rather, the question is whether the gender-based classification is itself substantially related to the achievement of the asserted governmental interest. Thus, the Government's task in this case is to demonstrate that excluding women from registration substantially furthers the goal of preparing for a draft of combat troops. Or to put it another way, the Government must show that registering women would substantially impede its efforts to prepare for such a draft. Under our precedents, the Government cannot meet this burden without showing that a gender-neutral statute would be a less effective means of attaining this end. . . . In this case, the Government makes no claim that preparing for a draft of combat troops cannot be accomplished just as effectively by *registering* both men and women but *drafting* [emphasis in the original] only men if only men turn out to be needed. Nor can the Government argue that this alternative entails the additional cost and administrative inconvenience of registering women. This Court has repeatedly stated that the administrative convenience of employing a gender classification is not an adequate constitutional justification under [*Craig*] [cite omitted].

The fact that registering women in no way obstructs the governmental interest in preparing for a draft of combat troops points up a second flaw in the Court's analysis. The Court essentially reduces the question of the constitutionality of male only *registration* to the validity of a hypothetical program for conscripting only men [emphasis in the original]. The Court posits a draft in which *all* [emphasis in the original] conscripts are either assigned to those specific combat posts presently closed to women or must be available for rotation into such positions. By so doing, the Court is able to conclude that registering women would be no more than a "gestur(e) of superficial equality" [cite omitted], since women are necessarily ineligible for every position to be filled in its hypothetical draft. . . .

Nothing in the Senate Report supports the Court's intimation that women must be excluded from registration because combat eligibility is a prerequisite for *all* [emphasis in the original] the positions that would need to be filled in the event of a draft. . . . [T]he Department [of Defense] indicated that conscripts would also be needed to staff a variety of support positions having no prerequisite of combat eligibility, and which therefore could be filled by women. . . . In testifying about the Defense Department's reasons for concluding that women should be included in registration plans, [Assistant Secretary of Defense] Pirie stated:

> "It is in the interest of national security that, in an emergency requiring the conscription for military service of the Nation's youth, the best qualified people for a wide variety of tasks in our Armed Forces be available. The performance of women in our Armed Forces today strongly supports the conclusion that many of the best qualified people for some military jobs in the 18-26 age category will be women."

. . . . The Defense Department also concluded that there are no military reasons that would justify excluding women from registration. The Defense Department's position was described to Congress in these terms:

> "Our conclusion is that there are good reasons for registering (women). Our conclusion is *even more strongly that there are not good reasons for refus-*

> *ing to register them*" [cite omitted; emphasis in the original].

All four Service Chiefs agreed that there are no military reasons for refusing to register women, and uniformly advocated requiring registration of women. . . .

This review of the findings contained in the Senate Report and the testimony presented at the congressional hearings demonstrates that there is no basis for the Court's representation that women are ineligible for *all* [emphasis in the original] the positions that would need to be filled in the event of a draft. Testimony about personnel requirements in the event of a draft established that women could fill at least 80,000 of the 650,000 positions for which conscripts would be inducted. Thus, with respect to these 80,000 or more positions, the statutes and policies barring women from combat do not provide a reason for distinguishing between male and female potential conscripts; the two groups are, in the majority's parlance, "similarly situated." As such, the combat restrictions cannot by themselves supply the constitutionally required justification for the MSSA's gender-based classification. Since the classification precludes women from being drafted to fill positions for which they would be qualified and useful, the Government must demonstrate that excluding women from those positions is substantially related to the achievement of an important governmental objective.

The Government argues, however, that the "consistent testimony before Congress was to the effect that there is no *military need* [emphasis in the original] to draft women" [cite omitted]. And the Government points to a statement in the Senate Report that "[b]oth the civilian and military leadership agreed that there was no military need to draft women. . . . The argument for registration and induction of women ... is not based on military necessity, but on considerations of equity" [cite omitted]. . . . In my view, a more careful examination of the concepts of "equity" and "military need" is required.

. . . By "considerations of equity," the military experts acknowledged that female conscripts can perform as well as male conscripts in certain positions, and that there is therefore no reason why one group should be totally excluded from registration and a draft. Thus, what the majority so blithely dismisses as "equity" is nothing less than the Fifth Amendment's guarantee of equal protection of the laws which "required that Congress treat similarly situated persons similarly" [cite omitted]. Moreover, whether Congress could subsume this constitutional requirement to "military need," in part depends on precisely what the Senate Report meant by "military need."

. . . To be sure, there is no "military need" to draft women in the sense that a war could be waged without their participation. This fact is however, irrelevant to resolving the constitutional issue. . . .

It may be, however, that the Senate Report's allusion to "military need" is meant to convey Congress' expectation that women volunteers will make it unnecessary to draft any women. . . . But since the purpose of registration is to protect against unanticipated shortages of volunteers, it is difficult to see how excluding women from registration can be justified by conjectures about the expected number of female volunteers. I fail to see why the exclusion of a pool of persons who would be conscripted only *if needed* [emphasis in the original] can be justified by reference to the current supply of volunteers. . . . Thus, however the "military need" statement in the Senate Report is understood, it does not provide the constitutionally required justification for the total exclusion of women from registration and draft plans.

Recognizing the need to go beyond the "military need" argument, the Court asserts that "Congress determined that staffing noncombat positions with women during a mobilization would be positively detrimental to the important goal of military flexibility [cite omitted]. None would deny that preserving "military flexibility" is an important governmental interest. But to justify the exclusion of women from registration and the draft on this ground, there must be a further showing that staffing even a limited number of noncombat positions with women would impede military flexibility. I find nothing in the Senate Report to provide any basis for the Court's representation that Congress believed this to be the case.

. . . The testimony on this issue at the congressional hearings was that drafting a limited number of women is quite compatible with the military's need for flexibility. . . .

The specific finding by the Senate Report was that "[i]f the law required women to be drafted *in equal numbers* [emphasis in the original] with men, mobilization would be severely impaired because of strains on training facilities and administrative systems" [cite omitted]. There was, however, no suggestion at the congressional hearings that simultaneous induction of *equal* [emphasis in the original] numbers of males [sic] and female conscripts was either necessary or desirable.

The Senate Report simply failed to consider the possibility that a limited number of women could be drafted because of its conclusion that [a subsection] of the MSSA does not authorize drafting different numbers of men and women and its speculation on judicial reaction to a decision to register women. But since Congress was free to amend [the subsection], and indeed, would have to undertake new legislation to authorize any draft, the matter cannot end there. Furthermore, the Senate Report's

> speculation that a statute authorizing differential induction of male and female draftees would be vulnerable to constitutional challenge is unfounded. The unchallenged restrictions on the assignment of women to combat, the need to preserve military flexibility, and the other factors discussed in the Senate Report provide more than ample grounds for concluding that the discriminatory means employed by such a statute would be substantially related to the achievement of important governmental objectives. Since Congress could have amended [the MSSA] to authorize differential induction of men and women based on the military's personnel requirements, the Senate Report's discussion about "added burdens" that would result from drafting equal numbers of male and female draftees provides no basis for concluding that the total exclusion of women from registration and draft plans is substantially related to the achievement of important governmental objectives.
>
> . . . the Senate Report established that induction of a large number of men but only a limited number of women, as determined by the military's personnel requirements, would be substantially related to important governmental interests. But the discussion and findings in the Senate Report do not enable the government to carry its burden of demonstrating that *completely* [emphasis in the original] excluding women from the draft by excluding them from registration substantially furthers important governmental objectives.
>
> In concluding that the Government has carried its burden in this case, the Court adopts "an appropriately deferential examination of *Congress'* [emphasis in the original] evaluation of (the) evidence" [cite omitted]. The majority then proceeds to supplement Congress' actual findings with those the Court apparently believes Congress could (and should) have made. Beyond that, the Court substitutes hollow shibboleths about "deference to legislative decisions" for constitutional analysis. . . .
>
> Furthermore, "(w)hen it appears that an Act of Congress conflicts with (a constitutional) provisio(n), we have no choice but to enforce the paramount commands of the Constitution. We are sworn to do no less. We cannot push back the limits of the Constitution merely to accommodate challenged legislation" [cite omitted]. In some 106 instances since this court was established it has determined that congressional action exceeded the bounds of the Constitution. I believe the same is true of this statute. In an attempt to avoid its constitutional obligation, the Court today "pushes back the limits of the Constitution" to accommodate an Act of Congress.

Only two justices—Justices Marshall and Brennan—were willing to use their judicial pens to strike down the "ancient canard" that sees "military women" as an oxymoron. No wonder, then, that women's rights advocates were saddened when Justice Brennan resigned from the Court in July 1990 and that they were devastated when Justice Marshall resigned a year later. All women (and men) should have been devastated by the implications of the majority's decision in *Rostker*—although they were not—because it could be argued that the Court had not only pushed back the limits of the Constitution but had also pushed backed as well the progress that women had been making in evolving new roles for themselves. The question arising from so many previous decisions is equally relevant here again: Was the majority opinion the result of sound legal thinking or stereotypical and traditional thinking—in this case, the old-fashioned stereotypical rejection of women as soldiers? Perhaps not since reading the majority and dissenting opinions in *Bradwell* have we read majority and dissenting opinions as directly opposed as these. Which is the legally sound decision? Is this a demonstration of judicial activism, and if so, which justice is the activist? Who advocates the status quo and who advocates change?

Whenever a group of people is disqualified from fulfilling a "fundamental civic obligation," such as jury duty or the draft, there is serious reason to question just how much the nation at large values the members of that group. Perhaps no case covered so far in this volume signals more clearly the low regard in which the Court (if not the nation) seemed to hold women. Despite volumes of expert testimony in support of women's valuable contributions to the armed forces, even if not in combat positions, the Court elected to endorse a continued restriction on women's ability to play a role in defending their country. In so doing, the Court cavalierly dismissed the contributions of all past, present, and future military women—if not of women altogether. The stereotypical image of men capable of fighting the good fight but women capable only of tearfully waving the men good bye remained intact. But what the Court could not or would not recognize about women's abilities, the future would. Although the presence of women in combat areas in the Gulf War was not trouble free (we had our first female prisoner of war), women were widely lauded for their contributions to that offensive.[4]

It would be five more years before another major women's rights case came before the Court, but the year following *Rostker* brought two important events in the course of women's struggle for equality. On September 25, 1981, Sandra Day O'Connor became the first female justice of the United States Supreme Court. More than one-hundred years after the Supreme Court had denied Myra Bradwell access to the bar, a token female penetrated the all-male Supreme Court! But the victory was not as all-encompassing as it might have been. Despite her sex, Justice O'Connor has not yet proven to be a strong and consistent champion of women's rights. Her appointment did, nevertheless, serve to suggest anew to many, and affirm for others, that women were indeed capable, competent, intelligent, and rational individuals.

The second event in the year following *Rostker* was a complete defeat for women. At the end of June 1982, the ten-year ratification period for the Equal Rights Amendment (ERA) expired, and so did the ERA, having failed to win ratification votes from two-thirds of the state legislatures. The proposed amendment would have simply stated that "equality of rights under the law shall not be denied or abridged by the United States or by any state on account of sex," and this one sentence promise of sexual equality, which some saw as women's savior, was lost to history.[5] Although the ERA never became federal law, national sentiment seemed to support it. In the years leading up to the ratification deadline, public opinion polls consistently showed the public in support of the amendment. Unfortunately for women, it was legislators, not those queried in public opinion polls, who had the final say. A number of states did, however, add ERA amendments to their state constitutions.

Basing their expectations on the activity of the late 1970s, many may have concluded that the 1980s would provide smooth sailing for women's struggle for equal rights and self-determination because the course appeared clearly charted, with only the timeframe in doubt. That, obviously, proved wrong. In view of both the clear outcomes and consequences in two of the three cases of the early 1980s—and the fact that these decisions came at the end, and not the beginning, of a more than century-old battle in the Court—this period must be seen as less than kind to women's struggle for equality. (And that is an understatement.)

The Court had resurrected the ancient canards of women as timid, weak, nonaggressive, irrational, and in need of protection by others, and it had stamped those canards with the approval of the nation's highest court. After so many years of struggle in the courts to expose the fallacies of such thinking, and a brief period of seeming success when the justices seemed to be beginning to recognize those fallacies, this new endorsement of the old canards sounded to women like the clang of prison doors closing again.

Some light, however, had managed to shine through the prison windows during the early eighties. And although the Court avoided the question of the validity of equal or even comparable worth, it had in *Gunther* given women some increased ability to obtain a just—and equitable—salary. Thus, women had gained somewhat in their economic standing but had clearly lost ground (in *Michael M.*) in their personal lives and, perhaps most important of all, had lost (in *Rostker*) in the civic arena. In that arena, women were still clearly second class citizens.

NOTES

1. Justice Stewart authored his own concurring opinion as well. Justice Blackmun authored a concurring opinion, in which he termed the statute a "sufficiently reasoned" measure for addressing the problem. He then went on to explore the question of the female's complicity in statutory rape. For the text of both of these opinions, see *Michael M. v. Superior Court of Sonoma County*, 101 S.Ct. 1200, 1208-1213 (1981) .

2. Though he relegated it to a footnote, Justice Rehnquist pointed out an interesting fact in the legislative history of Title VII, and one that is so reminiscent of behavior one-hundred years earlier that it throws into question just how much progress the U.S. had made. He noted the following:

> Indeed, Title VII was originally intended to protect the rights of Negroes. On the final day of consideration by the entire House, Representative Smith added an amendment to prohibit sex discrimination. It has been speculated that the amendment was added as an attempt to thwart passage of Title VII [*County of Washington v. Gunther*, 101 S.Ct. 2242, 2258, footnote 4 (1981)].

Despite efforts to use the entitlement of women as a scare tactic, the bill passed both houses of Congress. It might be concluded, consequently, that many were no longer threatened by the thought of women's rights.

3. Justice White authored a short dissent, in which Justice Brennan joined, questioning a number of the majority's conclusions but not the validity of the assumption that women should not be allowed in combat positions.

4. Although women are still ineligible to be drafted, Congress and the Executive Branch have been studying the question of lifting the combat restriction.

5. The remaining sections of the Equal Rights Amendment would have given Congress the power to enforce the proposed amendment and to stipulate when it should take effect.

11

The End of the Line

The law is the last result of human wisdom acting upon human experience for the benefit of the public.

Samuel Johnson
Anecdotes

The second half of the eighties and the move into the nineties would prove to be yet another uneven period in the history of women's struggle for equality. Six major women's rights cases, or so-called women's rights cases, came before the Court in those years.[1] Not varied in scope, they focused on two growing areas of women's litigation. Three addressed concerns surrounding women's employment, and three addressed women's access to abortion.

The abortion cases all involved laws that in some way sought to hinder women's access to abortion. One such law restricted the use of public medical facilities and their employees in the performance of "nontherapeutic" abortions.[2] Another barred professionals who received federal monies from providing abortion counseling or referrals or from suggesting in any way that abortion was an appropriate method of birth control (commonly referred to as the "gag rule" decision).[3] The third required a compulsory presentation on abortion at the medical office, a twenty-four-hour waiting period before having the abortion, and the consent of a parent or judge before a teenager could have an abortion.[4] In each case, the Court upheld the restrictions as constitutional.

Again, not denying the importance to women's self-determination (which is, after all, the ultimate goal of women's struggle for equality) of the right to choose for themselves whether or not to have an abortion, these cases, as was true earlier of *Roe*, still were not cast in the language of an equal protection challenge.[5] Thus, they do not seem consistent with the theme of this book. Accordingly, as important as they are to the course of women's struggle for independence and equity, they will not be discussed here.

SEXUAL HARASSMENT

The first case of the late 1980s that actually did continue the struggle for women's equity addressed, both in language and substance, a concern held by the great majority of women and one that should be the concern of every working woman. This is the issue of sexual harassment in the workplace.

It may seem surprising that the Supreme Court did not hear its first sexual harassment case until 1986 since sexual harassment is neither a new nor uncommon behavior; estimates are that the vast majority of women workers have been the victim of some form of sexual harassment. Even more startling, the behavior itself was not labeled "sexual harassment" until the mid-1970s. But the fact that sexual harassment cases are of such recent origin really should not be so surprising; after all, it is difficult for one to allege that she has been the victim of something for which people long had no broadly accepted name. And even after the term *sexual harassment* came into usage, the nature of what fell under this heading did not immediately become crystal clear.

Now, however, there is some general agreement as to what constitutes sexual harassment: any remark or overt behavior of a sexual nature in the context of a work situation that has the effect of making a woman uncomfortable on the job, impeding her ability to do her work, or interfering with her employment opportunities. Sexual harassment can take the form of looks, touches, jokes, innuendoes, gestures, direct propositions, and other forms of behavior. It can run the gamut from direct demands for sex to having to work in an office where pictures of naked women are displayed. This behavior and atmosphere are more and more widely viewed as coercive because they occur in the context of a woman's work environment, thereby influencing, if not in fact threatening, her job security and job satisfaction. Although these specifications were not so clear before the Supreme Court spoke on the issue, spelling them out here should prove helpful.

The person who brought the case was Mechelle Vinson, and the path that took her from job applicant to a party in a case before the Supreme Court illuminates just what harm she claimed to have suffered. In 1974, Vinson inquired about employment at a Meritor Savings Bank branch in Washington, D.C., managed by a man named Sidney Taylor. She completed an application, returned it the next day, and later that day Taylor called her to say she was hired. For four years, she worked with Taylor as her supervisor, rising ultimately from teller-trainee to assistant branch manager. As a trainee, Vinson had categorized Taylor as "fatherly," but after she rose in rank, he took her to dinner and suggested having sex. After an initial refusal, she consented out of fear of losing her job. Over the next several years, Vinson and Taylor had sex an estimated forty to fifty times, usually at the bank. In addition, Vinson said, Taylor forcibly raped her a number of times and occasionally fondled her in public in the bank. In 1977, she found a steady boyfriend, and Taylor's behavior stopped. All this time, Vinson said in her claim to the courts, she had not reported the harassment or used the bank's complaint procedure for fear of Taylor and losing her job.

In September 1978, Vinson told Taylor she was taking indefinite sick leave, and on November 1 she was fired for excessive sick leave. Vinson then filed suit in federal district court for the District of Columbia against both Taylor and Meritor Bank, claiming that the sexual harassment she had suffered during her tenure at the bank violated her rights under Title VII of the Civil Rights Act of 1964. The district court ruled against Vinson, saying that any sexual relationship between her and Taylor was voluntarily engaged in by both parties and that Vinson had not participated out of fear for her job. The district court also freed the bank from culpability, saying that it had never been informed of any problem.

The circuit court that heard the appeal, however, reversed the district court's decision. It relied on an earlier decision of its own (but in a case decided after the district court's trial of the Vinson case); that decision had cited Title VII's identification of two kinds of sexual harassment. One type involves making job benefits dependent on sexual favors, and the second simply involves an offensive and hostile working environment. Believing that Vinson had indeed been a victim of the latter form of sexual harassment, and believing that the lower court had not even considered that option, the circuit court remanded the case to the district court for further consideration.

In addition, the circuit court challenged the lower court on another important issue. It questioned the conclusion that Vinson's participation had been voluntary, wondering how behavior can be said to be voluntary when it is made a condition of keeping a job or advancing to a better one.

Finally, the circuit court found the bank liable as well for sexual harassment by its supervisory personnel, even though the bank claimed it had not known about the harassment; since Taylor was an agent of his employer, the bank, it too was liable, the circuit court held. The case was remanded to the district court, but when the appeals court denied a request to rehear the case, the bank appealed to the Supreme Court.

There is no doubt that the unanimous Supreme Court decision in *Meritor Savings Bank, F.S.B. v. Vinson*, 106 S.Ct. 2399 (1986), was a victory for women's rights in the workplace. The decision changed the theory, if not the practice, of what is and is not acceptable treatment of women—and men—in the workplace. In that regard, this decision is very much akin to *Reed* in that both altered a set of assumptions about women and how they can be treated, at least in the eyes of the law. Both decisions implied that women deserve fair, equal, and decent treatment and consideration.

Justice Rehnquist authored the majority opinion affirming the circuit court's decision and was joined in that opinion by Chief Justice Burger and Justices O'Connor, Powell, Stevens, and White. There were two concurring opinions: Justice Marshall wrote one, with Justices Blackmun, Brennan and Stevens joining him, and Justice Stevens wrote another, simply noting that because he saw no inconsistency between the majority opinion and that of Justice Marshall, he joined both.

After reviewing the facts of the case and its path from the district court to the Supreme Court, Justice Rehnquist discussed briefly the addition of sex discrimination to Title VII of the Civil Rights Act of 1964, noting that it was a last-minute decision. As a result, he said, the Court was left with "little legislative history to guide us in interpreting the Act's prohibition against discrimination based on 'sex'" [*Meritor Savings Bank, F.S.B. v. Vinson*, 106 S.Ct. 2399, 2404 (1986)]. He then proceeded with a straightforward opinion, one perhaps unexpected in view of his previous negative attitudes in various cases involving women's rights.

Meritor Savings Bank, F.S.B. v. Vinson
106 S.Ct. 2399 (1986)
Justice Rehnquist, for the Court

> [Vinson] argues, and the Court of Appeals held, that unwelcome sexual advances that create an offensive or hostile working environment violate Title VII. Without question, when a supervisor sexually harasses a subordinate because of the subordinate's sex, that supervisor "discriminate[s]" on the basis of sex. [Meritor Bank] apparently does not challenge this proposition. It contends instead that in prohibiting discrimination with respect to "compensation, terms, conditions, or privileges" of employment, Congress was concerned with what [Meritor Bank] describes as "tangible loss" of "an economic character," not "purely psychological aspects of the workplace environment. . ." [cite omitted].
>
> We reject [Meritor Bank's] view. First, the language of Title VII is not limited to "economic" or "tangible" discrimination. The phrase "terms, conditions, or privileges of employment" evinces a congressional intent "'to strike at the entire spectrum of disparate treatment of men and women'" in employment [cite omitted]. [Meritor Bank] has pointed to nothing in the Act to suggest that Congress contemplated the limitation urged here.
>
> Second, in 1980 the [Equal Employment Opportunity Commission] issued guidelines specifying that "sexual harassment," as there defined, is a form of sex discrimination prohibited by Title VII. . . . The EEOC guidelines fully support the view that harassment leading to noneconomic injury can violate Title VII.
>
> In defining "sexual harassment," the guidelines first describe the kinds of workplace conduct that may be actionable under Title VII. These include "[u]nwelcome sexual advances, requests for sexual favors, and other verbal or physical conduct of a sexual nature" [cite omitted]. Relevant to the charges at issue in this case, the guidelines provide that such sexual misconduct constitutes prohibited "sexual harassment," whether or not it is directly linked to the grant or denial of an economic *quid pro quo*, where "such conduct has the purpose or effect of unreasonably

interfering with an individual's work performance or creating an intimidating, hostile or offensive working environment" [cite omitted].

In concluding that so-called "hostile environment" (i.e., non *quid pro quo*) harassment violates Title VII, the EEOC drew upon a substantial body of judicial decisions and EEOC precedent holding that Title VII affords employees the right to work in an environment free from discriminatory intimidation, ridicule, and insult [cite omitted] .... [T]he Court of Appeals for the Fifth Circuit held that a Hispanic complainant could establish a Title VII violation by demonstrating that her employer created an offensive work environment for employees by giving discriminatory service to its Hispanic clientele. The court explained that an employee's protections under Title VII extend beyond the economic aspects of employment:

> "[T]he phrase 'terms, conditions or privileges of employment' in [Title VII] is an expansive concept which sweeps within its protective ambit the practice of creating a working environment heavily charged with ethnic or racial discrimination. . . . One can readily envision working environments so heavily polluted with discrimination as to destroy completely the emotional and psychological stability of minority group workers. . ." [cite omitted].

Courts applied this principle to harassment based on race, [cites omitted], religion [cite omitted], and national origin [cite omitted]. Nothing in Title VII suggests that a hostile environment based on discriminatory sexual harassment should not be likewise prohibited. The guidelines thus appropriately drew from, and were fully consistent with, the existing caselaw.

Since the guidelines were issued, courts have uniformly held, and we agree, that a plaintiff may establish a violation of Title VII by proving that discrimination based on sex has created a hostile or abusive work environment. As the Court of Appeals for the Eleventh Circuit wrote. . . :

> "Sexual harassment which creates a hostile or offensive environment for members of one sex is every bit the arbitrary barrier to sexual equality at the workplace that racial harassment is to racial equality. Surely, a requirement that a man or woman run a gauntlet of sexual abuse in return for the privilege of being allowed to work and make a living can be as demeaning and disconcerting as the harshest of racial epithets."

. . . Of course, as the courts . . . recognized, not all workplace conduct that may be described as "harassment" affects a "term, condition or privilege" of employment within the meaning of Title VII [cite omitted]. . . . For sexual harassment to be actionable, it must be sufficiently severe or pervasive "to alter the conditions of [the victim's] employment and create an abusive working environment" [cite omitted]. [Vinson's] allegations in this case—which include not only pervasive harassment but also criminal conduct of the most serious nature—are plainly sufficient to state a claim for "hostile environment" sexual harassment.

The question remains, however, whether the District Court's ultimate finding that [Vinson] "was not the victim of sexual harassment" [cite omitted] effectively disposed of [Vinson's] claim. The Court of Appeals recognized, we think correctly, that this ultimate finding was likely based on one or both of two erroneous views of the law. First, the District Court apparently believed that a claim for sexual harassment will not lie absent an economic effect on the complainant's employment. . . . ("It is without question that sexual harassment of female employees in which they are asked or required to submit to sexual demands as a *condition to obtain employment or to maintain employment or to obtain promotions* falls within protection of Title VII.") [emphasis in the original] Since it appears that the District Court made its findings without ever considering the "hostile environment" theory of sexual harassment, the Court of Appeals' decision to remand was correct.

Second, the District Court's conclusion that no actionable harassment occurred might have rested on its earlier "finding" that "[i]f [Vinson] and Taylor did engage in an intimate or sexual relationship. . . , that relationship was a voluntary one" [cite omitted]. But the fact that sex-related conduct was "voluntary," in the sense that the complainant was not forced to participate against her will, is not a defense to a sexual harassment suit brought under Title VII. The gravamen of any sexual harassment claim is that the alleged sexual advances were "unwelcome" [cite omitted]. While the question whether particular conduct was indeed unwelcome presents difficult problems of proof and turns largely on credibility determinations committed to the trier of fact, the District Court in this case erroneously focused on the "voluntariness" of [Vinson's] participation in the claimed sexual episodes. The correct inquiry is whether [Vinson] by her conduct indicated that the alleged sexual advances were unwelcome, not whether her actual participation in sexual intercourse was voluntary.

[Meritor Bank] contends that even if this case must be remanded to the District Court, the Court of Appeals erred in one of the terms of its remand. Specifically, the Court of Appeals stated that testimony about [Vinson's] "dress and personal fantasies" [cite omitted], which the District Court apparently admitted into evidence, "had no place in this litigation . . ." [cite omitted]. While "voluntariness" in the sense of consent is not a defense to such a claim, it does not follow that a complainant's sexually provocative speech or dress is irrelevant as a matter of law in determining whether he or she found particular sexual advances unwelcome. To the contrary, such evidence is obviously relevant.... While the District Court must carefully weigh the applicable considerations in deciding whether to admit evidence of this kind, there is no *per se* rule against its admissibility.

. . . Finding that "the bank was without notice" of Taylor's alleged conduct, and that notice to Taylor was not the equivalent of notice to the bank, the [district] court concluded that the bank therefore could not be held liable for Taylor's alleged actions. The Court of Appeals took the opposite view, holding that an employer is strictly liable for a hostile environment created by a supervisor's sexual advances, even though the employer neither knew nor reasonably could have known of the alleged misconduct. The court held that a supervisor, whether or not he possesses the authority to hire, fire, or promote, is necessarily an "agent" of his employer for all Title VII purposes, since "even the appearance" of such authority may enable him to impose himself on his subordinates.

. . . [Vinson], not surprisingly, defends the position of the Court of Appeals. Noting that Title VII's definition of "employer" includes any "agent" of the employer, she also argues that "so long as the circumstance is work-related, the supervisor is the employer and the employer is the supervisor" [cite omitted]. Notice to Taylor that the advances were unwelcome, therefore, was notice to the bank.

[Meritor Bank] argues that respondent's failure to use its established grievance procedure, or to otherwise put it on notice of the alleged misconduct, insulates petitioner from liability for Taylor's wrongdoing. A contrary rule would be unfair, [Meritor Bank] argues, since in a hostile environment harassment case the employer often will have no reason to know about, or opportunity to cure, the alleged wrongdoing.

The EEOC . . . contends that courts formulating employer liability rules should draw from traditional agency principles. Examination of those principles has led the EEOC to the view that where a supervisor exercises the authority actually delegated to him by his employer, by making or threatening to make decisions affecting the employment status of his subordinates, such actions are properly imputed to the employer whose delegation of authority empowered the supervisor to undertake them [cite omitted]. Thus, the courts have consistently held employers liable for the discriminatory discharges of employees by supervisory personnel, whether or not the employer knew, should have known, or approved of the supervisor's action [cite omitted].

. . . In [a sexual harassment claim based on the hostile environment definition], the EEOC believes, agency principles lead to

> "a rule that asks whether a victim of sexual harassment had reasonably available an avenue of complaint regarding such harassment, and, if available and utilized, whether that procedure was reasonably responsive to the employee's complaint. If the employer has an expressed policy against sexual harassment and has implemented a procedure specifically designed to resolve sexual harassment claims, and if the victim does not take advantage of that procedure, the employer should be shielded from liability absent actual knowledge of the sexually hostile environment (obtained, *e.g.*, by the filing of a charge with the EEOC or a comparable state agency). In all other cases, the employer will be liable if it has actual knowledge of the harassment or if, considering all the facts of the case, the victim in question had no reasonably available avenue for making his or her complaint known to appropriate management officials" [cite omitted].

As [Vinson] points out, this suggested rule is in some tension with the EEOC guidelines, which hold an employer liable for the acts of its agents without regard to notice. . . .

This debate over the appropriate standard for employer liability has a rather abstract quality about it given the state of the record in this case. [Lacking a complete transcript of the trial], [w]e do not know at this stage whether Taylor made any sexual advances toward respondent at all, let alone whether those advances were unwelcome, whether they were sufficiently pervasive to constitute a condition of employment, or whether they were "so pervasive and so long continuing . . . that the employer must have become conscious of [them]" [cite omitted].

We therefore decline the parties' invitation to issue a definitive rule on employer liability, but we do agree with the EEOC that Congress wanted courts to look to agency principles for guidance in this area. . . . Congress' decision to define "employer" to include any "agent" of an employer, . . . surely evinces an intent to place some limits on the acts of employees for which employers under Title VII are to be held responsible. For this reason, we hold that the Court of Appeals erred in concluding that employers are always automatically liable for sexual harassment by their supervisors. . . . For the same reason, absence of

> notice to an employer does not necessarily insulate that employer from liability. . . .
>
> Finally, we reject [Meritor Bank's] view that the mere existence of a grievance procedure and a policy against discrimination, coupled with respondent's failure to invoke that procedure, must insulate petitioner from liability. While those facts are plainly relevant, the situation before us demonstrates why they are not necessarily dispositive. Petitioner's general nondiscrimination policy did not address sexual harassment in particular, and thus did not alert employees to their employer's interest in correcting that form of discrimination. . . . Moreover, the bank's grievance procedure apparently required an employee to complain first to her supervisor, in this case Taylor. Since Taylor was the alleged perpetrator, it is not altogether surprising that respondent failed to invoke the procedure and report her grievance to him. [Meritor Bank's] contention that respondent's failure should insulate it from liability might be substantially stronger if its procedures were better calculated to encourage victims of harassment to come forward.

Two important points in Justice Rehnquist's opinion help clarify the legal content of sexual harassment. First, by upholding the bifurcated notion of sexual harassment—one form linked directly to economic rewards and another form linked to the quality and tone of the work environment—the Court acknowledged, and thereby respected, what every victim of sexual harassment knows and what few perpetrators and nonparticipants or nonvictims know: Sexual harassment is a serious personal invasion. The Court, in essence, recognized that sexual harassment is an assault—an assault on a woman's (or a man's) wallet, mind, body, and general well-being. And when that assault is severe and pervasive, the Court said, it will not be tolerated. Thus, the Court affirmed the concept that women—and, indeed, all employees—must be given a supportive and nonthreatening environment in which to work. As simple as it sounds, and as obvious as it may appear to many, this concept needed to be made explicit by the Court. Unfortunately, many women did not then, and many still do not, work in such an environment.

The opinion's second important element lies in Justice Rehnquist's statement that it is not the "involuntary" nature of the victim's behavior that must be assessed, but how "unwelcome" the victim finds the harasser's behavior. As was noted earlier, in certain situations the notion of "voluntary" appears questionable, if not moot—patently true when an aspiring underling faces her or his superior. When the same superior who writes the annual performance review that determines future raises and promotions demands compliance from an underling, how "voluntary" is that underling's agreement to the superior's sexual demands? How coercive is that situation? To prove, however, that a particular sexual advance was "welcome" or "unwelcome", though difficult, is still much less complex; definition of what is welcome or unwelcome leaps out of the nature of the situation at hand, and the same underling who lacks the true freedom to comply "voluntarily" with her/his superior's request can easily acknowledge whether that compliance was done happily and readily (read "welcomed") or unhappily and not readily (read "unwelcomed").

This opinion did not, however, give 100 percent protection to female victims of sexual harassment (or male victims of sexual harassment, it must be added, since there are such cases and almost certain to be more as an increasing number of women rise to management ranks). The opinion certainly made clear that the behavior of both alleged victim and perpetrator could be scrutinized, and the alleged harasser could attempt to offer proof to show that the woman had welcomed his advances. Moreover, the Court left room for employers to dispute their liability for the actions of their employees. The decision informed employers that although they were not automatically liable for the actions of their employees, they were not automatically free from liability simply because they were unaware of the problem or because they had not instituted a no-harassment policy and a grievance system for handling allegations of discrimination.

In substantiating his argument that a hostile work environment is a form of discrimination barred under Title VII and that sex harassment creates such a hostile environment, Justice Rehnquist cited a number of judicial opinions (as well as those of the EEOC). He referred to a case before the Fifth Circuit Court of Appeals in which an Hispanic had claimed that she was the victim of a hostile work environment and had won on the basis of Title VII's prohibition against discrimination based on ethnicity.[6] That case was heard in 1971, seven years after Title VII was enacted. (The Supreme Court had declined to hear an appeal of that case.) Eight more years passed before a sexual harassment case was heard in the Ninth Circuit Court of Appeals and nine years before a sexual harassment case began making its way to the Supreme Court.

So again the question asked so frequently earlier in this book. Why did the sex harassment issue (in this instance) take so long to make its way through the federal courts? The suggestion was made earlier that part of the answer is that the concept of sex harassment was so novel and unclear that getting it recognized and clarified took time. That aside, however, consider the following: Only seven years after Title VII outlawed discrimination in the workplace on the basis of race, ethnicity, and sex, the first case based on a claim of ethnic harassment, the case of the Hispanic, was won. Yet it was fifteen years—more than double the time it took to win the first ethnic harassment case—before a sexual harassment case was won. Could it have had something to do with the fact that the behavior now labeled "sexual harassment" was stereotypically viewed as both "natural" to men and "flattering" to women, while racial, religious, and ethnic origin harassment could <u>only</u> be seen in one way: as neither natural or flattering to any of the parties involved? In fact, it could be seen only as hostile.

Justice Marshall, and those who concurred with him, agreed with the Court in outcome and rationale that sexual harassment in the workplace did violate Title VII. Where they broke with the Court, however, was in looking at the liability of employers. Justice Marshall believed that "general Title VII law, like that supplied by federal labor law, [holds] that the act of a supervisory employee or agent is imputed to the employer" [*Meritor Savings Bank,*

F.S.B. v. Vinson, 106 S.Ct. 2399, 2410 (1986)]. He went on to note that "every Court of Appeals that has considered the issue has held that sexual harassment by supervisory personnel is automatically imputed to the employer when the harassment results in tangible job detriment to the subordinate employee" [*Meritor Savings Bank, F.S.B. v. Vinson,* 106 S.Ct. 2399, 2410 (1986)]. Justice Marshall concluded that there is [*Meritor Savings Bank, F.S.B. v. Vinson,* 106 S.Ct. 2399, 2411 (1986)]:

> no justification for a special rule, to be applied *only* [emphasis in the original] in "hostile environment" cases, that sexual harassment does not create employer liability until the employee suffering the discrimination notifies other supervisors. No such requirement appears in the statute, and no such requirement can coherently be drawn from the law of agency.
>
> . . . I would apply in this case the same rules we apply in all other Title VII cases, and hold that sexual harassment by a supervisor of an employee under his supervision, leading to a discriminatory work environment, should be imputed to the employer for Title VII purposes regardless of whether the employee gave "notice" of the offense.

As was his norm, Justice Marshall, once again, was urging more expansive protections for women and seemed to recognize the inherent difficulties present when an employee is subject to sexual harassment from her (or his) superior. Although his views did not always receive widespread support among his fellow justices, some of them in this case made their way into the thinking of the majority opinion—fortunately for women (and male) workers. And that majority opinion, despite a degree of vagueness at one or two points, was a major factor in forcing a redefinition of what was and was not legally acceptable behavior in the workplace. In adopting the notion of a "hostile environment," the Court was also accepting the reality that sexual harassment could not be limited to physical assaults on a person's body but must just as well include assaults on a person's mind. With that acceptance, thousands of women's long-standing complaints were legitimated; the Court had finally recognized what women had all along known was true.

AFFIRMATIVE ACTION

Less than ten months after deciding *Vinson,* the Court handed down its decision in *Johnson v. Transportation Agency, Santa Clara County, California,* 107 S.Ct. 1442 (1987). (It was, it should be noted, a slightly different Court that heard *Johnson.* No longer was it simply Justice Rehnquist, but Chief Justice Rehnquist, elevated to the post when Chief Justice Burger resigned. And the new member of the Court was Antonin Scalia, assessed by most legal observers as an outstanding legal scholar but also an extremely conservative one.) The subject matter in this new case was just as controversial, perhaps even more controversial, as that in *Vinson,* for *Johnson* challenged the legitimacy of affirmative action for women.

In 1978, seeking both to prohibit new discrimination and remedy past practices of discrimination, the Board of Supervisors of the Santa Clara, California, Transit District adopted an affirmative action plan for the County Transportation Agency. Intended to achieve the long-term goal of "a work force whose composition reflected the proportions of minorities and women in the area labor force," the plan stated that "in making promotions to positions within a traditionally segregated job classification in which women have been significantly underrepresented, the [County Transportation] Agency is authorized to consider as one factor the sex of a qualified applicant" [*Johnson v. Transportation Agency, Santa Clara County, California*, 107 S.Ct. 1442, 1446 (1987)]. The plan did not specify that a certain number of positions must be set aside for minority or women workers; in other words, there was no quota to be met. The plan simply allowed for sex (or race) to be taken into account as one factor in considering promotions to job categories in which women (and/or minorities) had been historically "poorly" represented.

Paul Johnson was one of twelve applicants for promotion to the job of "road dispatcher," which was classified as a "skilled craft." In fact, at the time of this case, there were no women road dispatchers at all and no women in the entire job category of "skilled craft." Nine of the twelve applicants were found to qualified for the job, including both Johnson and a woman named Diane Joyce. Johnson had begun working for the county in 1976 as a road yard clerk, having previously worked in the private sector, including positions as a supervisor and dispatcher. In 1974, he unsuccessfully applied for a road dispatcher position, and in 1977 transferred to the position of road maintenance worker, where he occasionally worked as a dispatcher.

Joyce had begun working for the county in 1970 as an account clerk. In 1974, she, too, unsuccessfully applied for the job of road dispatcher but was told she was ineligible because she had not been a road maintenance worker. In 1975, she transferred to road maintenance worker, becoming the first woman to hold that job. During her years in this position, she, too, occasionally worked as a road dispatcher. Like all the other qualified candidates, Johnson and Joyce were interviewed by a two-person board; Johnson tied for second with a score of 75, and Joyce was next with a score of 73. The seven applicants who scored well enough on the first interview went on to a second interview by three agency supervisors; they recommended Johnson for the promotion.

In the period between the two interviews, Joyce contacted the county affirmative action office; she feared that her second interview would not be a "disinterested" one since she had had past run-ins with two of the three supervisors who would conduct the interview. In fact, one had described her as "a 'rebel-rousing, skirt-wearing person'" [*Johnson v. Transportation Agency, Santa Clara County, California*, 107 S.Ct. 1442, 1448 ftnt. 5 (1987)]. The county affirmative action office contacted the Transportation Agency's affirmative action officer who, in turn, contacted the agency's director, who would make the ultimate decision as to the hire. The director ultimately chose Joyce for the promotion, saying: "'I tried to look at the whole picture, the combination of her qualifications and Mr. Johnson's qualifications, their test scores, their expertise, their background, affirmative action matters, things like that. . . . I believe it was a combination of all those.'" [*Johnson v. Transportation Agency, Santa Clara County, California*, 107 S.Ct. 1442, 1448 (1987)].

Johnson filed a complaint with the Equal Employment Opportunity Commission (EEOC), claiming that he had been denied promotion on the basis of sex and, therefore, in violation of Title VII. In March 1981, after its review, the EEOC issued Johnson a right-to-sue letter, a necessary formality for bringing the case to court, and he promptly filed suit in a federal district court in California. He claimed that he was the more qualified candidate and that the reason he was passed over was because he was a male and Joyce was a female. The district court agreed that sex had been the determining factor and then looked at the nature of the affirmative action plan that allowed for sex to be considered as a factor. After analyzing the plan, the court declared it invalid because it was not set up to be a temporary remedy, a criterion for affirmative actions plans previously established by the Supreme Court in *Steelworkers v. Weber*, 99 S.Ct. 2721 (1979), a case that had looked at the use of an affirmative action plan to redress a racial imbalance.

The county appealed the district court decision to the Ninth Circuit Court of Appeals, and that court disagreed with the lower court, finding that the plan was seeking to achieve, but not maintain, a proportional work force; since there were no promotional "quotas," the absence of a termination deadline was not crucial. Further, the circuit court noted that the plan "had been adopted, . . . to address a conspicuous imbalance in the Agency's work force, and neither unnecessarily trammeled the rights of other employees, nor created an absolute bar to their advancement" [*Johnson v. Transportation Agency, Santa Clara County, California*, 107 S.Ct. 1442, 1449 (1987)]. Again the case was appealed—this time to the Supreme Court.

The outcome was a six-to-three decision upholding the county's affirmative action plan and the promotion of Joyce rather than Johnson. Justice Brennan authored a straightforward opinion for the majority, joined by Justices Blackmun, Marshall, Powell, and Stevens; Justice Stevens filed a separate concurring opinion, and Justice O'Connor also wrote a separate concurring opinion. Justice Scalia filed a dissenting opinion, joined by Chief Justice Rehnquist and Justice White, and Justice White wrote a short separate dissenting opinion.

What is perhaps most noteworthy about all the opinions written in conjunction with *Johnson* is not what they contain but what they omit. What is missing is a discussion of stereotypes. For over a century, the Court had discussed and evaluated sex stereotypes, flip-flopping back and forth as to their validity. Yet it took only a few years, or so it seems, for the Court finally to move beyond the need to continue that discussion, to simply accept sex stereotypes as invalid, to turn its attention to means of combatting them, and thereby to begin to remedy the heritage left by long reliance on such stereotypes. The Court's turnaround is well evidenced in the majority opinion in *Johnson*; there the tone clearly accepts the reality of the legacy of discrimination, without the need for continued debate. Where the debate did continue, however, was on how best to redress that legacy.

Justice Brennan's majority opinion focuses narrowly on the legalities of the affirmative action plan as constructed and operating, and not broadly on the philosophical merits of the need for affirmative action plans in general. This can be taken as further proof that women's rights litigation had come a long way—at least in process if not in outcome. Justice Brennan noted that as with any petitioner, Johnson had the burden of establishing a *prima facie* case of sex discrimination—he had to demonstrate that sex had been used as a criterion in making the promotion decision. With that established, the burden then shifted to the employer "to articulate a nondiscriminatory rationale for its decision" [*Johnson v. Transportation Agency, Santa Clara County, California*, 107 S.Ct. 1442, 1449 (1987)]. The Court, like the circuit court, cited its decision in *Weber* as precedent. In that case, the Court had held that "taking race into account [in employee selection decisions] was consistent with Title VII's objective of 'breaking down old patterns of racial segregation and hierarchy'" [*Johnson v. Transportation Agency, Santa Clara County, California*, 107 S.Ct. 1442, 1450 (1987)]. And since the affirmative action plan in *Weber* did not "unnecessarily tramel the interests of the white employees," did not let white employees go in order to replace them with black employees, did not create an "absolute bar to the advancement of white employees," and was a temporary measure to redress racial imbalance rather than to maintain racial balance, the Court had found that particular affirmative action plan to be within the law. This was the standard to which the Court subjected Johnson's appeal.

Johnson v. Transportation Agency, Santa Clara County, California
107 S.Ct. 1442 (1987)
Justice Brennan, for the Court

The first issue is therefore whether consideration of the sex of applicants for Skilled Craft jobs was justified by the existence of a "manifest imbalance" that reflected underrepresentation of women in "traditionally segregated job categories" [cite omitted]. In determining whether an imbalance exists that would justify taking sex or race into account, a comparison of the percentage of minorities or women in the employer's work force with the percentage in the area labor market or general population is appropriate in analyzing jobs that require no special expertise, ... Where a job requires special training, however, the comparison should be with those in the labor force who possess the relevant qualifications.... The requirement that the "manifest imbalance" relate to a "traditionally segregated job category" provides assurance both that sex or race will be taken into account in a manner consistent with Title VII's purpose of eliminating the effects of employment discrimination, and that the interest of those employees not benefiting from the plan will not be unduly infringed....

It is clear that the decision to hire Joyce was made pursuant to an Agency plan that directed that sex or race be taken into account for the purpose of remedying underrepresentation. The

Agency Plan acknowledged the "limited opportunities that have existed in the past" [cite omitted] for women to find employment in certain job classifications "where women have not been traditionally employed in significant numbers" [cite omitted]. As a result, observed the Plan, women were concentrated in traditionally female jobs in the Agency, and represented a lower percentage in other job classifications than would be expected if such traditional segregation had not occurred. Specifically, 9 of the 10 Para-Professionals and 110 of the 145 Office and Clerical Workers were women. By contrast, women were only 2 of the 28 Officials and Administrators, 5 of the 58 Professionals, 12 of the 124 Technicians, none of the Skilled Craft Workers, and 1—who was Joyce—of the 110 Road Maintenance Workers. (cite omitted) The Plan sought to remedy these imbalances through "hiring, training and promotion of . . . women throughout the Agency in all major job classifications where they are underrepresented" [cite omitted].

As an initial matter, the Agency adopted as a benchmark for measuring progress in eliminating underrepresentation the long-term goal of a work force that mirrored in its major job classifications the percentage of women in the area labor market. Even as it did so, however, the Agency acknowledged that such a figure could not by itself necessarily justify taking into account the sex of applicants for positions in all job categories. . . . The Plan therefore directed that annual short-term goals be formulated that would provide a more realistic indication of the degree to which sex should be taken into account in filling particular positions. . . . These goals were to take into account factors such as "turnover, layoffs, lateral transfers, new job openings, retirements and availability of minorities, women and handicapped persons in the area work force who possess the desired qualifications or potential for placement. . . . From the outset, therefore, the Plan sought annually to develop even more refined measures of the underrepresentation in each job category that required attention.

As the Agency Plan recognized, women were most egregiously underrepresented in the Skilled Craft job category, since *none* [emphasis in the original] of the 238 positions was occupied by a woman. In mid-1980, when Joyce was selected for the road dispatcher position, the Agency was still in the process of refining its short-term goals for Skilled Craft Workers in accordance with the directive of the Plan. This process did not reach fruition until 1982, when the Agency established a short-term goal for that year of 3 women for the 55 expected openings in that job category—a modest goal of about 6% for that category.

We reject [Johnson's] argument that, since only the long-term goal was in place for Skilled Craft positions at the time of Joyce's promotion, it was inappropriate for the Director to take into account affirmative action considerations in filling the road dispatcher position. The Agency's Plan emphasized that the long-term goals were not to be taken as guides for actual hiring decisions, but that supervisors were to consider a host of practical factors in seeking to meet affirmative action objectives, including the fact that in some job categories women were not qualified in numbers comparable to their representation in the labor force.

By contrast, had the Plan simply calculated imbalances in all categories according to the proportion of women in the area labor pool, and then directed that hiring be governed solely by those figures, its validity fairly could be called into question. This is because analysis of a more specialized labor pool normally is necessary in determining underrepresentation in some positions. If a plan failed to take distinctions in qualifications into account in providing guidance for actual employment decisions, it would dictate mere blind hiring by the numbers, for it would hold supervisors to "achievement of a particular percentage of minority employment or membership . . . regardless of circumstances such as economic conditions or the number of available qualified minority applicants. . ." [cite omitted].

The Agency's Plan emphatically did *not* [emphasis in the original] authorize such blind hiring. It expressly directed that numerous factors be taken into account in making hiring decisions, including specifically the qualifications of female applicants for particular jobs. Thus, despite the fact that no precise short-term goal was yet in place for the Skilled Craft category in mid-1980, the Agency's management nevertheless had been clearly instructed that they were not to hire solely by reference to statistics. . . .

Furthermore, in considering the candidates for the road dispatcher position in 1980, the Agency hardly needed to rely on a refined short-term goal to realize that it had a significant problem of underrepresentation that required attention. Given the obvious imbalance in the Skilled Craft category, and given the Agency's commitment to eliminating such imbalances, it was plainly not unreasonable for the Agency to determine that it was appropriate to consider as one factor the sex of Ms. Joyce in making its decision. The promotion of Joyce thus satisfies the first requirement enunciated in *Weber*, since it was undertaken to further an affirmative action plan designed to eliminate Agency work force imbalances in traditionally segregated job categories.

We next consider whether the Agency Plan unnecessarily trammeled the rights of male employees or created an absolute bar to their advancement. . . . [T]he Plan sets aside no positions for women. The Plan expressly states that "[t]he 'goals' established for each Division should not be construed as 'quotas' that must be met" [cite omitted]. Rather, the Plan merely authorizes that consideration be given to affirmative action concerns when evaluating qualified applicants. As the Agency Director testified, the sex of Joyce was but one of numerous factors he took into account in arriving at his decision. . . . [T]he Agency Plan requires women to compete with all other qualified applicants. *No* persons are automatically excluded from consideration; *all* are able to have their qualifications weighed against those of other applicants [emphasis in the original].

In addition, petitioner had no absolute entitlement to the road dispatcher position. Seven of the applicants were classified as qualified and eligible, and the Agency Director was authorized to promote any of the seven. Thus, denial of the promotion unsettled no legitimate, firmly rooted expectation on the part of [Johnson]. Furthermore, while [Johnson] in this case was denied a promotion, he retained his employment with the Agency, at the same salary and with the same seniority, and remained eligible for other promotions.

Finally, the Agency's Plan was intended to *attain* a balanced work force, not to maintain one [emphasis in the original]. The Plan contains 10 references to the Agency's desire to "attain" such a balance, but no reference whatsoever to a goal of maintaining it. The Director testified that, while the "broader goal" of affirmative action, defined as "the desire to hire, to promote, to give opportunity and training on an equitable, non-discriminatory basis," is something that is "a permanent part" of "the Agency's operating philosophy," that broader goal "is divorced, if you will, from specific numbers or percentages" [cite omitted].

The Agency acknowledged the difficulties that it would confront in remedying the imbalance in its work force, and it anticipated only gradual increases in the representation of minorities and women. It is thus unsurprising that the Plan contains no explicit end date, for the Agency's flexible case-by-case approach was not expected to yield success in a brief period of time. Express assurance that a program is only temporary may be necessary if the program actually sets aside positions according to specific numbers. . . . In this case, however, substantial evidence shows that the Agency has sought to take a moderate, gradual approach to eliminating the imbalance in its work force, one which establishes realistic guidance for employment decisions, and which visits minimal intrusion on the legitimate expectations of other employees. Given this fact, as well as the Agency's express commitment to "attain" a balanced work force, there is ample assurance that the Agency does not seek to use its Plan to maintain a permanent racial and sexual balance. . . .

We therefore hold that the Agency appropriately took into account as one fact the sex of Diane Joyce in determining that she should be promoted to the road dispatcher position. The decision to do so was made pursuant to an affirmative action plan that represents a moderate, flexible, case-by-case approach to

> effecting a gradual improvement in the representation of minorities and women in the Agency's work force.

As previously noted, there is nothing in this opinion that should cause anyone to gasp for air in disbelief. Nevertheless, it is still possible to quibble with some of the conclusions reached, such as the statement that Johnson's denial of promotion uprooted his "firmly rooted expectation." And it is possible to ask what concern lies behind the Court's repeated references to the impermissibility of using an affirmative action plan to maintain racial and sexual balance once the earlier imbalance has been corrected.

On the whole, however, there do not seem to be any hidden messages in this opinion, nor is there any evidence of giving with one hand while taking away with the other—so common in earlier Court opinions in women's rights litigation. Rather, there seems to be a straightforward endorsement of using carefully constructed—and, yes, limited (and therein may perhaps lie a taking away)—affirmative action plans to increase women's initial participation in employment areas that had historically, for whatever reason, been unavailable to them.[7] And so one more barrier to women's full participation in the workplace fell, although other barriers still remained.

The two concurring opinions by Justices Stevens and O'Connor and the major dissenting opinion by Justice Scalia are examples of good legal posturing, but for the most part do not add too much of our knowledge of the Court's views on affirmative action. Justice Scalia does make one interesting argument, however; his highly legalistic opinion accuses the Court of ignoring precedent and turning the thrust of Title VII completely around, changing it from a weapon for antidiscrimination to one for discrimination. The following excerpt from his opinion makes this point clearly. In reading the first part, remember the Court's explanation in *Rawlinson* as to why it rejected the state's claim that Rawlinson should have produced comparative statistics for *actual* applicants for guard positions.

Johnson v. Transportation Agency, Santa Clara County, California
107 S.Ct. 1442 (1987)
Justice Scalia, dissenting

> In fact, however, today's decision goes well beyond merely allowing racial or sexual discrimination in order to eliminate the effects of prior societal *discrimination* [emphasis in the original]. The majority opinion often uses the phrase "traditionally segregated job category" to describe the evil against which the plan is legitimately (according to the majority) directed. As originally used in [*Weber*], that phrase described skilled jobs from which employers and unions had systematically and intentionally excluded black workers—traditionally segregated jobs, that is, in the sense of conscious, exclusionary discrimination [cite omitted]. But that is assuredly not the sense in which the phrase is used here. It is absurd to think that the nationwide failure of road maintenance crews, for example, to achieve the Agency's

ambition of 36.4% female representation is attributable primarily, if even substantially, to systematic exclusion of women eager to shoulder pick and shovel. It is a "traditionally segregated job category" *not* in the *Weber* sense, but in the sense that, because of longstanding social attitudes, it has not been regarded *by women themselves* as desirable work [emphasis in the original]. Or as the majority opinion puts the point, quoting approvingly the Court of Appeals: "'A plethora of proof is hardly necessary to show that women are generally underrepresented in such positions and that strong social pressures weigh against their participation'" [cite omitted]. . . . There are, of course, those who believe that the social attitudes which cause women themselves to avoid certain jobs and to favor others are as nefarious as conscious, exclusionary discrimination. Whether or not that is so (and there is assuredly no consensus on the point equivalent to our national consensus against intentional discrimination), the two phenomena are certainly distinct. And it is the alteration of social attitudes, rather than the elimination of discrimination, which today's decision approves as justification for state-enforced discrimination. This is an enormous expansion, undertaken without the slightest justification or analysis. . . .

Today's decision does more, however, than merely reaffirm *Weber*, and more than merely extend it to public actors. It is impossible not be aware that the practical effect of our holding is to accomplish *de facto* what the law . . . forbids anyone from accomplishing *de jure*: in many contexts it effectively *requires* employers, public as well as private, to engage in intentional discrimination on the basis of race or sex [emphasis in the original]. . . . [I]f . . . employers are free to discriminate through affirmative action, without fear of "reverse discrimination" suits by their nonminority or male victims, they are offered a threshold defense against Title VII liability premised on numerical disparities. Thus, after today's decision the *failure* to engage in reverse discrimination is economic folly, and arguably a breach of duty to shareholders or taxpayers, wherever the cost of anticipated Title VII litigation exceeds the cost of hiring less capable (though still minimally capable) workers [emphasis in the original]. (This situation is more likely to obtain, of course, with respect to the least skilled jobs—perversely creating an incentive to discriminate against precisely those members of the nonfavored groups *least* likely to have profited from societal discrimination in the past.) It is predictable, moreover, that this incentive will be greatly magnified by economic pressures brought to bear by government contracting agencies upon employers who refuse to discriminate in the fashion we have not approved. A statute designed to establish a color- blind and gender-blind workplace has thus been converted into a powerful engine of racism and sexism, not merely *permitting* intentional race- and

> sex-based discrimination, but often making it, through operation of the legal system, practically compelled.
>
> It is unlikely that today's result will be displeasing to politically elected officials. . . . Nor will it displease the world of corporate and governmental employers. . . . In fact, the only losers in the process are the Johnsons of the country, for whom Title VII has been not merely repealed but actually inverted. The irony is that these individuals—predominantly unknown, unaffluent, unorganized—suffer this injustice at the hands of a Court fond of thinking itself the champion of the politically impotent.

Though not as unemotional and levelheaded as his brethren, Justice Scalia may be right: The decision in *Johnson* may have turned Title VII into a *potential* tool for discrimination—and this is something clearly deserving of reflection. On a further point Justice Scalia is no doubt right: There is a difference between discrimination that results from a "conscious, exclusionary" process and discrimination based on self-selection reflecting long-held stereotypical social attitudes. And, as the Court had noted before, there is a difference between facially neutral laws that unintentionally end up discriminating and laws that are facially neutral but are intentionally discriminatory. All of these examples, however, can, and do, end up harming women. How, then, is it possible to let one version stand but not another?

In one pronouncement in his opinion, however, Justice Scalia was clearly wrong: In saying that the Court was fond of thinking of itself as the "champion of the politically impotent", he was most certainly off-base. Women, long politically impotent (though slowly gaining strength), surely could not have thought of the Court as their champion for the first one-hundred years of their legal struggle. And it is doubtful that even today women would be lining up to raise that banner over the Court.

FETAL PROTECTION

The Court's composition had changed yet again between *Johnson* and the last case in this book's historical review. Justice Rehnquist was well ensconced as Chief Justice, and Justice Scalia's reputation as a staunch conservative had been amply proven. But two new men had taken their seats on the Court. In 1987 Justice Powell, many of whose later opinions had been becoming more moderate or even liberal, resigned and was replaced by Anthony M. Kennedy, a member of the Ninth Circuit Court of Appeals generally counted as a moderate-to-strong conservative. Then when Justice Brennan resigned in 1990, he was replaced by David H. Souter of New Hampshire. This was clearly not an even exchange since Justice Brennan, a true "champion of the politically impotent," was being replaced by a little-known state court judge generally assumed to lean to the right. For those keeping score under broad attitudinal labels, the "conservatives" now clearly outnumbered the "liberals."

The final case to be included in this book's review of women's struggle for self-determination was heard by the Court in October 1990 and decided in March 1991. It involved a challenge to a fetal protection policy, a highly controversial issue not only between unions and employers but within labor and feminist circles as well, frequently splitting traditional allies.

Fetal-protection policies, in general, are designed to keep workers who are of childbearing age out of jobs that might endanger their procreative abilities or might harm their potential fetus. In this case [*International Union, UAW v. Johnson Controls*, 111 S.Ct. 1196 (1991)], labor unions challenged a sex-specific fetal protection policy that limited job access for women at Johnson Controls, a manufacturer of batteries. Lead is a key ingredient in making batteries, and it is widely believed that long-term exposure to lead is correlated with a number of health risks, including loss of procreative power and possible harm to fetuses.

Prior to 1977, no women worked in battery manufacturing at Johnson Controls; however, in June 1977 that changed as Johnson Controls implemented a new policy to bring itself in line with the amended Civil Rights Act of 1964. The policy governing females employed in work involving exposure to lead read as follows [*International Union, UAW v. Johnson Controls*, 111 S.Ct. 1196, 1199 (1991)]:

> [P]rotection of the health of the unborn child is the immediate and direct responsibility of the prospective parents. While the medical profession and the company can support them in the exercise of this responsibility, it cannot assume it for them without simultaneously infringing their rights as persons.
>
> . . . Since not all women who can become mothers wish to become mothers (or will become mothers), it would appear to be illegal discrimination to treat all who are capable of pregnancy as though they will become pregnant.

In short, women wishing to work in jobs that involved exposure to lead were allowed to do so but had to sign a consent form acknowledging that they were aware of the risks involved. In 1982, however, after a number of pregnant employees were discovered to have elevated levels of lead in their blood, Johnson Controls changed policy again, reverting back to its earlier policy of exclusion. The new policy read: "[I]t is [Johnson Controls'] policy that women who are pregnant or who are capable of bearing children will not be placed into jobs involving lead exposure or which could expose them to lead" [*International Union, UAW v. Johnson Controls*, 111 S.Ct. 1196, 1200 (1991)]. Any woman able to document medically that she was unable to bear children could be exempted from this prohibition.

The mentality surrounding this case is so reminiscent of *Muller* that it is hard to believe that it was not *Muller*'s contemporary but rather came more than eighty years later. Johnson Controls was obviously to a large degree seeking to protect itself from later suits for damages from women contending that exposure to lead had cost them their ability to bear children. But also, like the state of Oregon before it, Johnson Controls was still acting on the assumption that a man was capable of making tough decisions for himself, but a woman was not and therefore was in need of outside guidance and protection. Johnson Controls took on the role of parent, treating the adult as a child and telling the woman what was good or not good for her and what she could and could not do. Thus, we see once more a theme threaded constantly throughout this book: a woman's procreative ability—so often proclaimed as her special contribution and glory—also becomes singularly her burden and society's excuse for treating her as not equal to a man, less able to bear the responsibility of self-determination.

The outcome of this case, however, would ultimately differ from the outcome in *Muller*; this time the Court was not persuaded by the argument that "we're doing it for the welfare of the next generation." In April 1984, the United Auto Workers (UAW) union had filed suit in a Wisconsin federal district court charging that the company's sex-based fetal protection policy discriminated on the basis of sex and therefore was in violation of Title VII of the Civil Rights Act of 1964. The suit was ultimately certified as a class action suit on behalf of past, present, and future UAW members affected by the policy at nine Johnson Controls' plants. Among the original individuals suing were three people who drew even further the parallels between this case and *Muller*. They were a woman who opted for sterilization rather than lose her job, a fifth year old divorced woman who was transferred out of the lead-exposure job and suffered a consequent loss in pay, and a man who had been denied a request for a leave of absence so that he might lower his blood lead level enough to try fathering a child.

Both the district court for Wisconsin and, on appeal, the circuit court ruled in favor of Johnson Controls, relying on a "business necessity defense." This is a classification of legal defense that allows business firms to argue that a particular practice under attack was adopted out of necessity to preserve or enhance the well-being of the company. In this case, the legitimacy of the business necessity defense focused on a three part inquiry [*International Union, UAW v. Johnson Controls*, 111 S.Ct. 1196, 1201 (1991):

> . . . whether there is a substantial health risk to the fetus; whether transmission of the hazard to the fetus occurs only through women; and whether there is a less discriminatory alternative equally capable of preventing the health hazard to the fetus.

This defense, the circuit court held, "balance[s] the interests of the employer, the employee and the unborn child in a manner consistent with Title VII" [*International Union, UAW v. Johnson Controls*, 111 S.Ct. 1196, 1201 (1991)]. The circuit court, unlike the district court, also took up the issue of whether the company's policy fit as well into a defense of establishing a bona fide occupational qualification. And the circuit court concluded that it did, saying "that industrial safety is part of the essence of respondent's business, and that the fetal protection policy is reasonably necessary to further that concern" [*International Union, UAW v. Johnson Controls*, 111 S.Ct. 1196, 1201 (1991)].

Thus far there is nothing to distinguish the content or the outcome in *Johnson Controls* from *Muller*. But as noted above, the distinction came with the Supreme Court's response to the case. A unanimous Court decided against Johnson Controls, although it did not hand down a unanimous opinion. Justice Blackmun wrote the opinion of the Court, being joined by

Justices Marshall, O'Connor, Souter, and Stevens. Justice White, on behalf of himself, Chief Justice Rehnquist, and Justice Kennedy, wrote an opinion that concurred with the judgment of the Court and with part but not all of the opinion, and Justice Scalia concurred in the judgment of the Court but not in the reasoning.

Justice Blackmun's majority opinion saw two points that needed to be addressed. One was "the important and difficult question whether an employer seeking to protect potential fetuses, may discriminate against women just because of their ability to become pregnant" [*International Union, UAW v. Johnson Controls*, 111 S.Ct. 1196, 1202 (1991)]. The second point was the need to resolve differences of opinion among several circuit courts on the question of whether a sex-based fetal protection policy could qualify as a bona fide occupational qualification (BFOQ). Justice Blackmun began his analysis of these two issues by questioning whether the district and circuit courts had been correct in believing that a sex-based fetal protection policy was facially neutral.

International Union, UAW v. Johnson Controls
111 S.Ct. 1196 (1991)
Justice Blackmun, for the Court

The [Circuit Court] assumed that because the asserted reason for the sex-based exclusion (protecting women's unconceived offspring) was ostensibly benign, the policy was not sex-based discrimination. That assumption, however, was incorrect.

First, Johnson Controls' policy classifies on the basis of gender and childbearing capacity, rather than fertility alone. [Johnson Controls] does not seek to protect the unconceived children of all its employees. Despite evidence in the record about the debilitating effect of lead exposure on the male reproductive system, Johnson Controls is concerned with the harms that may befall the unborn offspring of its female employees. . . . Johnson Controls' policy is facially discriminatory because it requires only a female employee to produce proof that she is not capable of reproducing.

Our conclusion is bolstered by the Pregnancy Discrimination Act of 1978 (PDA), . . . in which Congress explicitly provided that, for purposes of Title VII, discrimination "on the basis of sex" includes discrimination "because of or on the basis of pregnancy, childbirth, or related medical conditions." "The Pregnancy Discrimination Act has now made clear that, for all Title VII purposes, discrimination based on a woman's pregnancy is, on its face, discrimination because of her sex" [cite omitted]. In its use of the words "capable of bearing children" in the 1982 policy statement as the criterion for exclusion, Johnson Controls explicitly classifies on the basis of potential for pregnancy. Under the PDA, such a classification must be regarded, for Title VII purposes, in the same light as explicit sex discrimination. [Johnson

Controls] has chosen to treat all its female employees as potentially pregnant; that choice evinces discrimination on the basis of sex.

We concluded above that Johnson Controls' policy is not neutral because it does not apply to the reproductive capacity of the company's male employees in the same way as it applies to that of the females. Moreover, the absence of a malevolent motive does not convert a facially discriminatory policy into a neutral policy with a discriminatory effect. . . . The beneficence of an employer's purpose does not undermine the conclusion that an explicit gender-based policy is sex discrimination . . . and thus may be defended only as a BFOQ. . . .

Under [Title VII], an employer may discriminate on the basis of "religion, sex, or national origin in those certain instances where religion, sex, or national origin is a bona fide occupational qualification reasonably necessary to the normal operation of that particular business or enterprise" [cite omitted]. We therefore turn to the question whether Johnson Controls' fetal protection policy is one of those "certain instances" that come within the BFOQ exception. . . .

The working of the BFOQ defense contains several terms of restriction that indicate that the exception reaches only special situations. The statute thus limits the situations in which discrimination is permissible to "certain instances" where sex discrimination is "reasonably necessary" to the "normal operation" of the "particular" business. Each one of these terms—certain, normal, particular—prevents the use of general subjective standards and favors an objective, verifiable requirement. But the most telling term is "occupational"; this indicates that these objective, verifiable requirements must concern job-related skills and aptitudes.

The concurrence defines "occupational" as meaning related to a job [cite omitted]. According to the concurrence, any discriminatory requirement imposed by an employer is "job-related" simply because the employer has chosen to make the requirement a condition of employment. In effect, the concurrence argues that sterility may be an occupational qualification for women because Johnson Controls has chosen to require it. This reading of "occupation" renders the word mere surplusage. "Qualification" by itself would encompass an employer's idiosyncratic requirements. By modifying "qualification" with "occupational," Congress narrowed the term to qualifications that affect an employee's ability to do the job.

Johnson Controls argues that its fetal-protection policy falls within the so-called safety exception to the BFOQ. Our cases have stressed that discrimination on the basis of sex because of safety concerns is allowed only in narrow circumstances. In [*Rawlinson*], this Court indicated that danger to a woman herself does not justify discrimination. . . . We there allowed the employer to hire only male guards in contact areas of maximum-security male penitentiaries only because more was at stake than the "individual woman's decision to weigh and accept the risks of employment" [cite omitted]. We found sex to be a BFOQ inasmuch as the employment of a female guard would create real risks of safety to others if violence broke out because the guard was a woman. Sex discrimination was tolerated because sex was related to the guard's ability to do the job—maintaining prison security. We also required in [*Rawlinson*] a high correlation between sex and ability to perform job functions and refused to allow employers to use sex as a proxy for strength although it might be a fairly accurate one. . . .

We stressed that in order to qualify as a BFOQ, a job qualification must relate to the "essence," . . . or to the "central mission of the employer's business" [cite omitted].

The concurrence ignores the "essence of the business" test and so concludes that "the safety to fetuses in carrying out the duties of battery manufacturing is as much a legitimate concern as is safety to third parties in guarding prisons. . ." [cite omitted]. By limiting its discussion to cost and safety concerns and rejecting the "essence of the business" test that our case law has established, the concurrence seeks to expand what is now the narrow BFOQ defense. . . . The concurrence attempts to transform this case into one of customer safety. The unconceived fetuses of Johnson Controls' female employees, however, are neither customers nor third parties whose safety is essential to the business of battery manufacturing. No one can disregard the possibility of injury to future children; the BFOQ, however, is not so broad that it transforms this deep social concern into an essential aspect of batterymaking.

Our case law . . . makes clear that the safety exception is limited to instances in which sex or pregnancy actually interferes with the employee's ability to perform the job. This approach is consistent with the language of the BFOQ provision itself, for it suggests that permissible distinctions based on sex must relate to ability to perform the duties of the job. Johnson Controls suggests, however, that we expand the exception to allow fetal-protection policies that mandate particular standards for pregnant or fertile women. We decline to do so. Such an expansion contradicts not only the language of the BFOQ and the narrowness of its exception but the plain language and history of the [PDA].

The [Pregnancy Discrimination Act's] amendment to Title VII contains a BFOQ standard of its own: unless pregnant employees differ from others "in their ability or inability to work," they must be "treated the same" as other employees "for all employment-related purposes" [cite omitted]. This language clearly sets forth Congress' remedy for discrimination on the basis of pregnancy and potential pregnancy. Women who are either pregnant or potentially pregnant must be treated like others "similar in their ability . . . to work" [cite omitted]. In other words, women as capable of doing their jobs as their male counterparts may not be forced to choose between having a child and having a job. . . .

[H]istory counsels against expanding the BFOQ to allow fetal-protection policies. . . . [E]mployers may not require a pregnant woman to stop working at any time during her pregnancy unless she is unable to do her work. Employment late in pregnancy often imposes risks on the unborn child, . . . but . . . the employer may take into account only the woman's ability to get her job done. . . . With the PDA, Congress made clear that the decision to become pregnant or to work while being either pregnant or capable of becoming pregnant was reserved for each individual woman to make for herself.

We conclude that the language of both the BFOQ provision and the PDA which amended it, as well as the legislative history and the case law, prohibit an employer from discriminating against a woman because of her capacity to become pregnant unless her reproductive potential prevents her from performing the duties of her job. . . . [A]n employer must direct its concerns about a woman's ability to perform her job safely and efficiently to those aspects of the woman's job-related activities that fall within the "essence" of the particular business.

We have no difficulty concluding that Johnson Controls cannot establish a BFOQ. Fertile women, as far as appears in the record, participate in the manufacture of batteries as efficiently as anyone else. Johnson Controls' professed moral and ethical concerns about the welfare of the next generation do not suffice to establish a BFOQ of female sterility. Decisions about the welfare of future children must be left to the parents who conceive, bear, support, and raise them rather than to the employers who hire those parents. . . .

Johnson Controls argues that it must exclude all fertile women because it is impossible to tell which women will become pregnant while working with lead. This argument is somewhat academic in light of our conclusion that the company may not exclude fertile women at all; it perhaps is worth noting, however, that Johnson Controls has shown no "factual basis for believing that all or substantially all women would be unable to perform safely and efficiently the duties of the job involved" [cite omitted]. Even on this sparse record, it is apparent that Johnson Controls is concerned about only a small minority of women. Of the eight pregnancies reported among the female employees, it has not been shown that any of the babies have birth defects or other abnormalities. The record does not reveal the birth rate for Johnson Controls' female workers but national statistics show that approximately nine percent of all fertile women become pregnant each year. The birthrate drops to two percent for blue

> collar workers over age 30 [cite omitted]. Johnson Controls' fear of prenatal injury, no matter how sincere, does not begin to show that substantially all of its fertile women employees are incapable of doing their job. . . .
>
> Our holding today that Title VII, as so amended, forbids sex-specific fetal-protection policies is neither remarkable nor unprecedented. Concern for a woman's existing or potential offspring historically has been the excuse for denying women equal employment opportunities. . . . Congress in the PDA prohibited discrimination on the basis of a woman's ability to become pregnant. We do no more than hold that the Pregnancy Discrimination Act means what it says.
>
> It is no more appropriate for the courts than it is for individual employers to decide whether a woman's reproductive role is more important to herself and her family than her economic role. Congress has left this choice to the woman as hers to make.

Contrary to the Court's own assessment of what it did, its opinion in *Johnson Controls* does seem remarkable, given that for decades the ability to bear children had been used as an excuse to limit women's access to jobs and wages. As was noted earlier, though the case was strikingly similar to *Muller* in its facts—women facing restricted work opportunities because of their child-bearing potential—there was an equally striking difference in the Court's position and the outcome of the case. Change had indeed occurred in the ensuing eighty-plus years.[8]

The Court had come to recognize the special problem that Montagu pointed out so long ago—that women are damned in so many subtle and not-so-subtle ways for their ability to have children. And if the Court did not finally and completely put this particular problem to rest, it did reduce it substantially in one major area. The Court signaled to the nation that a woman's capacity for childbearing did not automatically rob her of her ability to think, to weigh information, or to make intelligent and rational decisions in her own best interest or the best interest of any present or future "other" for whom she might be responsible. In so doing, the Court granted women an enlarged sphere of self-determination.

As this review closes, it is clear that the Court had, indeed, come a long way in its views of women and their struggles for equality and self-determination. But although the Court was willing to expand women's horizons, it was not yet an across-the-board expansion or one without some significant limitations. The Court was willing to give women considerable control in making decisions about employment, not only decisions affecting themselves but even affecting present and future offspring. It was less willing to do the same, however, with respect to decisions about women's bodies. As noted at the beginning of this chapter, in three abortion cases before it in the late 1980s and early 1990s, the Court consistently upheld laws limiting a woman's right to make her own decisions and increasing the extent to which others could intrude into her process of self-determination.

The fact that the Court was inconsistent—or even schizophrenic—in its response to women's struggles for equal rights and self-determination should not be surprising. Justices have, in the past, demonstrated ambivalent decision-making patterns in other major areas of the law, willing to grant expanded rights in some instances but not in others. Thus, the Rehnquist Court was simply following the lead of its predecessors, selecting where, when, and how it would champion the rights of women.

Johnson Controls closes this history not only chronologically but also serendipitously. It shows how tenaciously entrenched ideas, ideas long and widely held, can eventually be overturned. More than a century after it first stamped its approval on stereotypical notions that worked to restrict a woman's access to her choice of professions, the U.S. Supreme Court had moved far enough forward to reject those same stereotypical notions and to affirm a woman's right to make her own decisions about where and how she would work. Nevertheless, this path from nay sayer to yea sayer was not without its potholes and pitfalls, and women still have far to go on this path before reaching their ultimate destination.

NOTES

1. In fact, there was a seventh case bearing on women's rights. *Price Waterhouse v. Hopkins*, 109 S.Ct. 1775 (1989), involved Ann Hopkins' Title VII claim that she was denied partnership at the prestigious accounting firm because of sex discrimination. Although the case is replete with suggestions of stereotypical thinking, there was no clear outcome (there was no majority opinion), and it appears to be a very weak and narrow decision. Thus, it is not covered here.

2. *Webster v. Reproductive Health Services*, 109 S.Ct. 3040 (1989).

3. *Rust v. Sullivan*, 111 S.Ct. 1759 (1991).

4. *Planned Parenthood of Southeastern Pennsylvania et al. v. Robert P. Casey et al.*, 112 S.Ct. 2791 (1992).

5. Though not phrased in the language of an equal protection challenge, the majority opinion in *Casey et al.* came closest to fitting the language of such cases, addressing the question of whether the restrictions placed an undue burden on women seeking abortions. It should be noted, however, that at the same time that the Court, in a five-to-four decision, affirmed the twenty-four hour waiting period and the need for minors to have parental or judicial consent, it struck down a requirement that wives notify their husbands of their intent to have an abortion. The Court majority also assailed the government for continually bringing before it cases attempting to overturn *Roe* and affirmed its basic commitment to a constitutional right to abortion—albeit with restrictions.

6. *Rogers v. EEOC*, 454 F.2d 234 (CA5 1971).

7. Discussion of the relative merits of affirmative action is an intentional omission. Because volumes of pages of others' writings have been devoted to the matter, interested readers would be better served by reading them, rather than reading what would have to be a very condensed review here.

As a starting point, see the September 1992 issue (volume 523) of *The Annals of the American Academy of Political and Social Science*.

8. The rest of the Court, although in agreement with the judgment, did not go along with the opinion. Justice White, who was joined by Chief Justice Rehnquist and Justice Kennedy, agreed that Johnson Controls' sex-specific fetal-protection policy overtly discriminated against women. They disagreed, however, with the majority opinion's narrow interpretation of a BFOQ, which would exclude the possibility of a legal sex-specific fetal-protection policy. Justice Scalia, in an opinion noticeably shorter than usual, acknowledged that his was in general agreement with the majority opinion, but with several reservations. The most striking, for the purposes of this review, noted the following:

> "I think it irrelevant that there was 'evidence in the record about the debilitating effect of lead exposure on the male reproductive system' [cite omitted]. Even without such evidence, treating women differently 'on the basis of pregnancy' constitutes discrimination 'on the basis of sex,' because Congress has unequivocally said so. . . [*International Union, UAW v. Johnson Controls*, 111 S.Ct. 1196, 1216 (1991)].

12

Conclusion

> *All persons born or naturalized in the United States, and subject to the jurisdiction thereof, are citizens of the United States and of the State wherein they reside. No state shall make or enforce any law which shall abridge the privileges or immunities of citizens of the United States; nor shall any State deprive any person of life, liberty, or property, without due process of law; nor deny to any person within its jurisdiction the equal protection of the laws.*
>
> Amendment 14
> *The Constitution of the United States*

As we move into the third century of America's struggle for equality of the sexes, we can look back and see a path that is characterized by slow and erratic moves forward. And we can look ahead to a future that still needs to bring further advances. We have followed Oliver Wendell Holmes' suggestion offered at the opening of this book and traced the law's treatment of women as they have struggled for equal rights, seeing both what that treatment was and what it has become. Yet the law must move forward even more if it is truly to treat the sexes equally. To know where it still must move, we must be clear as to where it presently is.

In the first chapter of this book, a number of questions offered a guide for routine reflection as the reader moved through the chapters. Other questions were identified as those that the reader should be able to answer at the end of the book—if not definitively, at least with a first draft of responses. This second group of questions asked about such things as the scope of the Constitution's protections for women, the status of women as defined by the Supreme Court as the ultimate arbitrator of U.S. law, and the nature and quality of those actions of the U.S. Supreme Court that helped to define both the status of women and the scope of constitutional protections granted them. It is time now for the reader to respond; in so doing, it should be possible to see clearly how the law presently defines "equality," where the law still must go, and how it might be moved there.

In this quest, we must consider—among many other items—the following points:

- Whether the Court has really, and finally, abandoned its reliance on stereotypes;
- Whether the Court continues to judge a discriminatory law facially neutral and therefore acceptable simply because the resulting discrimination was unintended;
- Whether the Court continues to accept special treatment, which "protects" women, in lieu of equal treatment, which may, in fact, remove those protective kid gloves; and
- Whether the Court has moved beyond laws that reflect what is "pretty nearly" convenient—as Justice Holmes described them—to what is fair and just.

Unfortunately, the answers to these questions are still not simple and easy to come by, for in none of these areas has the Court engaged in any clear *and* consistent behavior. In none of these areas has the Court completely abandoned practices that lead to women's being treated less than equal to men.

Nonetheless, even though the Court has thus far refused or had been unable to abandon completely the modes of thinking that have so long hampered women's progress and restricted their lives, the status of women has changed. Through most of the battle for equality, a battle that has lasted over two centuries, there was little interest in or willingness to grant women much of anything in terms of political, economic, or civil status—but progress did eventually come, albeit slowly.

Yet another question pushes forward. Did this progress come haphazardly, *nolens volens*, or, at bottom, did it come in what could be characterized as a very considered and deliberate chiseling away of the cage that confined women? Did the Court very consciously and purposefully preserve the most sacred stereotypes for the last to fall? If we carefully examine the areas of confinement that were dismantled and those that were retained, we see that the retained areas appear to be those resting upon the bedrock of sex and gender stereotypes. To dismantle those areas requires dismantling the essence of those stereotypes.

Women may now be lawyers and police officers, and they may work in a bar even if their father or husband does not own the establishment. But women may not work in situations in which the stereotypical notion of the frailty of their sex can be used as the basis for arguing that they would endanger others or themselves—as in combat or in male penal institutions.

Women, even those as young as eighteen, are now deemed rational enough to vote, to sit on a jury and judge others, and to negotiate their own terms of employment. But those notions of women as rationally competent individuals fall by the wayside when confronted with a central core of our stereotypical notions—that the male is the active player in sexual relationships while the female is passive. Thus, young women may not be culpable in a situation of statutory rape because they are not deemed rational enough to understand the implications of willingly engaging in sexual intercourse with a male. Holding them culpable might suggest that women are equal partners with men in sex, and this is antithetical to the stereotypical understanding of sex as the man's prerogative and interest and the woman's act of mere compliance.

Women's struggle for equal rights is ultimately the struggle to destroy effectively and completely our country's belief in stereotypes. It is a struggle for individual self-determination rather than societal determination based upon group assessments rather than individual characteristics. And though many would assert that men have long held that right to self-determination, others would argue that men, too, are penalized by stereotypical thinking. After all, the conceptualizations that allowed men to be given, early on, the right to be a lawyer or to work in a bar or to negotiate their own hours of employment reflected not the actual and individual characteristics of the men seeking those opportunities but rather society's expectations based on stereotypical notions of what is male. We have long thought woman disadvantaged but have myopically failed to recognize that men were equally so. (Ironically, this may be the one place where true equality of the sexes has long existed.)

In our effort to correct women's disadvantage, we have engaged in further discrimination, often considered justified because it was benignly intended. Now that we can look back and see the results of all discrimination—both that perpetrated with the intention of restricting opportunity and that followed with the intention of enlarging it—we must question whether there really is such a thing as good or benign discrimination.

Despite the progress made, we are still light years away from giving women true equality with men. As long as laws tell women when and how they may control their bodies, but no similar laws dictate to men, there is no such thing as equality. As long as women are excluded from combat simply because they are female while men are automatically eligible simply because they are male, there is no equality. As long as laws limit women as to where and how they may work if they also want to be mothers but no such laws exist for fathers and would-be fathers, there is no equality.

Equality of the sexes will come only when we treat people on the basis of their individual characteristics, not categorically on the basis of their sex. Equality will come only when we give all individuals, regardless of sex, the respect that acknowledges them as intelligent, rational individuals capable of making decisions in the best interest of themselves, their families (both present and future), their friends, and their society. Only then, when we respond to each other as individuals—and not as a member of a particular group—does equality exist. Only then do all benefit, men as well as women.

In an 1862 message to Congress, President Abraham Lincoln so wisely noted that "in giving freedom to the slave, we assure freedom to the free—honorable alike in what we give and what we preserve." As it was with race, so it is with sex. As often noted in these pages, when we give full equality to women, we simultaneously ensure it for men.

Not yet there, we are at least on the way.

Bibliography and Suggested Readings

Adkins v. Children's Hospital, 43 S.Ct. 394 (1923).

Andolsen, Barbara Hilkert. 1986. *"Daughters of Jefferson, Daughters of Bootblacks": Racism and American Feminism.* Macon, Ga.: Mercer University.

Anonymous. 1991. Background: Sexual harassment. *CQ Researcher,* 1(13): 545-550.

Anonymous. 1971. Myra Bradwell (1931-1894). *Women's Rights Law Reporter,* 1(1): 5-6.

Ballou, Patricia, ed. 1986. *Women: A Bibliography of Bibliographies,* 2nd edition. Boston: G. K. Hall.

Bass, Stuart & Slavin, Nathan. 1991. Avoiding sexual discrimination litigation in accounting firms and other professional organizations: The impact of the Supreme Court decision in *Price Waterhouse v. Ann B. Hopkins. Women's Rights Law Reporter,* 13(1): 21-38.

Bator, Paul. 1986. Equality as a constitutional value. *Harvard Journal of Law and Public Policy,* 9(1): 21-24.

Bennett-Alexander, Dawn. 1987. The Supreme Court finally speaks on the issue of sexual harassment: What did it say? *Women's Rights Law Reporter,* 10(1): 65-78.

Bergold, Laurel. 1976. The changing legal status of American women. *Current History,* (70): 206-210, 230-231.

Binion, Gayle. 1991. Toward a feminist regrounding of constitutional law. *Social Science Quarterly*, 72(2): 207-220.

Black, Donald. 1989. *Sociological Justice*. New York: Oxford.

Blier, Ruth. 1984. *Science and Gender: A Critique of Biology and Its Theories on Women*. New York: Pergamon.

Bolner, James Sr. 1984. The Burger Court and equal protection: Exercises in legal pragmatism. *Southern University Law Review*, 10: 241-262.

Bradwell v. Illinois, 83 US (16 Wall.) 442 (1873).

Caban v. Mohammed, 99 S.Ct. 1760 (1979).

Califano v. Goldfarb, 97 S.Ct. 1021 (1977).

Califano v. Webster, 97 S.Ct. 1192 (1977).

Cardozo, Benjamin. 1949 (1921). *The Nature of the Judicial Process*. New Haven, Conn: Yale University Press (1949).

Carter, Lief. 1985. *Contemporary Constitutional Lawmaking*, New York: Pergamon.

____1979. *Reason in Law*. Boston: Little Brown.

Catt, Carrie Chapman & Shuler, Nettie Roger. 1969 (1926). *Woman Suffrage and Politics: The Inner Story of the Suffrage Movement*. Seattle: University of Washington.

Chafe, William. 1972. *The American Woman: Her Changing Social, Economic, and Political Roles, 1920-1970*. New York: Oxford University.

Chafetz, Janet Saltzman. 1978. *Masculine, Feminine or Human? An Overview of the Sociology of Gender Roles*. Itasca, Ill.: F.E. Peacock.

Civil Rights Cases, 3 S.Ct. 18 (1883).

Cleveland Board of Education v. La Fleur, 94 S.Ct. 791 (1974).

Cole, David. 1984. Strategies of difference: Litigating for women's rights in a man's world. *Law and Inequality*, 2(33): 33-96.

Conway, Jill. 1982. *The Female Experience in Eighteenth and Nineteenth Century America: A Guide to the History of Women*. New York: Garland.

Cook, Beverly. 1978. The Burger Court and women's rights 1971-1977. In *Women in the Courts*, ed. Winifred Hepperle & Laura Crites, pp. 47-83. Williamsburg, Va.: National Center for State Courts.

Cott, Nancy, ed. 1972. *Root of Bitterness: Documents of the Social History of American Women*. New York: Dalton.

County of Washington v. Gunther, 101 S.Ct. 2242 (1981).

Cox, Archibald. 1987. *The Court and the Constitution*. Boston: Houghton Mifflin.

Craig v. Boren, 97 S.Ct. 451 (1976).

DeCrow, Karen. 1974. *Sexist Justice*. New York: Random House.

Dothard v. Rawlinson, 97 S.Ct. 2720 (1977).

Douglas, William O. 1949. *The Record of the Association of the Bar of the City of New York*, 4: 153-154.

Dred Scott v. John F. A. Sanford, S.C. (19 How) 691 (1857).

DuBois, Ellen Carol. 1978. *Feminism and Suffrage: The Emergence of an Independent Women's Movement in America 1848-1869*. Ithaca, N.Y.: Cornell University Press.

Eisenstadt v. Baird, 92 S.Ct. 1029 (1972).

England, Paula, & Bahar, Norris. 1985. Comparable worth: A new doctrine of sex discrimination. *Social Science Quarterly*, 66 (Sept.): 629-643.

Epstein, Cynthia Fuchs. 1991. In praise of women warriors. *Dissent*, 38(3): 421-422.

Evan, William. 1974. *Law and Sociology: Exploratory Essays*. Westport, Conn.: Greenwood.

Ex parte Lockwood, 14 S.Ct. 1082 (1894).

Fausto-Sterling, Anne. 1985. *Myths of Gender: Biological Theories About Women and Men*. New York: Basic Books.

Feldberg, Roslyn. 1984. Comparable worth: Toward theory and practice in the United States. *Signs*, 10(Winter): 311-328.

Firestone, Juanita. 1992. Occupational segregation: Comparing the civilian and military work force. *Armed Forces and Society*, 18(Spring): 363-381.

Fiske, Susan; Bersoff, Donald; & Borgida, Eugene. 1991. Social science research on trial: Use of sex stereotyping research in *Price Waterhouse v. Hopkins*. *American Psychologist*, 46 (Oct.): 1049-1070.

Frontiero v. Richardson, 93 S.Ct. 1764 (1973).

Geduldig v. Aiello, 94 S.Ct. 2485 (1974).

Ginsburg, Ruth Bader. 1975. Gender and the Constitution. *University of Cincinnati Law Review*, 44(1): 1-42.

____1973. Comment: *Frontiero v. Richardson*. *Women's Rights Law Reporter*, 1(5): 2-4.

Goesaert v. Cleary, 69 S.Ct. 198 (1948).

Graham, Hugh Davis. 1992. The origins of affirmative action: Civil rights and the regulatory state. *The Annals of the American Academy of Political and Social Science*, 523 (Sept.): 50-62.

Gruberg, Martin. (1968) *Women in American Politics*, Oskosh, Wisc.: Academia Press.

Gundersen, Joan. 1987. Independence, citizenship, and the American revolution. *Signs*, 13(1): 59-77.

Gurko, Miriam. 1974. *The Ladies of Seneca Falls: The Birth of the Woman's Rights Movement*. New York: Macmillan.

Halpern, Stephen & Lamb, Charles, eds. 1982. *Supreme Court Activism and Restraint*. Lexington, Mass.: Lexington Books.

Hamilton, Charles. 1992. Affirmative action and the clash of experiential realities. *The Annals of the American Academy of Political and Social Science*, 523 (Sept.): 10-18.

Hoff-Wilson, Joan. 1987. The unfinished revolution: Changing legal status of U.S. women. *Signs*, 13(1): 7-36.

____1979. The legal status of women in the late nineteenth and early twentieth centuries. *Human Rights*, 6: 125-133.

Holmes, Oliver Wendell, Jr. 1891. *The Common Law*. Boston: Little, Brown & Co.

Hoyt v. Florida, 82 S.Ct. 159 (1961).

Hubbard, Ruth; Henifin, Mary Sue & Fried, Barbara, eds. 1982. *Biological Woman—the Convenient Myth: A Collection of Feminist Essays and a Comprehensive Bibliography*. Cambridge, Mass.: Schenkman.

Hughes, Marija Matich, ed. 1977. *The Sexual Barrier: Legal, Medical, Economic, and Social Aspects of Sex Discrimination*. Washington: Hughes Press.

Hymowitz, C., & Weissman, M. 1978. *A History of Women in America*. New York: Bantam.

International Union, UAW v. Johnson Controls, 111 S.Ct. 1196 (1991).

Johnston, John D., Jr., & Knapp, Charles L. 1971. Sex discrimination by law: A study in judicial perspective. *New York University Law Review*, 46 (October): 675-747.

Kahn v. Shevin, 94 S.Ct. 1734 (1974).

Kanowitz, Leo. 1969. *Women and the Law: The Unfinished Revolution*. Albuquerque, N.M.: University of New Mexico.

Kaye, Judith. 1991. Women in law: The law can change people. *New York University Law Review*, 66(6): 1929-1939.

Kerber, Linda. 1992. The paradox of women's citizenship in the early republic: The case of *Martin v. Massachusetts*, 1805. *American Historical Review*, 97(2): 349-378.

____1977. From the Declaration of Independence to the Declaration of Sentiments: The legal status of women in the early republic 1776-1848. *Human Rights*, 6: 115-124.

Kolbert, Kathryn. 1989. *Webster v. Reproductive Health Services*: Reproductive freedom hanging by a thread. *Women's Rights Law Reporter*, 11(3&4): 153-162.

Kornblum, Lori. 1984. Women warriors in a men's world: The combat exclusion. *Law and Inequality*, 2: 351-445.

Lasser, William. 1988. *The Limits of Judicial Power: The Supreme Court in American Politics*. Chapel Hill, N.C.: University of North Carolina.

Lefcourt, Carol, ed. 1984. *Women and the Law*. New York: Clark Boardman.

Levitan, Sar, & Belous, Richard. 1979. *More than Subsistence: Minimum Wages for the Working Poor*. Baltimore, Md.: Johns Hopkins University.

Lipset, Seymour. 1992. Affirmative action and the American creed. *The Wilson Quarterly*, 16 (Winter): 52-62.

____1992. Equal chances versus equal results. *The Annals of the American Society of Political and Social Science*, 523 (Sept.): 63-74.

Livernash, Robert. 1980. *Comparable Worth: Issues and Alternatives*. Washington, D.C.: Equal Employment Advisory Council.

Lochner v. New York, 25 S.Ct. 539 (1908).

Martin, Fenton & Goehlert, Robert, eds. 1990. *The U.S. Supreme Court: A Bibliography*. Washington, D.C.: Congressional Quarterly.

Martin, Susan. 1980. *Breaking and Entering: Policewomen on Patrol*. Berkeley, Calif.: University of California.

Meritor Savings Bank, F.S.B. v. Vinson, 106 S.Ct. 2399 (1986).

Mezey, Susan Gluck. 1984. Gender equality in education: A study of policymaking by the Burger Court. *Wake Forest Law Review*, 20 (Winter): 793-817.

Michael M. v. Superior Court of Sonoma County, 101 S.Ct. 1200 (1981).

Millman, Marcia & Kanter, Rosabeth Moss. 1975. *Another Voice: Feminist Perspectives on Social Life and Social Science*. Garden City, N.Y.: Anchor/Doubleday.

(Virginia) Minor (& Francis Minor, her husband) v. (Reese) Happersett, S.C. 21 Wall. 162 (1875).

Montagu, Ashley. 1952. *The Natural Superiority of Women*, 3rd edition. New York: Collier, 1974.

Moore, Brenda. 1991. African-American women in the U.S. military. *Armed Forces and Society*, 17 (Spring): 363-384.

Muller v. Oregon, 28 S.Ct. 324 (1908).

Orr v. Orr, 99 S.Ct. 1102 (1979).

Parsons, Talcott, ed. 1947. *Max Weber: The Theory of Social and Economic Organization*. New York: Oxford University.

____1964. *Social Structure and Personality*. New York: Free Press.

Personnel Administrator of Massachusetts v. Feeney, 99 S.Ct. 2282 (1979).

Petersen, Cheryl. 1982. Doing time with the boys: An analysis of women correctional officers in all-male facilities. In *The Criminal Justice System and Women*, ed. B. Price & N. Sokoloff, pp. 435-460. New York: Clark Boardman.

Pettinga, Gayle-Lynn. 1987. Rational basis with bite: Intermediate scrutiny by any other name. *Indiana Law Journal*, 62(3): 779-803.

Pfeffer, Leo. 1965. *This Honorable Court: A History of the United States Supreme Court*. Boston: Beacon.

Planned Parenthood of Southeastern Pennsylvania et al. v. Robert P. Casey et al., 112 S.Ct. 2791 (1992).

Plessy v. Ferguson, 16 S.Ct. 1138 (1896).

Pogrebin, Letty Cottin. 1980. *Growing Up Free: Raising Your Child in the 80s.* New York: McGraw.

Price Waterhouse v. Hopkins, 109 S.Ct. 1775 (1989).

Reed v. Reed, 92 S.Ct. 251 (1971).

Roe v. Wade, 93 S.Ct. 705 (1973)

Rogers v. EEOC, 454 F.2d 234 (CA5 1971).

Rossi, A., ed. 1973. *The Feminist Papers: From Adams to de Beauvoir.* New York: Bantam Books.

Rostker v. Goldberg, 101 S.Ct. 2646 (1981).

Rust v. Sullivan, 111 S.Ct. 1759 (1991).

Sachs, Albie & Hoff-Wilson, Joan. 1978. *Sexism and the Law: A Study of Male Beliefs and legal Bias in Britain and the United States.* New York: Free Press.

Salmon, Marylynn. 1986. *Women and the Law of Property in Early America.* Chapel Hill, N.C.: University of North Carolina.

Scales, Ann. 1980-1981. Towards a feminist jurisprudence. *Indiana Law Journal,* 56(3): 375-444.

Schlesinger v. Ballard, 95 S.Ct. 572 (1975).

Schneir, M., ed. 1972. *Feminism: the Essential Historical Writings.* New York: Vintage.

Schur, Edwin. 1968. *Law and Society, A Sociological View.* New York: Random House.

Simon, Rita James, ed. 1968. *The Sociology of Law: Interdisciplinary Readings.* San Francisco: Chandler.

Sinclair, Andrew. 1965. *The Better Half: The Emancipation of the American Woman.* New York: Harper & Row.

Slaughter-House Cases, 83 U.S. (16 Wall.) 394 (1873).

Smart, Carol. 1989. *Feminism and the Power of Law.* London: Routledge.

Stanton, Beth Lynn. 1981. Sexual harassment: A bibliography. *Capital University Law Review,* 10(3): 697-708.

Stanton, Elizabeth Cady & Gage, Matilda Joslyn, eds. 1970 (reprint). *History of Woman Suffrage, Volumes 1-6.* New York: Source Books.

Stanton v. Stanton, 95 S.Ct. 1373 (1975).

Steelworkers v. Weber, 99 S.Ct. 2721 (1979).

Sternhell, Carol. 1986. Life in the mainstream. *Ms.* July: 48-51, 86-91.

Taylor v. Louisiana, 95 S.Ct. 692 (1975).

Wald, Patricia. 1989. Breaking the glass ceiling: Will we ever rid the legal profession of "the ugly residue of gender discrimination"? *Human Rights*, 16 (Spring): 40-43+.

Washington v. Davis, 96 S.Ct. 2040 (1976).

Weber, Max. 1919. Science as a vocation. In *From Max Weber: Essays in Sociology*, ed. H. H. Gerth & C. Wright Mills, pp. 129-156. New York: Oxford University, 1946.

Webster v. Reproductive Health Services, 109 S.Ct. 3040 (1989).

Weidner, Paul. 1980. The Equal Protection Clause: The continuing search for judicial standards. *University of Detroit Journal of Urban Law*, 57: 867-917.

Weinberger v. Wiesenfeld, 95 S.Ct. 1225 (1975).

Wertheimer, Barbara. 1977. *We Were There: The Story of Working Women in America*. New York: Pantheon Books.

West Coast Hotel Co. v. Parrish, 57 S.Ct. 578 (1937).

Wright, J. Skelly. 1968. The role of the Supreme Court in a democratic society: Judicial activism or restraint? *Cornell Law Review*, 54 (Nov.): 1-28.

Index

About the Author

LAURA A. OTTEN, Ph.D., is Assistant Professor of Criminal Justice and Women's Studies at LaSalle University. She was instrumental in developing the university's Women's Studies Program, and she served as its second Director.